MW00412406

Wildlife of
Southern Africa

Martin B. Withers and David Hosking

Princeton University Press • Princeton and Oxford

DEDICATION

To our parents
Eric & Dorothy Hosking and Ben & Margaret Withers,
who encouraged our love of the natural world,
of Africa and of the camera.

PRINCETON POCKET GUIDES

Coral Reef Fishes: Indo-Pacific and Caribbean, Revised Edition
Ewald Lieske and Robert Myers

Wildlife of the Galápagos
Julian Fitter, Daniel Fitter, and David Hosking

Wildlife of East Africa
Martin B. Withers and David Hosking

The Kingdon Pocket Guide to African Mammals
Jonathan Kingdon

Reptiles and Amphibians of East Africa
Stephen Spawls, Kim M. Howell, and Robert C. Drewes

Wildlife of Southern Africa
Martin B. Withers and David Hosking

Published in the United States, Canada, and the Philippine Republic
by Princeton University Press,
41 William Street, Princeton, New Jersey 08540

nathist.press.princeton.edu

Published by arrangement with HarperCollins Publishers Ltd

First published in the United Kingdom in 2011 by HarperCollins Publishers,
77–85 Fulham Palace Road, London W6 8JB

Library of Congress Control Number: 2011926276
ISBN: 978-0-691-15063-5

Collins uses papers that are natural, renewable and recyclable products made from
wood grown in sustainable forests. The manufacturing processes conform to the
environmental regulations of the country of origin.

Edited and designed by Tom Cabot/Ketchup

Printed and bound in Hong Kong by Printing Express Ltd

16 15 14 13 12 11
10 9 8 7 6 5 4 3 2 1

Contents

Acknowledgements

The authors owe a debt of gratitude to countless people for their help in bringing this project to fruition. They would like to thank John Tinning for his help, particularly with the butterfly section of this guide, as well as Chris Mattison, Gianpiero & Paola Ferrari, Peter Steyn, Gill Wheeler, Shem Compion & Minette van den Berg of C4 Images & Safaris, Peter & Inge Hennes, Vernon Swanepoel, Villiers Steyn, Wilderness Safaris, Graham Armitage at Sigma UK Ltd and the many Hosking Tours clients who have made our travels to Southern Africa such a delight.

We would like to express our appreciation and thanks to the staff of HarperCollins Publishers, particularly to Julia Koppitz and Myles Archibald.

Lastly, we owe a huge debt of thanks to Sally Withers for her help with proofreading the text and to Jean Hosking and all her staff at the Frank Lane Picture Agency, for their help in sourcing the pictures for this guide.

Martin B. Withers FRPS
David Hosking FRPS, FBNA

Picture Credits

The authors would like to thank the Frank Lane Picture Agency (FLPA) for their assistance in the compilation of the photographs used in this book. All the photographs are by the authors with the exception of those listed below.

L. Batten – Great Shearwater; **N. Bowman** – Klaas's Cuckoo, Red-fronted Tinkerbird, Desert Cisticola, Yellow-breasted Apilis, Brimstone Canary; **R. Brooks** – Spotted Crake, Gt Reed Warbler, Lr Grey Shrike; **C. Brown** – Cape Clapper Lark; **R. Chittenden** – Baillon's Crake; **S. Compion** – African Honey Bee, Peringuey's Adder, Great White Shark, Cape Cobra, Cape Vulture, Bearded Vulture, Jackal Buzzard, Cape Shoveler, Fulvous Duck, Yellow Canary, Sharpe's Grysbok; **W. Dennis** – Little Sparrowhawk, African Grey Rhebok, Red Duiker, Blue Duiker; **Y. Eshbol** – Sooty Falcon; **M. Gore** – Cape Weaver; **V. Grafhorst** – Monotonous Lark; **P. Heard** – Cape Bulbul, Puff Adder, Red Locust, Dune Ant; **J. Holmes** – Shy Albatross, Great-winged Petrel; **M. Hosking** – Wahlberg's Eagle; **J. Karmali** – Yellow-crowned Bishop, Yellow-throated Petronia; **G. Lacz** – Aardwolf; **F. Lane** – Springhare; **H. Lansdown** – Red-tailed Tropicbird; **Minden, Hiroya Minakuchi** – Bottlenose Dolphin; **Mark Moffett** – Darkling Beetle; **C. Marshall** – Cape Clawless Otter; **C. Mattison** – Cape Cormorant, Brown House Snake; **W. T. Miller** – Red-faced Mousebird, Orange River White-eye, Swee Waxbill; **Panda Photo** – Cory's Shearwater; **P. Perry** – Crested Guineafowl, Temminck's Courser, Dusky Sunbird, Civet, Brown Hyaena; **A. Riley** – Red-chested Cuckoo; **M. Schuyl** – Cape Wagtail, Humpback Whale; **J. & C. Sohns** – Bennett's Woodpecker, Amethyst Sunbird, Gt Double Collared Sunbird; **D. Smith** – Red-winged Francolin, African Palm Swift, Village Indigobird; **P. Steyn** – White-rumped Swift; **C. & T. Stuart** – Lr Bushbaby, Suni, Common Caco, Common Green Mantis; **J. Tinning** – Amur Falcon, House Martin, Grass Jewel, African Monarch, Natal Acraea, Neobule Acraea, Yellow Pansy, Long-tailed Blue, Brown Veined White, Common Joker, Painted Lady, Blue Pansy, Striped Policeman; **R. Tidman** – Antarctic Prion, White-chinned Petrel, European Storm Petrel, Long-tailed Jaeger, Antarctic Tern, Black Tern, Knysna Turaco, Alpine Swift; **T. Whittaker** – Common River Frog; **W. Wisniewski** – African Black Oystercatcher, Pomarine Jaeger, Cape Rock Thrush; **M. Woike** – Lr Spotted Eagle; **A. V. Zandbergen** - African Goshawk, Diderick's Cuckoo, Lichtenstein's Hartebeest, Raucous Toad.

Preface

The main purpose of this book is to provide travellers with an easy to use reference and identification guide to many of the most commonly seen species likely to be encountered while visiting the National Parks and Reserves of Southern Africa. The number of species found within the region is vast. The species included in this guide are based on our own experiences and observations. We request travellers to appreciate that a book giving complete coverage would have to extend to many volumes.

The text and photographs have been combined to provide a full diagnostic description of each species featured, within the limitations of space. However, it should be remembered that in many instances, particularly with birds, variations in colour and detail could be quite marked within a species as a result of age, sex and distribution. Wherever possible we have attempted to bring any such differences to the attention of the reader.

Photography Notes

Pre-Planning

You will have given a lot of thought to the planning of your safari, so it is well worth spending a little time considering how to record what you see and where you go. There are bound to be some memorable moments that you will want to share with family and friends on your return home. You need to consider whether you want still images and/or video and how you will store the images while on safari and when you get back home. It is very important that you understand how your equipment works before you depart and that all the storage systems work, so take some time to familiarise yourself with how it all functions, including the transfer of data onto your home computer.

Time spent researching the areas you will be visiting, how they may differ during the year and establishing what flora and fauna you are likely to see, will help you to decide what will be the best equipment to use.

Make sure you have adequate insurance cover for all your equipment. Ensure that your policy fully covers equipment for loss or damage in all the countries you plan to visit. Keep a checklist of all the equipment you are taking and remember most cameras and lenses have serial numbers and these will be required should you have to make a claim. If any of your equipment is stolen you should report it to the local police and obtain a statement confirming the report of the theft, as some insurance companies will not settle any claim without such confirmation.

Cameras

The choice of modern day cameras is vast, but, when buying you can begin to narrow down the search by deciding how much you want to spend and whether your interest is in 'stills' or 'video'. If it is to be 'stills' then you have to decide between an Single Lens Reflex (SLR), a camera that has interchangeable lens or a compact, which does not. A common option that now applies to many compacts and some SLRs is Digital Single Lens Reflex (DSLR), where the conventional viewfinder has been replaced by a LCD viewing screen, making the camera body much smaller. LCD screen's are slowly being replaced by Active Matrix Organic Light-emitting Diode (AMOLED). As well as being brighter and sharper, they use less power and are slimmer than LCDs.

There is a very good choice of SLR brands to choose from: talk to friends, visit your local camera shop, search the web and see what other people are using to help you decide. Most top brands have two or three levels of SLR which are usually price and function related. Pay particular attention to the sensor that is used to record the image, its size and the number of pixels and whether the camera automatically cleans the sensor; this is so important – dust can get to the sensor each time you change a lens and any dust that enters and settles on the sensor will show on every image until the sensor is cleaned. Top of the range SLR cameras use a full frame sensor similar in size to 35 mm film: other sensor sizes are smaller – 1.6 , 1.3, or the Micro Four Thirds (MFT). While the smaller sensors have the advantage of the subject size being bigger in the recording area, the disadvantage is cramming lots of pixels in to a smaller area. Entry and mid level SLR cameras are likely to have 10 to 18 million pixel sensors, while the top level full frame sensor may have 25 million pixels. If you are interested in underwater photography check that an underwater housing is available for the SLR model you choose.

Entry level cameras offer an impressive array of options, they are priced competitively, often being cheaper than the top end compact cameras. Camera body construction is usually plastic which is fine provided you do not throw them around, and they are usually smaller than the mid level models. The sensor size is generally 1.6.

The mid level SLRs are the most popular: with a mix of basic and advanced options they are often used by professionals as their main camera or as a back-up to their top level model. The construction is much more robust and they often retain some of the useful features of their entry level cousin, such as a 'pop up' flash, a handy extra missing from professional top level models.

Top level models are expensive but offer outstanding performance and quality. They are usually water and dust resistant with a full frame or 1.3 sensor and have the very best auto focus

and metering technology. The down side is the size and weight, which can be double that of the entry level models.

When it comes to compact cameras the choice is vast. Many mobile phones come with a built in camera: some are very basic in quality but can be fine for sending images to another mobile, while others can record good quality images that can be downloaded at home and printed. Make sure that the internal memory is going to hold enough images or that it will take memory cards. Also check the battery life; some safari locations will not have charging facilities.

Almost all compact cameras will have some form of zoom lens, which is ideal for composition where you can make your subject bigger or smaller. This change in subject size is normally achieved 'optically' by the lens increasing or decreasing in size. However, some compact cameras achieve this 'digitally' by cropping of the sensor: this does not produce the best results, so look for a compact that uses an optical zoom.

Some compacts have a fixed focal length lens: these are usually combined with other features for the dedicated photographer, so are best avoided unless you are adventurous.

Other considerations are battery life and whether spare batteries are easily available and what type of memory cards it uses: avoid any compact that does not accept plug in memory cards and relies on solid state internal memory. Some compacts have image stabilisation, which is a great way of reducing image blur, particularly in low light. For those who may want to take their compact swimming, look for one that is waterproof; these come in different levels from shower proof, to light submersion, to full underwater capabilities. Underwater housings are also available for some compact models and these are very popular with divers.

Supplementary lenses can be added to some compact cameras and camcorders: these either magnify faraway action or widen the image. They are fitted by screwing onto the built in lens.

There are a number of options for recording moving subjects. The conventional video recorder, which uses magnetic tape to record on to, or the mini disc system. These have largely been replaced by solid state camcorders which are small and light with footage being saved directly to internal electronic storage and/or removable memory cards.

All the new camcorders shoot in high definition HD: some video is saved in 'advanced video coding high definition' (AVCHD), which is used by many professional film makers but may not be compatible with some cheaper computer software programs. The other commonly used method is H.264, sometimes known as MPEG4, which saves footage more efficiently, thereby using less memory. Check what memory cards are available, what the battery life is and the cost of spare batteries. Look at what optics are available, 5x or 10x zoom are normal but some go up to 35x which is great for capturing faraway wildlife action.

Another 'must have' option is Image Stabilisation: not only is this available for camcorders and compacts but also some SLR lenses and camera bodies. Camera shake is a big problem on all image recording equipment and more so with the bigger zooms or longer focal length lenses. There are two ways of reducing shake – optical or electronic. Optical stabilisation suspends the lens within the casing, so it can move slightly to counteract movement, and is most commonly found in SLR lenses and some compacts and camcorders where the lens is built in. Electronic stabilisation retains a border round the edge of the sensor used to create the image; should the camera move, the image is 'shifted' into that region to counteract the shake.

There is a lot of crossover technology between SLRs, compacts and camcorders. It is quite common for the latest SLRs to also take video clips, which is great if you mainly want stills but also want to record the odd bit of action, and the same is possible with compacts and mobile phone recorders. Many camcorders also have the option to record still images and some of the very latest cameras allow photo quality freeze framing, with pre-10-second record memory, so you will never miss the action.

Lenses

If you choose the SLR option you will need to think about what interchangeable lenses to take with you. To some extent this will be dictated by which manufacturer made your camera, although there are some very good independent manufacturers who make lenses to fit most makes and also produce some unique lens designs. While on safari there will be a wide variety of photographic opportunities that you need to be prepared for.

Your lens options can be broken down into three areas: short, medium and long. There are zoom or fixed focal length lenses to fit all three categories. Zoom lenses have many advantages, one lens can cover many different situations. While for the very best optical results a fixed focal length is considered the best it greatly limits composition and may involve carrying many more lenses. Lenses with image stabilisation (IS) may be more expensive but in a bumpy safari vehicle IS can make a big difference. Look also for lenses that use diffractive optics, they are 25% smaller and lighter than conventional lenses.

Short lens zooms come in many different combinations starting at about 8–16 mm and some cover a huge range such as 18–250 mm. It worth remembering that some of these lenses are not compatible with full frame sensor cameras.

Medium zoom lenses tend to be 70-300 mm to 100-400 mm. Some lenses have wide apertures such as f 2.8 and are compatible with teleconverters, so a 70-200 mm f 2.8 with a 2x converter becomes a 140-400 mm f 5.6.

The options available in long range lenses are far fewer. For the best results 400 mm, 500 mm or 600 mm fixed focal length lenses, often combined with 1.4 or 2x converters, are the preferred choice of most professional photographers. If your budget does not stretch to these expensive lenses, look at the long zoom lenses made by some of the independent manufacturers such as the 150-500 mm or even the 50-500 mm. Image stabilisation comes into its own with these long lenses where movement is magnified, so if you have a choice go for a lens with stabilisation.

One other specialist lens option worth remembering is macro. If you are interested in photographing the world in close-up, look at the shorter 70 mm macro lens for plants and the longer 180 mm for subjects that move, such as insects.

Choose wisely and you could manage with just two or three lenses and cover most focal lengths from 8 mm to 600 mm.

Memory

The memory card is the equivalent of film and stores the information which makes up your picture digitally. Whatever camera you use it will require one of these removable cards. There are a number of different kinds: the commonest types are Compact Flash (CF), Secure Digital (SD), XD picture and the memory stick.

The picture information is stored as either a '0' or a '1' so it is not possible to have a bad quality card, but it is possible to corrupt this information, so buy well known brand names. The card capacity is measured in megabytes (MB) or gigabytes (GB). The more GB you have the more images can be stored. However, storing too many images on one card is not a good idea, just in case there is a problem, so take a good number of compatible cards. These can be stored in purpose-made cases which hold two or four cards and will protect them from dust and damp conditions.

Memory cards come in different speeds; this is the time it takes to transfer the picture information onto the card and from the card to your computer. This is known as 'reading' and 'writing' and is measured in Kbits/sec or Mbits/sec. The main advantage of the faster cards is the speed at which this information is moved around. If you are taking lots of pictures in quick succession, you don't want to be held up by a slow transfer rate.

The most common reason for a card becoming corrupt is when the card is removed from the camera or when the camera is turned off while it is still writing or reading to the card. Treat the card with care: do not squash or drop it and keep the connecting terminals free from dust.

There are a number of options for viewing, editing and backing up your images while on safari. Probably the best option is a laptop, then you can have all the software programs from home for editing while on safari. Make sure you have lots of memory space and a card reader. A USB portable hard drive is a useful extra back-up, as is a DVD and/or Blu-ray writer. The down side of travelling with a laptop is the extra weight and space, plus you can find yourself taking pictures all day and editing all night!

A multimedia storage viewer will copy most card formats and has a LCD screen for viewing. They are small, light and run on rechargeable batteries so are very convenient. Look for one with a good size memory capacity.

Technique

For the most part, the secret to successful photography lies in the ability to master and control several major factors – those of exposure, lighting, depth of field, definition and composition. If all these factors are successfully mastered you will be producing many pleasing pictures.

Raw or Jpeg

The most common formats for recording your images are Jpeg or Raw. You will have the option to select the one you prefer in your camera set up. Jpeg is very popular because it is a very space efficient way of recording your images; however, it does this by using varying degrees of compression to reduce the file sizes at the expense of fine image detail. Raw files contain all the data collected by the sensor and give more flexibility for post correction of exposure, colour and sharpening. Raw is the preferred shooting format of most professional photographers.

ISO and Noise

ISO determines how sensitive the image sensor is to the amount of light present. It affects the shutter speed/aperture combinations you can use to obtain correct exposure. However, the price you pay for using a high ISO is 'noise'. This is apparent by the presence of colour speckles where there should be none. For example, you might notice faint pink, purple and other colour speckles amongst the otherwise blue sky. At ISO settings up to 400 very little noise is noticeable, so keep the ISO below 400 and save the higher settings for occasions when there is no alternative.

Exposure

Your camera will have a mode dial, giving you lots of options to automate your exposure. It is worth remembering that obtaining the correct exposure is a combination of aperture and shutter speed settings. Aperture controls the depth of field by making the aperture of the lens iris larger or smaller and the shutter controls the length of time the light is allowed to pass through the aperture. If you set the mode dial to 'Av', you set the aperture and the camera works out how long to allow light through. Tv works in the opposite way – you set the shutter speed and the camera determines the aperture – while 'P' allows the camera to work both settings out for you. 'M' is totally manual, so you have to determine both the shutter speed and the aperture. Some mode dial's will have little symbols as well: select a flower or mountain symbol and the camera will give a small aperture, which will give great depth of field; use the running person symbol and the camera will use a faster speed to stop the movement.

While these automatic modes are generally very accurate, there are occasions when they will let you down. For example, when photographing white birds, or light coloured animals against a dark background or, alternatively, a dark animal against a light background. Under such lighting conditions knowledge in the use of +/- compensation is required. In the case of white/light subjects against dark backgrounds the metering system may well be influenced to a great extent by the dark areas, thereby over exposing your main subject. This will require you to underexpose to retain detail in the important white/light subject areas by using - compensation. Conversely, in the case of dark subjects against light skies or backgrounds, the light areas may well over influence the metering, resulting in a silhouette of the main subject. This problem will require you to overexpose in order to obtain detail in the shadow or dark areas of your subject: use the + compensation. Do remember to cancel any over or under exposure settings before moving on to the next situation.

In cases where determining the correct exposure is in doubt, it is advisable to 'bracket' your exposures. For example, if your metering system indicates an exposure of 1/60th at f 8, take one picture at this setting, then two further exposures either side of it (i.e. 1/60th at f 5.6 and 1/60th at f 11). Some cameras will have an auto bracketing option; if not use the +/-. One of the resulting exposures should produce what you require, but experience with your own equipment under these difficult conditions is the only real answer.

The LCD monitors on digital cameras will give an instant indication of what your pictures look like and badly exposed results can be deleted and retaken.

Lighting

During the course of a single day in Southern Africa, the lighting conditions experienced can vary tremendously. The conditions experienced in the early morning are often the most pleasing, the low angle of the sun producing wonderful soft lighting, with excellent modelling of the subject. These lighting conditions are often repeated in late afternoon with the addition of a warm glow towards sunset. From late morning to mid afternoon lighting conditions can be very challenging, with the sunlight often directly overhead, resulting in rather flat lighting effects.

In most cases, standard portraits of birds and mammals are taken with the sunlight behind the photographer, thereby fully lighting the subject. It is always worth experimenting with other lighting arrangements, particularly side or back lighting. These lighting conditions often produce spectacular and unusual pictures of even the most common animal species.

Depth of Field

The range of 'f' stops available on each individual lens determines depth of field. In most landscape pictures, taken with wide-angle or standard lenses, there is a necessity for maximum depth of field, to render as much of the foreground, middle and far distance as sharp as possible. To achieve this result, it is necessary to select a small aperture (f 16 or f 22). This will consequently result in a slow shutter speed, so ensure you use a tripod or some other means of support, to reduce the risk of picture failure as a result of camera shake.

For individual images of birds or mammals, using longer lenses, it is often better to select a large aperture (f 5.6 or f 4). This will result in the background being thrown well out of focus, which in turn will help to isolate your main centre of interest, be it bird or mammal. The use of a large aperture, in these circumstances, will also help to eliminate background distractions by rendering them out of focus.

Don't forget that you can check the depth of field created by any given 'f' stop by using the depth of field button on your camera body. This button allows you to preview the finished image and to adjust it to your own satisfaction prior to making any exposure.

Definition

The success or failure of any photograph is dependent to a great extent on definition. On the whole, modern lenses are produced to a high standard and give excellent definition; any lack of focus is usually attributable to other causes. The most frequent cause is, undoubtedly, due to camera shake during exposure (see Camera Supports). Another cause can be movement of the subject during exposure; this can be lessened to a great extent by the use of a fast shutter speed.

It is, however, worth remembering that in some instances movement of the subject during exposure can often result in a pleasing pictorial image (i.e. animals running, flocks of birds flying etc.).

Composition

Unlike many elements of a photograph which are automatically undertaken by the camera itself, composition demands an active input from the photographer. It is, therefore, in your own interest to be fully conversant with the factors relating to good composition.

Many newcomers to photography tend to produce all of their images in a horizontal format. Cameras work equally well when turned through 90 degrees! Do remember to fully utilise the possibilities of a vertical format.

Also remember to consider changing your viewpoint on occasions, don't always photograph from a standing position and explore the possibilities of photographing a subject

by kneeling or even lying on the ground. On game drives don't always photograph from the open roof of the vehicle, use the windows occasionally, it can often add impact and provide better scale to the resulting pictures.

In the case of bird or mammal portraits, having decided on your format and viewpoint, you need to concentrate on the size and placement of your subject within the picture area. Generally speaking most subjects need room to move or look into the picture space, so avoid cropping your image too tightly, unless of course it is your intention to show a close-up of the subject's head.

Try to avoid placing your subject in the centre of the picture space: instead consciously divide the space into 'thirds', both vertically and horizontally, and place your main point of interest where the lines cross. Do pay attention to the line of the horizon, particularly in landscapes, and keep it along the 'thirds' – and at all costs keep it level.

When it comes to precise framing zoom lenses are very useful, allowing control over subject size and perspective. In some cases the size of the main subject can be quite small within the picture space, provided that the inclusion of more surroundings adds information or pictorial interest to the finished image.

By utilising a range of lenses it is often possible to secure an interesting sequence of images of a bird or mammal – 50 mm to show the creature in it's habitat, 200 mm or 300 mm to produce portraits, and 500 mm or 600 mm for depicting the head only.

The Moment of Exposure

Having located your subject, decided on the elements of exposure, lighting and composition, when do you press the shutter? This, of course, is very subjective but any animal or bird portrait will be greatly improved and have a 'sparkle of life' if you can make your exposure when a 'highlight' is visible in the eye of your chosen subject. This is particularly important if the eye of the subject being photographed is dark and surrounded by black fur or feather.

You should always attempt to maintain concentration when photographing any subject, remaining alert to the possibility of a yawn, scratch or wing-stretch, which may provide you with only a fleeting moment in which to capture the action.

Moving Subjects

Animals 'on the move' present the photographer with some interesting problems. Supporting the camera is a major concern, as the use of a tripod or monopod is usually too restricting for this type of work. Other than hand-holding the camera, a rifle stock, or shoulder pod is probably the only option available; either way you should endeavour to use the fastest shutter speed available, to minimise the risk of camera shake. Capturing any moving bird or mammal is best accomplished by 'panning'. This technique involves moving the camera in the same direction and at the same speed as the subject and taking the picture while the camera is still moving. Any resulting pictures will have a feeling of movement, showing the subject in sharp focus with the background blurred due to the motion of the panning camera.

Getting Close to Birds and Mammals

Whilst on safari the vast majority of your photography will be undertaken from a vehicle during game drives. Many opportunities also exist for wildlife photography on foot, within the grounds of safari lodges and at specially designated areas within the National Parks and Reserves.

At many of the lodges getting close to birds is often quite easy, due to the tame nature of many species. Others, however, require some knowledge of basic 'stalking' procedures to gain a close enough approach for a worthwhile image size in the finished pictures. Avoid walking straight towards your intended subject, as this is likely to cause it to fly away; a slow, angled approach is more likely to succeed. Watch your subject during your approach and should it appear concerned 'freeze' for a while until it again looks relaxed but avoid direct eye contact. A crouched approach during a 'stalk' can also be beneficial, the smaller you appear the less likely you are to frighten your intended subject. It is also a good idea to make use of any natural cover that the terrain may offer.

Many of the safari lodges provide food and water for the local bird population and these feeding areas can offer good photographic opportunities. Even if the bird tables themselves are non-photogenic you can attempt to photograph birds on natural perches as they make their way to and from the feeding areas.

You should exercise considerable caution when 'stalking' mammal species; remember they are wild animals and can be extremely dangerous. Never try to tempt monkeys or baboons to come closer with food items: this is a sure way to get badly bitten.

Camera Bags

A good quality camera bag that will protect expensive camera equipment from damage, dust and rain is essential for the travelling photographer. There are many well-designed camera rucksacks and bags on the market today. In selecting a suitable bag, resist the temptation to purchase one that is too big you will only feel obliged to fill it! With ever-tightening controls and restrictions being imposed by airlines on the size and weight of cabin baggage, the smaller the better. Waist-mounted camera and lens pouches can help to spread the load. Stuff bags, sold in most camping shops, in varying sizes, offer an additional form of protection from dust and rain.

Camera Supports

The commonest cause of picture failure is undoubtedly lack of definition as a result of camera shake. Overcoming this problem will increase your success rate enormously. Most camera instruction manuals give details of 'How to hold your camera' and it is well worth developing a good technique in this area, with elbows locked tightly into the body.

Whenever possible we would recommend the use of a tripod. There are many light, yet sturdy models on the market made from carbon-fibre which will fit comfortably into the

average suitcase or roll bag. Monopods are also a good means of steadying the camera, but they do require a little practice. On most photographic safaris the vast majority of filming will be undertaken from a vehicle during game drives; in most cases this precludes the use of a tripod or monopod. The best alternative for photographing from a vehicle is to employ the use of a beanbag – a very simple, but extremely effective method of camera support. Although beanbags are commercially available, they are not difficult to make. All that is needed is a section of cloth or canvas sewn to form a zippered bag of around 300 mm x 150 mm. This can be packed in your luggage and, on arrival at your chosen destination, be filled with rice, peas or beans. When the beanbag is placed on the roof of your safari vehicle it quickly moulds around your camera and lens, forming a very efficient support.

Rifle stock and pistol grip supports allow freedom of movement when attempting to photograph moving subjects, such as animals running, or birds in flight.

Flash

An electronic flashgun is well worth its place in your camera bag – not only to record any nocturnal creatures that you may encounter, but also as a 'fill in' to soften harsh shadows during the daytime and to light any close-up macro photography. Most modern day flashguns feature 'through the lens' (TTL) exposure control which will guarantee correct exposure automatically. Many of these flashguns also feature an infrared auto focus system, which overcomes the problem of focusing in the dark. In the absence of this facility, a head-mounted torch can prove invaluable, allowing you to illuminate your chosen subject while at the same time leaving both hands free to focus manually. There are restrictions on the use of flash in some parks.

Camera Accessories

A cable release is an excellent way of reducing camera shake and your camera should accept either an electronic or mechanical type. A wide camera strap with some degree of elasticity will help to distribute the weight of your camera and lens. A small hot shoe spirit level for checking straight horizons can be a great aid to landscape workers.

Batteries

As most digital camera's use rechargeable batteries, don't forget to pack chargers, leads and international plug adaptors and, where available, a car charger. Remember to have enough spare rechargeable batteries to allow for those days when mains electricity may not be available.

Care and Maintenance

As a general rule it is advisable to thoroughly check and clean all your camera bodies and lenses at the end of each day's shooting. All equipment used on safari is subject to the potentially damaging effects of sunlight, damp, rain and dust. Do remember to keep camera bags out of direct sunlight whenever possible. Remember that a single peace of dust or sand grain on the image sensor will show as a dark speck on every image. A rubber blower brush or mini vac sucking device is ideal for keeping the inside of your camera clean, while lens elements and filters are best cleaned with specially purchased cleaning fluid and tissues, alcohol or even fresh water could be used as a last resort. The outer casings of both cameras and lenses can be cleaned using an ordinary paintbrush. It is always worth having a supply of large plastic bags with you, into which you can seal your entire camera bag on the days when you are travelling from one location to another. This will greatly reduce the risk of dust entering the most sensitive parts of your camera.

Code of Conduct

The National Parks and Reserves of Southern Africa operate a strict Code of Conduct for both drivers and visitors. A short, simple list of dos and don'ts have been implemented to minimise disturbance to the birds and mammals, to lessen the impact of tourism on the environment and to ensure that all visitors experience safe and enjoyable safaris.

Please do not pressurise your driver into breaking Park regulations; you will be jeopardising his job and run the risk of expulsion from the Park. Please keep noise to a minimum, particularly when close to animals, and never leave the vehicle, sit or stand on the roof, or hang precariously from the windows. Never discard any form of litter: apart from being unsightly it can cause serious injury or even kill animals if ingested.

General Notes

Many people visiting Southern Africa express a wish to photograph the local people. Before doing so please obtain permission and be prepared for the possibility of paying for the privilege. On no account attempt to photograph military installations or personnel.

Notes

Sometimes identifying the vast number of animals and other subjects you photograph on safari can be a nightmare. Keeping detailed notes each day will be a great help later. Providing you have remembered to set the date and time on your camera, each digital image should have the information imbedded in the metadata, so that the images can be matched to your notes when captioning and key wording pictures on your return home. Unlike film, where you would physically have a slide or a print, digital images remain in a folder on your computer until you are ready to do something with them. The local supermarket can probably run a set of prints off from your safari folder. High quality display prints are easy to have made from your best images. Probably the nicest memento of your holiday would be to produce a photo-book. Many online companies offer this service: it is easy to down load the software, drop your pictures into pre-designed pages, add captions and text and then you can have as many copies printed as you want and the cost is often less than a set of prints.

Travel Tips and Checklist

- Travel Documents
- **Passport** - Expiry should be at least six months after date of your return)
- Other ID Documents

- **Visa** – if required
- **Flight Tickets**
- **Itinerary**
- **Foreign Currency**
- **Credit Cards** – inform your card company that you will be using your card overseas
- **Driving Licence**

Health and Medications

- **Personal medications** – Always carry them in your hand baggage, as hold baggage occasionally goes astray. Also pack additional tablets in case your return flight is delayed or cancelled. If you will be travelling with large amounts of prescriptive drugs, it may be advisable to take a copy of your prescription to prove you are registered to be in possession.
- **Malaria prophylactics** – if your destination is within an infected area.
- **Contact lenses or prescriptive spectacles** – along with cleaning fluid.
- **Insect repellent**
- **Medical history** – If you are travelling with a tour guide it may be worth supplying him/her with a brief history of any allergies, or other conditions which could be of concern to medics during an illness or emergency. These details can be supplied in a sealed envelope and returned to you at the end of your tour.
- **Stomach upsets** – Often occur when travelling to new destinations. You should take local advice about the quality of tap water and if there is any doubt buy bottled.

Useful Items

- Hat
- Sunscreen
- Sunglasses
- Head or hand torch
- Notebook and pens
- Maps
- Field Guides

Personal Items and Clothing
- Long sleeved cotton shirts
- Cotton trousers
- Fleece or Sweatshirt
- Wet-weather gear
- Walking boots or shoes
- Spare batteries and chargers
- Binoculars
- Beanbag
- Electrical adapters
- Camera
- Spare memory cards

National Parks & Reserves of Southern Africa

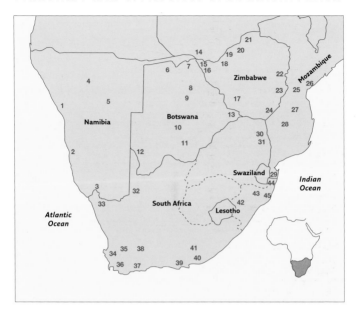

1	Skeleton Coast NP	**23**	Chimanimani NP
2	Namib-Naukluft NP	**24**	Gonarezhou NP
3	Fish River Canyon Park	**25**	Gorongosa NP
4	Etosha NP	**26**	Marromeu NP
5	Waterberg Plateau Park	**27**	Zinave NP
6	Moremi Game Reserve	**28**	Banhine NP
7	Chobe NP	**29**	Maputo Elephant Reserve
8	Nxai Pan NP	**30**	Kruger NP
9	Makgadikgadi Pans NP	**31**	Sabi Sand Game Reserve
10	Central Kalahari Game Reserve.	**32**	Augrabies Falls NP
11	Khutse Game Reserve	**33**	Richtersveld NP
12	Kgalagadi Transfrontier Park	**34**	West Coast NP
13	Northern Tuli Game Reserve and Mashatu	**35**	Cederberg Wilderness Area
		36	Cape of Good Hope Nature Reserve
14	Zambezi/Victoria Falls NP	**37**	De Hoop Nature Reserve
15	Kazuma Pan NP	**38**	Karoo NP
16	Hwange NP	**39**	Tsitsikarna NP
17	Matobo NP	**40**	Addo Elephant NP
18	Chizarira NP	**41**	Mountain Zebra NP
19	Matusadona NP	**42**	uKhahlamba Drakensberg NP
20	Charara Safari Area	**43**	Hluhluwe/Umfolozi Game Reserve
21	Mana Pools NP	**44**	Tembe Elephant Park
22	Nyanga NP	**45**	The Greater St Lucia Wetlands Park

Bibliography

The following books are recommended for further reference.

Branch, Bill, *Field Guide to Snakes and Other Reptiles of Southern Africa* (3rd rev. edn). Struik Publishers, Cape Town, 1998.

Brown, L.H., Urban, E.L., Newman, K., Fry, C. H., & Keith, S., *The Birds of Africa* (vols 1–7). Academic Press, London, 1982–2004.

Chittenden, Hugh, *Roberts Bird Guide: A Comprehensive Field Guide to Over 950 Bird Species in Southern Africa*. John Voelcker Bird Book Fund, Cape Town, 2007.

Cramp, S., *et al.* (eds), *Handbook of the Birds of Europe, the Middle East and North Africa: The Birds of the Western Palearctic* (vols 1–9). Oxford University Press, Oxford, 1977–96.

Hockey, Phil, Dean, W. R. J., & Ryan, P. G., *Roberts Birds of Southern Africa* (7th rev. edn). John Voelcker Bird Book Fund, Cape Town, 2005.

Hosking, D., & Withers, M., *Wildlife of Kenya, Tanzania & Uganda* (Collins Traveller's Guide). HarperCollins, London, 2007.

Kingdon, Jonathan, *The Kingdon Field Guide to African Mammals*. Christopher Helm, London, 2003.

Lieberman, Dan, & Loon, Rael, *Hidden Wonders: The Small 5005 of Southern Africa – Insects, Spiders, Frogs and Reptiles*. Jacana Media Ltd, Johannesburg, 2006.

Macfadyen, Duncan Neil, & Compion, Shem, *A Landscape of Insects*. Jacana Media Ltd, Johannesburg, 2009.

Schiotz, A., *Treefrogs of Africa*. Edition Chimaira, Frankfurt, 1999.

Unwin, Mike, *Southern African Wildlife: A Visitor's Guide*. Bradt Travel Guides, Chalfont St. Peter, 2003.

Zimmerman, D. A., Turner, D. A., & Pearson, D. J., *Birds of Kenya & Northern Tanzania* (3rd rev. edn). Christopher Helm, London, 2005.

Parts of a Bird

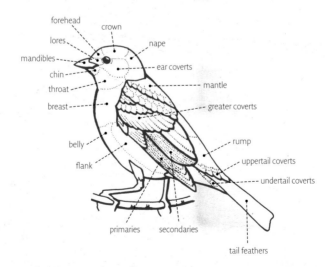

forehead
crown
lores
nape
mandibles
ear coverts
chin
throat
mantle
breast
greater coverts
belly
rump
flank
uppertail coverts
undertail coverts
primaries
secondaries
tail feathers

The Wildlife

Common Ostrich *Struthio camelus* Volstruis
It would be difficult to confuse this bird with any other African species. It is the world's largest bird, standing 2 to 2.5 m in height. It is a bird of open woodlands, scrub and desert plains. The male has mainly black plumage with white feathers forming the tail and the outer portion of the stunted wings. The head, neck and legs are grey/blue and are for the most part devoid of feathers. They have a stripe of red on the shins. The plumage of the female is a mixture of greys and browns, as are the head, neck and legs. A species that is often encountered in small groups. Several females will often lay eggs in the same nest and a 'major pair' will then undertake the raising of the brood. Incubation duties are undertaken by both the male and the female, the male usually doing the night shift.

African Penguin *Spheniscus demersus* Brilpikkewyn
The only resident species of penguin found in Southern Africa. The back, wings and face are black with a broad band of white running from the forehead around the side of the head and onto the breast; all of which is white, with the exception of a black band which extends from the front of the throat and runs down either side of the breast and onto the flanks. The lower breast and belly are also white. They nest on offshore islands as well as along some areas of mainland coast. They bray like donkeys and can be extremely noisy; as a result of this call they are often known as Jackass Penguins.

Little Grebe *Tachybaptus ruficollis* Kleindobbertjie
A common species found on areas of open water throughout the region, sometimes known as a Dabchick. The smallest grebe in Southern Africa with a rather dumpy appearance. The head is dark grey/brown with the sides and front of the neck being rufous/chestnut during the breeding season, much of this colour being lost during non-breeding periods. The back of the neck is dark grey/brown as are the back and wings. The rufous flanks and whitish rear end of the bird often have a fluffed-up appearance. There is a conspicuous pale gape patch at the base of the bill and the eyes are dark red.

Great Crested Grebe *Podiceps cristatus* Kuifkopdobbertjie
Found in areas of deep water where they live on fish, aquatic invertebrates and tadpoles. A large elegant grebe with a black head and crest, white cheeks and elongated ear coverts of rufous tipped with black. The longish neck is white at the front becoming brownish grey to the sides and rear. The back is brown and the flanks and tail, which have a fluffy appearance, are a mixture of brown and white. They are much paler during non-breeding periods. They have a most elegant courtship display, which often commences with head shaking leading to the pair treading water or paddling across the surface in unison.

Black-browed Albatross *Thalassarche melanophrys* Swartrugalbatros
The most common albatross to be found in coastal waters mainly during the winter months. A true ocean wanderer, travelling thousands of miles in search of food, often seen following fishing boats in the hope of gathering discarded items from the catch. A very large seabird with a wingspan up to 2.5 m. The plumage is mainly white on the body with grey on the hindneck becoming darker on the back and upper surface of the wing. The underwings are white, edged and tipped with black. They have a blackish eyebrow and an orange/yellow bill. Their numbers have been decreasing in recent years due mainly, it is thought, to the birds becoming accidental victims of long-line commercial fishing activities.

Shy Albatross *Thalassarche cauta* Bloubekalbatros
Even larger than the Black-browed Albatross this species is chiefly a winter visitor to coastal waters often coming closer to the shoreline than other species do. Its body is mainly white with a grey back, grey wings and a grey tail. The underside of the wings are white with a narrow dark grey border and wing tips. There is a distinctive black mark on the underside of the wing at a point where the wing and body join. They have a smudge of grey along the area of the eyebrow and a pale grey face. The bill is pale grey with a yellow tip. Like other albatross species there has been some reduction in numbers in recent years due possibly to the practices of the long-line fishing industry.

Southern Giant Petrel *Macronectes giganteus* Reusenellie

A bird of the open ocean, occasionally seen closer to shore, usually in the winter months. They often follow fishing vessels in search of discarded offal. They can also be found scavenging around seal colonies. A very large petrel, the size of a small albatross. There are two distinct forms, a light and a dark form. The dark form has grey/brown plumage which lightens around the area of the head and neck giving a mottled appearance. They generally become paler with age. The light form is almost entirely white in plumage with a varying amount of dark spots. Both forms have a light yellowish bill with a greenish tip. The eyes are usually pale but in some individuals can be dark brown.

Great-winged Petrel *Pterodroma macroptera* Langvlerkstormvoël

A visitor to African waters from where it takes squid, fish and crustaceans from the surface, mainly in the summer months. It will often attend trawlers and other fishing vessels to scavenge on any offal or other discards from the catch. A large petrel with uniform dark brown plumage, long wings which have a distinctive backward sweep and a large head with a short black bill. They often show a smudge of white around the base of the lower section of the bill. They travel vast distances and breed on islands throughout the southern oceans, as far afield as the northern coasts of New Zealand.

Antarctic Prion *Pachyptila desolata* Antarktiese Walvisvoël

This species is thought to be the commonest prion in South African waters, particularly in the south and west. A wanderer of the open oceans, they are often found close to the shoreline during periods of strong onshore winds. They will regularly follow fishing vessels in search of discards. They can often be found in large flocks. The plumage on the upperside is predominantly pale grey with a flush of blue. They have a prominent white eyebrow, a smudge of black from the rear of the eye across the ear coverts, with a white throat, breast and belly. A black line runs from the wing tips, along the front edge of the wing to the carpal joint, from where it sweeps across the wing to the inner, rear edge. There is a broad black band on the end of the tail. The bill is grey/blue.

White-chinned Petrel *Procellaria aequinoctialis* Bassiaan

A common non-breeding visitor to the southern and western oceans. Will often follow all manner of shipping, particularly fishing boats in search of fish scraps and any other discarded foodstuffs. They have a body length of around 55 cm and are smooth, powerful flyers. They also show a bold aggressive nature, squabbling with other species when food is found. The entire plumage is dark brown with the exception of a prominent white chin/throat patch. The underside of the primaries can have a silvery sheen. They have a wedge shaped tail and the slender bill is pale whitish/yellow.

Cory's Shearwater *Calonectris diomedea* Geelbekpylstormvoël

A relatively common summer visitor to the western waters of the region, quite often in large flocks. They feed on fish, crustaceans, offal and discards from fishing vessels; they also follow whales and ocean predators from where they scavenge food scraps. They are able to dive to depths of up to 15 m in pursuit of prey items. The plumage of the upperside is brown/grey, while the underside is white with the exception of the wing tips and edges which are bordered in brown. The bill is pale yellow with a dark tip.

Great Shearwater *Puffinus gravis* Grootpylstormvoël

A species that breeds on South Atlantic islands from where they migrate to waters off the west and south coasts of our region arriving in April/May. Like other closely related species they are attracted to the rich pickings found in the vicinity of fishing vessels where they often gather in sizeable flocks. They will often plunge dive for food. They can often be found gathered in large flocks, sitting on the water surface, resting. The plumage of the upperside is mainly brown, with the exception of a prominent white band at the base of the tail. The head is dark brown, the chin and throat are white which extends around the neck to form a collar towards the nape. The undersides are white with the wing tips and edges bordered with brown. The central belly area has a variable dark patch and the flanks are smudged with brown. The underside of the tail is brown.

Sooty Shearwater *Puffinus griseus* Malbaartjie

A common species in southern and western waters throughout the year, particularly during the winter months, when they become one of the most numerous seabirds in our region. They are often found out at sea in large flocks, where they readily mix with other species of shearwaters. They quite often feed from a swimming position, diving under the water and pursuing fish, squid and sand eels etc. They may also plunge dive from a flying position, usually arresting their dive momentarily just prior to breaking the water surface. They forage regularly behind fishing vessels for any discards. As its name suggests the plumage is almost entirely sooty brown, the only exception being the area of the underwing coverts which appear paler. They have a long blackish bill and dark brown eyes. The sexes are alike and juveniles look similar to adults.

Manx Shearwater *Puffinus puffinus* Swartbekpylstormvoël

This bird can be found in western and southern waters often associating with other shearwater species, particularly when feeding on discards from fishing vessels. They use several different feeding methods when at sea: they surface feed, taking shoaling fish close to the surface, and they often plunge dive and also engage in pursuit fishing to depths of several metres. The upperside of the bird is dark brown, while the chin, throat, cheeks, breast and belly are white. The underside of the wings are white, bordered in dark brown and with brown wing tips. The bill is slaty grey with a dark tip, the eyes are brown, the legs are pink and the feet are pale with a flush of yellow. The sexes are similar.

Red-tailed Tropicbird *Phaethon rubricauda* Rooipylstert

The most common tropicbird in the region, breeding along the coast of Mozambique and in colonies on oceanic islands, they may be encountered along the eastern coast and out into the waters of the Pacific Ocean. They often feed far out to sea on fish, squid and other sea organisms by surface feeding or diving. The plumage is predominately white with a flush of pink. They have black eyes and a black eyebrow smudge and the primaries are edged with black. The white tail has a long central red streamer, the bill is red and the legs and feet are black.

Wilson's Storm Petrel *Oceanites oceanicus* Gewone Stormswael

A small seabird species having a body length of about 18 cm and a wingspan of about 42 cm. Found singularly or in small flocks throughout the year in waters to the west and south. They are an extremely gregarious species being one of the commonest petrels in the region. They scavenge from fishing vessels but usually stay well clear of other larger species. They have a direct flight, gliding and zig-zagging across the water surface, hovering with their feet daintily paddling on the water surface when feeding. The plumage is almost entirely black with the exception of the very prominent white rump. The white extends onto the flanks and the under tail coverts. The tail is square, the legs are black and project beyond the tail when the bird is in normal flight. The feet are black with some yellow visible on the webbing.

European Storm Petrel *Hydrobates pelagicus* Europese Stormswael

The smallest petrel in the region. A common summer visitor in southern and western waters, particularly off the coast of Namibia. They can be seen in large flocks when feeding in the wake of fishing vessels. They have a very buoyant flight, gliding over the water surface, and when food is located they hover with wings raised and feet pattering on the water surface. The plumage is almost entirely black with the exception of a prominent white rump, extending on to the flanks and the undertail coverts. The upperwing coverts are faintly edged with white and the underwing coverts are similarly marked but more pronounced. The tail is not quite as square as Wilson's Storm Petrel, the bill is black, the eyes are dark and the legs and feet are black.

Great White Pelican *Pelecanus onocrotalus* Witpelikaan

A bird of lakes, estuaries and other types of open water both alkaline and saline. Fairly common in areas with suitable habitat. A very gregarious species found in large flocks, spending much of their time bathing and preening. They often fish in small flocks of about a dozen birds, forming themselves into an arc shape and swimming forward. Approximately every 20 seconds they all plunge their heads beneath the surface towards the centre of the arc. They seem to fish mainly in the early morning and the late afternoon. They are heavy birds, weighing around 12 kg, and usually need the aid of hot-air thermals to fly from place to place. The plumage is almost entirely pure white often with a flush of pink. The primary flight feathers are black, the tail is white and the large bill is yellow with a large pouch. The face is devoid of feathers and shows as pink skin, the eyes are dark brown and the legs and feet are yellowish pink.

Pink-backed Pelican *Pelecanus rufescens* Kleinpelikaan

Locally common in the north and east of our region, usually found in flocks on rivers, lakes and marshes. Smaller and generally greyer in appearance than the Great White Pelican. The entire plumage is greyish white, the face, throat and underparts are white. Occasionally the entire plumage has a flush of pink. The primary flight feathers are black, the bill is greyish yellow with a pinkish pouch and a small area of featherless pink skin is visible around the eyes. The legs and feet are reddish pink. The sexes are similar.

Cape Cormorant *Phalacrocorax capensis* Trekduiker

A resident, locally abundant species found along the whole of the west coast and from the Cape east to the Durban area. A very gregarious bird, often seen flying in long lines over the sea. They often feed in large groups, diving from the swimming position and pursuing their prey underwater. They nest in large colonies on cliff ledges and on flat ground on offshore islands. The plumage is almost entirely black with a sheen of blue and the edges of the wing feathers are metallic green. At the base of the bill is a yellow/orange patch, the bill, legs and feet are black and the eyes are grey/blue.

White-breasted Cormorant *Phalacrocorax lucidus* Witborsduiker

The largest of the African cormorants. A common bird throughout much of the region in both freshwater and marine habitats. They are usually encountered in large flocks. When feeding they pursue fish by swimming underwater, returning to the surface to swallow their catch. Their plumage is not fully waterproof and following bouts of fishing the plumage becomes waterlogged. They are then forced to dry out and can be seen standing for long periods with their wings open in a heraldic posture. The plumage is mainly dull brown/black with a white chin, throat and upper breast. They have a crest of erectile feathers on the crown and a white patch on the flanks during the breeding season. An area around the eye and the base of the upper mandible is yellow, the bill is grey at the base darkening towards the tip. The eyes are green and the legs and feet are black.

Cape Gannet *Morus capensis* Witmalgas

Fairly common in coastal areas throughout much of our region. They gather in large flocks when good fishing is available. On sighting food up to a metre or so below the surface, they fold their wings and plunge dive into the water at a steep angle. To witness a large flock feeding in this fashion is a truly memorable sight. Many hundreds can gather around fishing vessels as the catch is being landed. They breed in vast colonies along the coasts of Namibia and South Africa as well as on offshore islands. A very sleek bird with predominately pure white plumage with a yellow head and upper neck. The primary flight feathers are black, as are the secondaries and the tail. They have a pale cream eye, a greyish blue bill and black legs and feet.

African Darter *Anhinga rufa* Slanghalsvoël
A reasonably common bird frequenting freshwater lakes, swamps, rivers and marshes. They feed by swimming underwater and stabbing their prey with their spear-like bill. When fishing they often swim with just their head and long thin neck above the surface. Unlike most waterbirds their plumage contains no oil and they soon become waterlogged when fishing. As a result of this they are often to be seen perched in the sun with their wings spread open, drying off the feathers. The plumage is mainly dark brown/black. The head, crown and rear of the neck are black, the sides of the neck are a rich chestnut. The long, sharp bill is pale yellow/green, the eyes are golden yellow and the legs and feet are greyish brown.

Reed Cormorant *Phalacrocorax africanus* Reitduiker
A common resident in areas of freshwater lakes, rivers and swamps as well as in coastal regions. A small long-tailed cormorant found alone or in small groups, usually perching on overhanging branches and half submerged boulders. They feed mainly on fish, frogs and aquatic insects. The overall plumage colour is black with the feathers of the mantle, back, rump and wings being pale brown edged with black. An area of bare skin around the eyes is yellow/orange; the eyes themselves are ruby red. The bill is yellow and the legs and feet are black. The sexes are similar.

Goliath Heron *Ardea goliath* Reusereier
A widespread, locally common species found in lakes, rivers and other damp habitats. The largest of the world's herons, standing about 1.5 m tall. They are usually solitary and rarely wander far from water. The back, wings and tail are slate grey. The head is rufous as are the sides and the back of the neck. The front of the neck has a white band streaked with black running from the throat to the breast. The bill is grey on the upper mandible and yellow on the lower. The eyes are yellow and the legs and feet are dark grey/black. The sexes are similar.

Greater Frigatebird *Fregata minor* Grootfregatvoël
A rare visitor to the east coast. A very large bird with a wingspan in excess of 2 m. Almost unmistakeable in flight, with long, pointed wings bending backwards sharply at the carpal joints. The tail is very long and is deeply forked. They feed by taking items from the water surface, but will also harass other seabirds mercilessly until they disgorge their last meal. The plumage is black with a sheen of metallic bronze/green on the crown and the mantle. The males have an inflatable throat sac, which they inflate on the breeding grounds to attract females. The bill is blue/grey, the eyes are dark brown and the feet are red. Females are duller and have a grey throat, which merges into the white breast.

Grey Heron *Ardea cinerea* Bloureier
A common resident throughout the region in all but the most arid of habitats. They are usually encountered singularly or in small groups wading in shallow water taking fish, frogs, reptiles, crabs and other aquatic life forms. They will often stand motionless for long periods in the hope of ambushing prey. The plumage is mainly grey in colour with a black band running along the line of the eyebrow to the nape from where several plumes emerge. There is also a broken black line extending from the front of the throat down the entire length of the neck. They also have black shoulder patches which extend on to the sides of the breast. The belly is black as are the primary and secondary flight feathers. The bill and eyes are yellow and the legs and feet are a yellowish brown.

Black-headed Heron *Ardea melanocephala* Swartkopreier
A widespread, locally common resident found in damp grasslands, marshes and the edges of rivers and lakes. They feed on insects, frogs, reptiles, small mammals and birds up to the size of doves. The plumage is mainly slate grey with the head and the hindneck black. The tail and the primary and secondary flight feathers are dark slate grey. The upper portion of the bill is dark grey/black and the lower portion is yellowish green. The eyes are yellow, becoming red in the breeding season. The legs and feet are black. The sexes are alike.

Purple Heron *Ardea purpurea* Rooireier

A locally common resident frequenting lake and river margins and other damp, swampy habitats. Outside of the breeding season they are generally solitary, wading the shallow reed-fringed margins of lakes and rivers for fish, lizards, snakes, frogs and small birds and mammals. The plumage is similar to that of the Goliath Heron but the Purple Heron is barely half the size. The back, wings and tail are slate grey. There is a black line running from the forehead along the top of the head and on down the nape to the hindneck. A line also runs from the gape under the eye, across the lower face and on to and down the full length of the neck. The throat and front of the neck is white the latter edged with broken black lines. There are two plumes which emerge from the nape. There are shoulder patches of rufous as well as a deep rufous breast and belly. The primary and secondary flight feathers are black. The bill is deep yellow, the eyes are yellow and the legs and feet are dark brown, the soles of the feet are yellow.

Squacco Heron *Ardeola ralloides* Ralreier

A locally common resident around lakes, ponds, along rivers and in areas of swamps and marshes. A small dumpy little heron, usually solitary but suitable areas of habitat will find them in loosely associated flocks. They usually feed by slowly stalking in shallow water or vegetation along the water's edge, taking fish, crabs, frogs and a large variety of insects. The head and neck are buff streaked with black, brown and grey. The mantle and scapulars are dull buff. The tail and wings are white. The lower breast and belly are white. The bill is greenish yellow, the eyes are yellow and the legs and feet are yellowish green. During the breeding season they develop long white plumes with black edging from the nape and plumes of buff feathers from the mantle which lay over the wings and the tail. The streaking on the head and neck is also replaced with white feathers. The bill becomes blue with a black tip and the legs become redder. The sexes are similar.

Black Heron *Egretta ardesiaca* Swartreier

A bird of swamps, lake edges and marshes in the north and eastern parts of our region. Usually encountered in small to medium sized groups of up to fifty individuals, but quite often they can be solitary. They have a most unusual method of fishing, by making a canopy of their wings to shade the water surface. The reason for this behaviour is not certain, the canopy eliminates reflections making it easier for the bird to see below the water surface and the shade provided may attract small fish and other creatures. The plumage is entirely dark blue/black. They have plumes on the crown, the neck and the mantle. The bill is black, the eyes are yellow, the legs are black and the feet are yellow. The sexes are similar.

Black-crowned Night Heron *Nycticorax nycticorax* Gewone Nagreier

A common species often overlooked due to it being largely nocturnal. They inhabit lakes, rivers and marshes and spend much of the day roosting in waterside vegetation, sometimes in large flocks. The plumage is black, grey and white. The head, nape, mantle and scapulars are black. There are two or three long plumes, which extend from the crown during the breeding season. The wings, back and tail are mid grey. The face, neck, throat, breast and belly are white. The bill is grey, turning black in the breeding season. The eyes are ruby red and the legs and feet are yellow. The sexes are similar. Immature birds are dark brown, streaked and speckled with white and buff. The bill is orange/yellow and the legs and feet are dull green/yellow.

Green-backed Heron *Butorides striata* Groenrugreier

A common resident found mainly in the north and east of our region. A solitary heron encountered in mangroves, in estuaries, in vegetation along riverbanks and around lake edges. A small, dumpy heron that hunts by means of stalking along the water's edge or from a perch overhanging the water. They feed on fish, dragonflies, crabs, grasshoppers, frogs and reptiles. The plumage is generally dark with the head and nape black with a sheen of metallic green. There is a small white patch on the cheek and the neck is grey. The wings are glossy green and the back and tail are dark grey. The upper central part of the breast is rufous, the remainder of the breast and belly are grey. The upper section of the bill is grey and the lower section is yellowish, the eyes are yellow, the legs and feet are yellow with grey on the shins. The sexes are similar.

nmature

Cattle Egret *Bubulcus ibis* Veereier

The commonest of all Southern Africa's egrets. They are to be found throughout the region mainly in areas of open grassland and farmland, but they also favour the surrounds of lakes, marshes and floodplains. Compared to other egrets they are of short stocky build and are the smallest white-plumaged egrets in southern Africa. They readily associate with man and can be seen in large numbers following cattle herds, taking insects disturbed by the grazing herds. They will also follow herds of wild animals and are often found with Elephant and Buffalo herds. Quite often they will be seen perched on the backs of animals from where they can feed on ticks and gain a better vantage point. They nest in large colonies which are usually a mixture of breeding waterbirds. The plumage is white, often with a hint of buff on the crown and the nape. The bill and eyes are yellow. The legs and feet are yellowish. During the breeding season the feathers of the crown and nape become a rich buff colour and long ornamental plumes appear from the mantle and almost reach the tail. Smaller plumes appear from the foreneck and the breast.

Little Egret *Egretta garzetta* Kleinwitreier

A common resident species found in most water habitats both coastal and inland. Found throughout the region with the exception of the Namibian Deserts. Usually solitary but towards roosting times can gather into large flocks. They feed by walking or even running through shallow water in a seemingly random fashion, picking items from close to the water surface. They will also stand for long periods almost motionless, waiting for prey to wander within reach. They feed mainly on fish, frogs, shrimps and insects. They will often associate with man, gathering around fishing vessels as they unload their catches. They will also occasionally follow cattle herds, snapping up insects disturbed by the hooves of the animals as they graze. They nest in large colonies in trees and bushes; quite often these colonies are made up of several different species of egrets and herons. The plumage is all white. The bill is black, the eyes are yellow, the legs are black and the feet are greenish/yellow. There is a dark morph of Little Egret which has slate grey plumage. During the breeding season two or three plumes appear from the nape, while others appear from the foreneck, the breast and the mantle.

Great Egret *Ardea alba* Grootwitreier

A resident and winter visitor to areas of open water, swamps and marshes as well as coastal habitats. The largest of the egrets, having slender build with a long neck and long legs. Usually encountered singly or in small groups. They are active by day when they can be seen wading slowly through the water in search of fish, frogs, aquatic insects and small mammals. They may also be seen standing almost motionless for long periods in an upright position with their head and beak bent over the water waiting for prey items to wander within striking distance of the sharp, spear-like bill. The plumage is all white. There is a small black line which runs from the gape to just behind the eye. The bill is yellow in the non-breeding season becoming black during breeding times. The eyes are yellow and the long legs and feet are black. During the breeding season they develop long plumes from the scapulars which extend beyond the tail. Plumes also appear from the upper breast and foreneck.

Yellow-billed Egret *Egretta intermedia* Geelbekwitreier

A locally common species found in areas of freshwater lakes, marshes and swamps as well as in coastal habitats. They can be encountered singly or in scattered groups of up to 50 birds. At a distance it can be difficult to distinguish from the Great Egret, but it has a shorter bill, a thicker and shorter neck and shorter legs. They feed by slowly wading in shallow water, lunging forward when prey is sighted. Their prey consists mainly of fish, frogs and aquatic and terrestrial insects. They nest in large colonies usually in trees at the water's edge or in reed beds. These breeding colonies are usually a mixture of egret species. The plumage is all white. The bill is yellow becoming redder in the breeding season. The eyes are yellow becoming redder in the breeding season and the legs and feet are yellow on the tibia and black from the tarsal joint to the tip of the toes.

Little Bittern *Ixobrychus minutus* Kleinrietreier

Two populations of this species occur in Southern Africa, the resident population *I.m.payesii* and *I.m.minutes* which is a non-breeding winter-visiting population from the far north. A small thick set bittern and although secretive can be found in swamps, marshes and reedbeds. They feed by perching on reed stems or any vegetation overhanging the water surface, or by standing in shallow water and waiting patiently for prey items to move within reach. They are most active towards dusk. They feed mainly on fish, shrimps, frogs and aquatic insects. The plumage of the male has the crown, nape, scapulars and back black with a slight sheen of green. The face, neck, breast and belly are whitish buff. The wing coverts are creamy buff edged with white and the underwings are white. The resident population *I.m.payesii* shows rufous on the neck. The bill is greenish yellow, the eyes are yellow and the legs and feet are dull greenish yellow. The plumage pattern of the female is similar to the male but duller with the underparts streaked with dark buff and brown. The wing pattern is less striking and the wing coverts are browner. Juveniles are much like females but have more streaking on the underparts.

Dwarf Bittern *Ixobrychus sturmii* Dwergrietreier

An uncommon bittern of lakes, pools, rivers, streams, flooded grasslands and other wetland habitats fringed with reedbeds, trees and bushes in the north and east of our region. This is the smallest bittern in Southern Africa and is generally a very secretive species. They feed on fish, frogs and aquatic insects. They are usually to be found singly or in pairs and are for the most part nocturnal. The male has the crown, nape, mantle, back, tail and wings uniform bluish slate grey. The underwings are also bluish slate grey. The throat and breast are pale buff, heavily streaked with black. The belly is a darker buff heavily streaked with black. The relatively short bill is dark greenish yellow, the eyes are reddish and the legs are brown to the front and yellow to the rear. The feet are greenish yellow. The female is similar to the male but the plumage is paler.

Rufous-bellied Heron *Ardeola rufiventris* Rooipensreier

An uncommon resident in northern and eastern regions of Southern Africa. They are usually solitary and can be found in flooded grasslands, along the edges of lakes, streams and in reedbeds. They feed during the day as well as at night. They are thought to be partially migratory moving to and from areas of seasonal flooding. They feed on fish, amphibians and aquatic insects. When not feeding they often roost in trees far from water. The plumage of the male is dark slaty black on the head, neck, breast, back and wing coverts. The shoulders, belly, rump and tail are a rich chestnut red. The primary flight feathers are black. The bill is yellow/orange-red with a dark tip. The eyes are yellow and the legs and feet are orange yellow which contrasts strongly with the dark undersides when the bird is seen in flight. The plumage of the female is generally duller and lighter than the male, with a browner chin, throat and neck. The female also shows a white stripe from the chin to the foreneck. Juveniles are similar to females but have streaks of brown on the sides of the head, neck and breast.

Hamerkop *Scopus umbretta* Hamerkop

A very common resident throughout the region, frequenting wetland habitats usually singly or in pairs. It is a bird considered by many local people to be an ill omen and to have magical powers. These beliefs have given the birds a great deal of protection. They feed mainly on amphibians, fish and insects but have also been known to scavenge from local villages. They usually feed by standing in shallow water, occasionally stirring the bottom with their feet to dislodge any aquatic creatures that may provide a meal. They build enormous nests, usually in trees by the waterside. The finished nests can be as much as 1.6 m across and contain around ten thousand sticks. It is almost impossible to mistake this bird for any other. It has a heavy bill and a backward-flowing crest which gives the bird a distinctive hammer-shaped profile from which it gets its name. The plumage is a uniform pale brown, a little paler on the chin and throat. The primary flight feathers and the tail are a darker brown. The bill is black, the eyes are brown and the legs and feet are black. The sexes are similar, the male is slightly larger.

African Openbill   *Anastomus lamelligerus*   Oopbekooievaar
Locally common in northern and eastern regions of Southern Africa, they inhabit wetland areas in open country. They feed mainly on snails and mussels. The bill is highly developed to deal with such difficult prey. The top mandible is straight but the lower mandible is curved to such an extent that a gap between the two is easily visible. This adaptation makes easy work of opening molluscs. They usually travel in flocks but will disperse when feeding. The plumage is entirely black with a sheen of both green and purple. Feathers on the breast and mantle are long, giving them a loose, shaggy appearance. The bill is black at the tip becoming pale at the base. The eyes are brown, the legs and feet are black. The sexes are similar.

Black Stork   *Ciconia nigra*   Grootswartooievaar
An uncommon resident over much of the region. Usually found singly or in pairs in wetland habitats in highlands, where they feed on fish, crabs, reptiles, small mammals and nestling birds. When feeding they walk about slowly in shallow water stabbing at prey. They are most active by daylight and roost in large trees or on cliff faces. The head, neck, breast, back, wings and tail are black with a sheen of green and purple. The belly is white. They have a red orbital eye ring, the eyes themselves are dark brown and the legs and feet are red.

Yellow-billed Stork   *Mycteria ibis*   Nimmersat
Locally common in northern and eastern regions of Southern Africa, usually found singly or in pairs in a variety of wetland habitats, including freshwater lakes, coastal mudflats and flooded grasslands. They feed in shallow water, mainly for fish, frogs and aquatic insects. They have a most unusual method of catching prey; they place their bill in to the water almost to the nostril and with the bill slightly open they stir the muddy bottom with their foot; any aquatic creature that is disturbed is quickly despatched by snapping shut the bill. For the most part the plumage is white, often with a flush of pink. The wings and tail are black. The forward portion of the head is devoid of feathers, the bare skin being red in colour. The bill is yellow, the eyes are dark brown and the legs and feet are red. The sexes are similar, the female being slightly smaller.

Abdim's Stork   *Ciconia abdimii*   Kleinswartooievaar
An abundant, locally common species which breeds in East Africa and migrates south in November, staying in southern parts until returning north in April. They inhabit areas of open grasslands, cultivated farmland and pastures, where they feed on a variety of large insects including locusts, grasshoppers, beetles and other large insects. A small stork with predominantly black plumage with a sheen of purple. The breast, belly and underwings are white, the wings and tail are black with a greenish sheen. The bill is a dull greenish grey with a hint of red at the tip. The bare skin of the face is blue/grey, the eyes are yellow with a red orbital ring. The legs are dull greenish grey with red tarsal joints. The feet are red. The sexes are similar, females being slightly smaller

Woolly-necked Stork   *Ciconia episcopus*   Wolnekooievaar
An uncommon species found in the northern and extreme eastern parts of our region. A bird of both marine and freshwater habitats. During the summer months the populations are boosted in Namibia and Botswana by the arrival of non-breeding migrants from the north. They feed in swamps, ponds and floodplains taking large insects, fish, frogs and reptiles. The plumage of the breast, back and wings is black with a sheen of bluish purple. The face is white smudged with black. The belly is white. The most distinguishing feature is the neck which is white and as its name suggests has a woolly appearance. The bill is black, the eyes are blood red and the legs and feet are black.

White Stork   *Ciconia ciconia*   Witooievaar
A small population is resident year-round but numbers swell as migrants arrive from the north during the winter months. They can be found on areas of open grassland feeding on a multitude of large insects, reptiles and small mammals. The plumage is white on the head, neck, mantle, wing coverts, breast, belly and tail. The flight feathers are black. The bill is red, the eyes are dull red and the legs and feet are black. The sexes are similar.

Saddle-billed Stork *Ephippiorhynchus senegalensis* Saalbekooievaar

The tallest of Africa's storks, found in aquatic habitats in open country. They usually forage alone or in pairs, feeding on fish, frogs, small reptiles and some small mammals. Although they do not migrate, they do move from region to region as water levels fluctuate. The plumage is striking with the head and neck black and the mantle, breast belly and flight feathers white. The wing coverts, scapulars and tail are black with a sheen of green. The heavy, slightly upturned bill is bright red with a black band across the centre. There is also a yellow frontal shield at the base of the upper mandible. The eyes are dark brown in the male and bright yellow in the female. The legs are black with red feet and a red band encircling the tarsal joint.

Marabou Stork *Leptoptilos crumeniferus* Maraboe

A fairly common resident throughout a wide variety of habitats. They will scavenge from village and town rubbish dumps and from the kills of big cats and other predators. They will feed on pretty well any animal matter, including small mammals and birds, fish, frogs, and they have even been known to take and eat flamingos. A large heavily built stork with a bare neck and neck pouch which the males can inflate to attract females. The head is dull red mottled with black spots and smudges, the neck is buff and the breast and belly are white. The wings and tail are grey/black and the primary flight feathers are grey/black edged with white. The large bill is buff with dark mottling, the eyes are brown and the legs and feet are dark grey.

Greater Flamingo *Phoenicopterus ruber* Grootflamink

A locally common resident throughout Southern Africa, usually encountered in large flocks, often numbering thousands, on lakes, saltpans, tidal mudflats and in other freshwater and saline areas. They feed on small invertebrates and algae which they filter through the bill in shallow water. The largest of the flamingos, standing up to 1.6 m in height, they are unmistakable. In flight they have the head and neck outstretched to the front and their long legs stretched out to the rear. The plumage is predominantly white with a flush of pink. The wing coverts are bright scarlet pink and the flight feathers are black. The bill is pale pink with a black tip, the eyes are pale yellow and the legs and feet are bright pink. The sexes are similar.

Lesser Flamingo *Phoenicopterus minor* Kleinflamink

A locally common resident over much of the region. They inhabit large alkaline lakes, saltpans and occasionally coastal estuaries. They are rarely encountered in areas of freshwater except when bathing or drinking. They are extremely gregarious and are often encountered in their thousands. They breed in large colonies, building cone-shaped nests of mud and soda crystals in inaccessible areas way out in alkaline lakes. They feed mainly on microscopic algae which they filter through their highly specialised bill. Adults can be distinguished from the Greater Flamingo by their smaller size, just a metre high, by their darker rose pink plumage and by the dark blood red bill which has a black tip. The eyes are pale yellow and the legs and feet are bright red. The sexes are similar, but females are slightly smaller and lighter in colour.

African Spoonbill *Platalea alba* Lepelaar

A common bird in aquatic areas and, due to the spoon-shaped bill, is almost impossible to misidentify. Quite often found in groups of 6 to 30 wading through shallow water and feeding with a sweeping motion of the bill from side to side. They feed on small fish and aquatic insects. They breed in nests placed in reedbeds or in trees overhanging water; there are sometimes up to 250 pairs in a breeding colony. Other species such as cormorants, herons and darters often build in the same colony. The plumage is predominantly white with a hint of grey. The forehead and face are rich pink, the large bill is grey/pink, the eyes are pale blue and the legs and feet are rich pink. The sexes are similar, the male being slightly larger than the female.

Southern Bald Ibis *Geronticus calvus* Kalkoenibis

An uncommon resident favouring highland grasslands, cultivated fields, dry riverbeds and rocky slopes, often seen feeding on arid ground almost devoid of vegetation. They are usually encountered in loose flocks and take grasshoppers, crickets, beetles, ants, lizards, fish and a wealth of other creatures. They roost at night on ledges or in trees in groups of up to 150 individuals, often with Cattle Egrets and Sacred Ibis. They breed in colonies of up to 60 pairs or more in caves and on cliff ledges. The bare head is red and the bare face is pink/white. The nape and neck are loosely feathered, giving the appearance of a ruff, with metallic green and purple feathers. The rest of the plumage is dark metallic green with a flush of purple. The wing coverts show a hint of glossy copper and violet. The bill is red, the eyes are red and the legs and feet are also red.

African Sacred Ibis *Threskiornis aethiopicus* Skoorsteenveër

A common resident in all areas other than deserts. They are to be found mainly in areas of freshwater and cultivated farmland. They are quite gregarious and can be found feeding by probing in soft ground for worms, molluscs, crustaceans and amphibians as well as for surface-dwelling insects such as grasshoppers, beetles and crickets. Large numbers can be seen roosting in trees along river courses and lake edges. They also breed in colonies holding up to 2,000 pairs, in trees or on the ground in isolated river islands. An almost unmistakable large white bird with a long decurved bill. The plumage is predominately white, but with the unfeathered head and neck black. They have black scapular plumes that extend down the back and the tail. The bill is dark grey at the base, becoming black towards the tip, the eyes are dark brown and the legs and feet are black. The sexes are similar.

Hadeda Ibis *Bostrychia hagedash* Hadeda

A common species, particularly in the east of our region. They favour wet grasslands and wooded streams running through areas of open savannah. They also inhabit urban parks and residential gardens. They feed on large insects as well as reptiles and earthworms. They are found in pairs during the breeding season and in small daytime flocks of around 30 birds during non-breeding times. They normally roost in flocks, quite often mixing with herons and other ibis species. A very vocal species, particularly as they leave and return to roosts. Usually when in flight they emit a loud, raucous 'haa-daa-daa' – hence its name). They nest as solitary pairs in trees and bushes, usually close to water. The plumage is generally brown with metallic sheens of purple and green on the mantle and back as well as on the primary and secondary flight feathers and the wing coverts. They show a pale curved line from the base of the bill to the ear coverts. The sexes are similar.

Glossy Ibis *Plegadis falcinellus* Glansibis

An uncommon resident species inhabiting lakes, marshes and ponds as well as coastal lagoons. They are usually gregarious and in flocks of up to 30 birds, feeding by probing the muddy water margins with the decurved bill searching out worms, leeches, fish, frogs and insects. They nest in reedbeds and other waterside vegetation, often with other waterbird species. A small, slender ibis with the head, neck and shoulder areas dull, dark chestnut, the remainder of the plumage being a mixture of metallic greens and purples. The bill is brownish grey, the eyes are rich brown and the legs and feet are dark brown. The sexes are similar.

White-faced Duck *Dendrocygna viduata* Nonnetjie-eend

A very common resident found in lakes, large rivers, floodplains and many other wetland habitats. They are very gregarious during non-breeding seasons. They emit a continuous whistling sound. A long-necked duck with an upright stance, they feed mainly for a couple of hours after dawn and for a couple of hours prior to sundown. They feed by diving, surface feeding being most unusual. They have the crown, nape and hindneck feathers black, the forehead the face and the upper throat are white. The lower neck and upper breast are chestnut. The breast and flanks are barred with white and brown and the underbelly are dark brown. The wing coverts are mid-brown edged with white and the flight feathers are brown. The bill is black, the eyes are brown and the legs and feet are mid grey. The sexes are similar, the females being slightly smaller.

Yellow-billed Duck *Anas undulata* Geelbekeend

A common bird in areas of open water, coastal lagoons and meandering rivers. They feed mainly on aquatic creatures and vegetation in varying flock sizes from just a few too many hundreds, mainly in the early morning and late afternoon, swimming with their head and bill underwater or by up-ending, searching out plant matter and small aquatic animals. The overall plumage is blackish grey, the feathers being edged with pale grey giving the effect of streaking. The speculum is iridescent green. The very distinctive bill is yellow with a black central patch on the upper mandible. The eyes are yellow and the legs and feet are dull reddish brown.

Fulvous Duck *Dendrocygna bicolor* Fluiteend

A fairly common resident species in the east and north. A duck with an upright stance, quite gregarious outside of the breeding season. Found on inland waters with aquatic vegetation. They are generally crepuscular in feeding habits, spending much of the day preening and resting on the water's edge. They feed normally by dabbling in shallow waters but will also up-end in deeper water, eating seeds, fruits and aquatic plant life. The plumage has the forehead and crown rufous brown with a stripe of brown running from the crest to the mantle. The remainder of the neck, face and throat is buff brown with some white striations on the upper neck. The back and scapulars are dark brown with the feathers edged with buff brown. The upper tail coverts are white and the tail is black. The underparts are buff, becoming richer on the belly. From the flanks emerge long feathers/plumes of buff edged with white. The bill is grey, the eyes are brown and the legs and feet are greyish/black. The sexes are similar.

Cape Teal *Anas capensis* Teeleend

A reasonably common duck in areas with shallow lagoons, saltpans and tidal mudflats. Usually encountered in pairs or in small groups feeding by up-ending in search of aquatic creatures, seeds and vegetation. A small delicate-looking duck with the head and neck ash grey finely speckled with brown. The breast, flanks and underparts are ash grey with the central portion of the feathers dark brown, giving a spotted appearance. The wing feathers are brown edged with ash grey and the speculum is an iridescent green. The bill is pink towards the base, blending to grey at the tip. The eyes are pale orange brown and the legs and feet are pale orange. The sexes are similar.

Comb Duck *Sarkidiornis melanotos* Knobbeleend

A fairly common rather goose-like duck of the northern regions, frequenting lakes, ponds, marshes, floodplains and lagoons. The males are easily identified with a large black protuberance or comb on the upper mandible. The comb is much reduced in size during non-breeding times and is absent in the female. The head, neck and breast are white with a flush of yellow, the face and neck being randomly spotted with black. The underparts are greyish white. The back and wings are black with a wash of bluish green. The eyes are dark brown and the legs and feet are greyish brown.

African Black Duck *Anas sparsa* Swarteend

A common resident in east, southern and south western regions, where they prefer fast flowing rivers and streams. The body plumage is almost entirely black with just a little spotting on the back. The speculum is blue, bordered with bands of white and black, being most visible when the wing is fully spread in flight. The bill is grey with a hint of pink, the eyes are dark brown and the legs and feet are dull orange. The sexes are similar.

Northern Pintail *Anas acuta* Pylsterteend

An uncommon visitor to the northern regions, inhabiting coastal estuaries and inland waters. A most attractive long-necked duck with a long pointed tail, features that make it almost impossible to confuse with other duck species. The head, face and hindneck are chocolate brown with a vertical stripe running from the ear to the white of the neck. The breast and underparts are white with a wash of grey. The mantle and wing coverts are pale grey with fine dark grey vermiculations. The scapular feathers are elongated and have black centres with white edging. The bill is slate grey, the eyes are brown and the legs and feet are grey.

Garganey *Anas querquedula* Somereend

An uncommon vagrant to the northern region, usually found in shallow bodies of freshwater, they generally avoid coastal habitats. They feed by swimming with their heads underwater or by up-ending to reach aquatic plant material as well as small creatures. Outside of the breeding season they gather together into small groups. The head, neck and breast are whitish with fine dense mottling in dark brown. The male has a distinctive white patch curving from the front of the eye around the ear to the hindneck. The lower breast and belly are white marked with dark vermiculations. The scapulars are elongated with dark centres and paler edges and hang loosely over the flanks. The bill is greyish, the eyes are dark brown and the legs and feet are grey/black.

Southern Pochard *Netta erythrophthalma* Bruineend

A common resident bird of freshwater habitats. Their numbers are swelled during the early wet season by birds migrating from the north. They feed mainly during the early morning and late evening by up-ending or diving as well as by foraging in vegetation on the water margins. They feed on seeds, particularly those of water lilies, on duckweed and other aquatic vegetation as well as taking small insects. The plumage of the male is blackish on the forehead, nape and the rear of the neck, with the scapulars, back and tail a rich dark brown. The face and sides of the neck are a warm brown becoming darker from the lower neck to the underbelly. The flanks are a rich chestnut. The wing coverts are brown, the secondaries are white, being very prominent in flight and the primaries are brownish. The bill is pale slaty blue, the eyes are red and the legs and feet are greyish. The female is paler than the male and has a white patch at the front edge of the face and a white arc running from the rear of the eye around the ear.

Maccoa Duck *Oxyura maccoa* Bloubekeend

An uncommon duck of inland bodies of shallow freshwater, preferably with emergent vegetation. They feed by diving down to the muddy bottoms of lakes and ponds, where they gather seeds and invertebrates. Easily identified on the water by their squat appearance and by the stiff upward-pointing tail. The adult male has the head and upper neck black, the lower neck, breast and underparts are greyish brown and the back and upper tail coverts are rich chestnut. The short, broad bill is slate blue, the eyes are dark brown and the legs and feet are greyish brown. The female lacks the colourful plumage of the male and is predominately ashy brown with speckles and streaks.

Cape Shoveler *Anas smithii* Kaapse Slopeend

An uncommon resident usually to be found in small flocks during the non-breeding season. They frequent freshwater lakes and ponds and more rarely tidal estuaries and coastal lagoons. They usually feed by surface dabbling, taking mainly animal matter including snails, crustaceans and insects as well as some seed and water vegetation. The plumage of the head, neck and underparts is off-white, the feathers having dark centres giving a speckled effect, finer on the head and neck than elsewhere. The tail is dark brown, the wing coverts are slate blue, the speculum is bluish green edged with white and the long spatulate bill is black. The eyes are yellow in the breeding season and the legs and feet are orange; during non-breeding periods the eyes and the legs and feet are much duller.

Red-billed Teal *Anas erythrorhyncha* Rooibekeend

A common resident bird found in large flocks, particularly in non-breeding periods, on inland lakes, ponds and floodplains. They are very gregarious and can be encountered in flocks of thousands when conditions are favourable. They feed by night as well as by day, taking aquatic plants, seeds and various other forms of vegetation. The male has the top portion of the head from the base of the bill to just below the eye and extending to the nape and rear of the neck dark brown. The remainder of the head and face is buff/white. The neck, breast and underparts are buff/white with the central area of the feathers dark brown which gives a very speckled appearance. The feathers of the back, scapulars and wings are dark brown thinly edged with buff/white. The bill is pinkish red, the eyes are brown and the legs and feet are bluish grey. The sexes are similar.

Egyptian Goose *Alopochen aegyptiacus* Kolgans

A common widespread resident throughout the region with the exception of deserts. They can be found on inland bodies of water as well as estuaries and cultivated farmlands. They are often in conflict with farmers as a result of eating shoots of growing crops, as well as grasses and seeds. The head, neck and breast are grey with a chestnut patch surrounding the eye. The lower neck has a chestnut collar and the centre of the breast has an irregular chestnut patch. The mantle and scapulars are reddish brown and the tail is black. The wing coverts are white, with a black band towards the tips. The secondaries are brown with a sheen of metallic green; the primaries are black. The bill is pale pink, the eyes are orange and the legs and feet are pinkish red. The sexes are similar, the females being slightly smaller.

Spur-winged Goose *Plectropterus gambensis* Wildemakou

A common resident throughout much of the region, forming large flocks in the non-breeding season. Found on large inland waters and floodplains where they feed by grazing on grasses, grains and soft aquatic vegetation. A very large goose with predominantly black plumage, the wings having an iridescent wash of green. The front of the face is devoid of feathering, the bare skin being pinkish red as is the bill. The remainder of the face is white. There is a white stripe which extends from the centre of the lower neck and broadens out to cover the entire breast and belly. The eyes are dark brown and the legs and feet are reddish.

African Pygmy Goose *Nettapus auritus* Dwerggans

An uncommon resident in the north and east of our region. They inhabit areas of freshwater with emergent vegetation, particularly water lilies. A small duck which is often difficult to locate due to their habit of remaining motionless among the aquatic vegetation when threatened. The male has the forehead, face and throat white, the nape and hindneck being bottle green washed with metallic blues. The lower neck and flanks are chestnut, the breast and belly are white. The wings are metallic green and the tail is black. The bill is yellow with a black tip, the eyes are brown and the legs and feet are grey. The female is less colourful than the male.

Hottentot Teal *Anas hottentota* Gevlekte Eend

A locally common duck, which, at first glance, could be confused with the Red-billed Teal, but its smaller size and differing bill colour separate the two. They are usually to be found in shallow freshwater lakes, ponds and marshes. They feed mainly by immersing the head and bill under the surface of the water, taking a variety of vegetable matter and, to a lesser degree, aquatic animal life. The adult male has the top of the head, from level with the eye, blackish brown, the remainder of the head being buff/white. There is an area of mottling on the sides and back of the neck. The mantle and scapulars are dark brown edged with buff, giving a scaly appearance. The rump and tail coverts are pale brown with dark vermiculations. The breast and underparts are buff/white; the feathers having dark brown centres produce the effect of spotting; on the belly these spots merge to produce barring. The wing coverts are darkish brown with a strong wash of metallic green/blue. The flight feathers are black and the speculum is green. The bill is slate blue, the eyes are dark brown and the legs and feet are greyish/black.

European Honey Buzzard *Pernis apivorus* Wespedief

A non-breeding migrant from the north, mainly encountered in the north-east of our region during the period November/May. They inhabit well-wooded areas and are generally secretive. They eat a variety of insects including grasshoppers, locusts, wasps, termites and bees. The plumage can vary greatly, as there are several colour phases. The commonest phase have the head and neck whitish with fine brown speckling. The back, scapulars and wings are dark brown thinly edged with buff/white. The breast and belly are white with brown barring. The tail is brown with a broad blackish terminal band. In flight, the dark patches on the carpal joints and the slender long head are key features to identification. The bill is black and the eyes are yellow, as are the legs and feet. The sexes are similar.

Yellow-billed Kite *Milvus aegyptius* Geelbekwou

A common and widespread kite which was, until recently, considered to be a subspecies of the Black Kite. A very adaptable species being found in almost any habitat, from open grasslands and cultivated farmland to towns and villages where they will scavenge on rubbish dumps and general refuse associated with mankind. The plumage is predominantly brown with a flush of chestnut, the underparts are streaked with dark brown/black. The primary flight feathers are black. The tail is brown, forked and with faint broad barring. The bird uses its tail as a rudder, twisting it from side to side to maintain level flight. The bill is bright yellow, the eyes are brown and the legs and feet are yellow.

Black-shouldered Kite *Elanus caeruleus* Blouvalk

A common resident bird throughout the region, found in open grassland areas, cultivated farmland and on woodland edges and clearings. They feed on rodents, large insects and some reptiles and small birds. They hunt by perching above productive areas and diving down to the ground to grab prey; they also sometimes hover in a manner more associated with the kestrel, but only for short periods. The plumage is mainly grey with a white forehead, neck and underparts. The primary flight feathers are grey with black tips and the shoulders show a prominent patch of black. The bill is black with a yellow cere, the eyes are bright crimson and the legs and feet are yellow. The sexes are similar.

Osprey *Pandion haliaetus* Visvalk

An uncommon non-breeding migrant from the north, arriving in August/September and departing by May. They are likely to be encountered on inland lakes, estuaries and coastal lagoons. They feed almost entirely on fish, by plunging in to the water, to a depth of up to a metre. They can take fish weighing up to 3 kilos. The forehead is brown/black with a black band running through the eye and over the ear coverts to the hindneck. The crown, face, neck, breast and belly are white with some brown streaking around the lower neck. The back, wings and tail are brown, the wing feathers being edged with buff/white and the tail having broad dark bands. The bill is greyish, the eyes are bright yellow and the legs and feet are yellowish grey. The sexes are similar, the female being slightly larger then the male.

Black Kite *Milvus migrans* Swartwou

Very similar to the Yellow-billed Kite – it is only in recent years that DNA evidence has shown the two to be different species. The Black Kite is slightly larger, has less rufous in the plumage and often shows a paler head. The bill is black with a yellow cere, the eyes are yellow as are the legs and feet. They are non-breeding migrants to our region present from November to March. They inhabit a wide variety of habitats and often associate with people, scavenging from towns and villages. They will often be found at carcases along with other birds of prey and vultures. They also feed on the wing, catching dragonflies, termites and other flying insects. The sexes are similar.

African Fish Eagle *Haliaeetus vocifer* Visarend

A locally common resident associating with large bodies of water. They feed mainly on fish which they snatch from just below the surface in a swooping dive. They also take flamingos and other waterbirds and will scavenge in hard times, particularly immature birds. A large eagle with body feathering rich brown with darker flight feathers and the head, neck and tail are pure white. The bill is black with a yellow cere and facial patch, the eyes are brown and the legs and feet are golden yellow. The sexes are similar. Immature birds take four to five years to develop the full white head and neck of the adult.

Hooded Vulture *Necrosyrtes monachus* Monnikaasvoël

An uncommon resident found mainly in the north of the region, favouring areas of woodlands as well as grasslands and savannahs. Compared to other African vultures the hooded is slight in build and often seen on the periphery at carcasses taking scraps. They are very adaptable and feed on almost any animal matter from tiny termites to large insects and man-made refuse. Can be frequently encountered at rubbish dumps along with other scavengers. The head and most of the neck are devoid of feathers and pink in colour. They have a 'hood' of short grey downy feathers extending from the nape down the hindneck. The entire plumage is dark brown, the tail feathers being slightly darker. The slender bill is pinkish at the base with a black tip. The eyes are dark brown with a ring of pale whitish blue. The legs and feet are grey. The sexes are similar.

Palm-nut Vulture *Gypohierax angolensis* Witaasvoël

An uncommon resident mainly found in areas where oil palms are present in good numbers. They are unique among vultures and other birds of prey in having a mainly vegetarian diet, feeding for the most part on oil palm fruits and wild dates. They will, however, take fish, amphibians, crabs and small birds and mammals when fruits are in short supply. They feed mostly in the early morning and will rest up during the hottest part of the day in the canopy shade of a tree. They are sedentary, rarely moving far from their own territory. The head, neck, breast and belly are white, the primary flight feathers are white tipped with black and the back and upperwing coverts are white. The scapulars are black and the tail is black with a broad terminal white band. They have an orange/red patch of bare skin around the eyes, the bill is pale yellow, the eyes are yellow and the legs and feet are pinkish. The sexes are similar.

Egyptian Vulture *Neophron percnopterus* Egiptiese Aasvoël

One of the rarest vultures in the region, with most birds thought to be migrants from the central parts of Africa or from the Palearctic region. They occur in dry areas of grassland and savannah. They feed on carrion of all sorts but their slight build precludes them from taking a dominant role at carcasses, where larger species maintain control; they are forced to content themselves with snatching small scraps from the outer edges. They also eat termites and small insects. Their most remarkable feeding habit is that of using tools to smash into ostrich eggs. On finding an egg they will select a stone and throw it at the egg in the hope of cracking the shell. Although they are not very accurate, eventually they succeed in producing at least a crack into which they are able to insert their slim bill and extract the contents. They will also eat the eggs of smaller birds such as flamingos, by lifting them in their bill and smashing them on the ground. The plumage is predominantly off-white, with black flight feathers and a white wedge-shaped tail being distinctive features when the bird is in flight. They have loose feathering around the head. The bare skin of the facial region is yellow, the bill is yellow with a black tip, the eyes are brown and the legs and feet are yellow. The sexes are similar.

Bearded Vulture *Gypaetus barbatus* Baardaasvoël

Also known as the Lammergeier, this is one of the largest of Africa's vultures and can be found in the Drakensberg Mountains and the surrounding foothills, they are rarely found below an altitude of 1500 m. An uncommon resident. They are unique among vultures in their ability to fly high above rocks carrying animal bones which they drop to break into smaller pieces, before gathering up the fragments and swallowing. Some of the bone sections swallowed can be as long as 25 cm. Up to 90 per cent of their food intake can be in the form of bone marrow. They will also eat a variety of carrion when available, often feeding on dead domestic stock as well as carcasses of wild animals. In flight the wings are very long and they show a large diamond-shaped tail, which distinguishes it from all other vultures other than the Egyptian Vulture, which is only half the size. The forehead, face and crown are white with a black mask around the eyes extending to black bristles at the base of the bill. The neck, breast and underparts are white, often stained rufous by the birds' habit of dusting and bathing in areas rich in iron oxide. The back, wings and tail are black, the bill is yellowish, the eyes are yellow surrounded by a red ring and the legs and feet are greyish.

White-backed Vulture *Gyps africanus* Witrugaasvoël

The commonest vulture in Southern Africa, found in lightly wooded savannahs and grasslands in central and northern regions. A gregarious species which gather in large numbers at carcasses of dead livestock and game animals as well as at night-time roosts. They are one of the most aggressive species, continually squabbling to gain prime positions at the carcass. They gorge themselves almost to the point where they are unable to fly. Following a feeding session they will withdraw and rest on the ground, often lying down or adopting a pose with the wings spread out in a heraldic posture. They can remain in a resting position for many hours, slowly digesting the heavy meal. The head and long neck are covered in thin off-white downy feathers, with a ruff of similar downy feathers around the lower neck. The bare skin of the face is black. The mantle and scapulars are brown, the wing coverts are buff and the flight feathers are blackish brown. In stark contrast the back and tail are white. The plumage tends to lighten as the birds age. The heavy bill is black, the eyes are dark brown and the legs and feet are black. The sexes are similar.

Cape Vulture *Gyps coprotheres* Kransaasvoël

A locally common species throughout the region, found in areas of hills and mountains as well as on grasslands. They roost in large numbers on cliffs and mountain ledges. They are to be seen on carcasses of large dead animals, flying in from far distances to land within a few metres and bound towards the carcass in a very aggressive manner with feet held high and wings out stretched. Birds newly arrived at a carcass quite often take prime position immediately upon arrival. The head and neck are devoid of normal feathering, but have short, sparse whitish down, with a ruff of pale buff around the lower neck. The upperwing coverts, back and rump are buff/white. The breast and belly are pale buff, the primary flight feathers are blackish and the secondaries are blackish grey. The tail is black, the bill is black and the eyes are pale yellow. The legs and feet are greyish. The sexes are similar.

Lappet-faced Vulture *Torgos tracheliotus* Swartaasvoël

An uncommon resident in the northern parts of our region, found in areas of open grassland and sparsely covered savannahs. The largest of Africa's vultures and by far and away the most dominant species to be found on dead carcasses. Their presence at a newly dead carcass is often essential as they are usually required to open up the body using their large, heavy bill. They will also feed on termites and flamingo eggs and nestlings. They are generally solitary or in small groups. The large bill, the naked pink head and neck and the fleshy red/pink lappets on the sides of the face distinguish this species from any of the other vultures. They have a greyish/ brown ruff around the lower neck , the breast and belly are brown with white streaking and the flanks are white. The back, wings and tail are dark brown. The bill is yellowish, the eyes are dark brown and the legs and feet are grey with downy white thighs. The sexes are similar.

White-headed Vulture *Trigonoceps occipitalis* Witkopaasvoël

An uncommon resident mainly in northern regions, found in grasslands and in lightly wooded areas. Usually to be seen alone or in pairs and very often they are the first vulture species to arrive at a newly dead carcass. Their slight build and low wing loading means that they are able to take to the air in search of carrion earlier in the day than other species, being less dependent on hot air thermals than the larger vultures to get themselves airborne. Once the melee of feeding starts at a carcass the White-headed is reduced to gathering scraps from the periphery. They also eat termites and locusts as well as taking lizards and birds and their eggs, including those of flamingos. The crown is covered with a thick growth of white downy feathering slightly peaked at the rear. The bare skin of the face is pinkish with a wash of light blue. The upper breast is black, the lower portion and belly are white. The wing coverts are black, the secondaries are white and the primary flight feathers are black. In flight the thin white bar separating the primaries from the wing coverts is a diagnostic feature. The bill is red faintly tipped with black, the eyes are dark brown, the cere is bluish and the legs and feet are pink. The sexes are similar.

Black-chested Snake Eagle   *Circaetus pectoralis*   Swartborsslangarend

A locally common resident, found on open plains and in lightly wooded areas throughout much of Southern Africa. An eagle that mainly feeds on snakes, both small harmless species and large venomous varieties such as cobras and puff adders. They will also take lizards and some amphibians as well as small mammals and birds. They will hunt from elevated perches or from the wing, scanning the ground for any movement. They will occasionally hover for short periods while hunting. At a distance this eagle could be confused with the Martial Eagle, but is much smaller and lacks the spotting on the breast and belly that is so distinctive on the Martial. The head, neck, upper breast, back and upperwings are brownish black. The underwings are white with narrow bands of black. The tail is brown with three faint dark bars. The lower breast and belly are white. The bill is greyish at the base and dark at the tip, the eyes are bright yellow, and the legs and feet are pale grey. The sexes are similar.

Bateleur   *Terathopius ecaudatus*   Berghaan

A relatively common bird of prey in the northern part of our region. Found in areas of grassland and lightly wooded savannahs. They feed on a wide variety of birds and mammals, as well as reptiles and some carrion. They attack their larger prey by means of a fast downward stoop, often from a great distance. When seen high in the sky, the long wings and almost indiscernible tail make for easy identification. They will cover great distances in search of prey, occasionally following roads and tracks in the hope of picking up animal road-kills. They roost and nest in trees, often in pairs, and will occupy the same territory for many years. The head, neck, breast and belly are black. The back and tail are chestnut. The underwings are white with a black trailing edge, this edge being much wider in the male than in the female. The upperwing coverts are buff/grey and the flight feathers are black. The bare skin of the face and the cere are bright red, the base of the bill is yellow with a black tip, the eyes are dark brown and the legs and feet are red. Juveniles have a uniform mid-brown plumage with a greenish blue cere and will be 6 or 7 years old before attaining adult plumage.

Brown Snake Eagle   *Circaetus cinereus*   Bruinslangarend

The largest of the snake eagles, a locally common resident species found mainly in the northern parts of our region in woodland habitats. They are usually seen singly, hunting from treetops or other high perches, scanning the ground below for any prey movement. They feed mainly on snakes of all sizes and varieties but will also take lizards as well as gamebirds such as francolins. The entire plumage is mid-brown, with lighter areas on the underwings. The tail is dark brown with three grey bars and tipped with grey. The bill is dark at the tip becoming grey at the cere, the eyes are a piercing yellow and the legs and feet are greyish. The sexes are similar, the female being slightly larger.

African Marsh Harrier   *Circus ranivorus*   Afrikaanse Vleivalk

A locally common resident of swamps and marshes where they hunt for small rodents, birds, amphibians and flying insects caught on the wing. They usually hunt from just a metre or two above the ground. They breed in reedbeds or other aquatic vegetation in small loosely held territories. The plumage is generally browns, the upper parts being streaked with rufous, the underparts are off-white streaked with dark brown and becoming rufous on the thighs. The tail is brown with a series of dark bars. The wings are grey/brown with rufous on the secondaries and with black primary flight feathers. The bill is dark, the eyes are yellow and the legs and feet are yellow.

Montagu's Harrier   *Circus pygargus*   Blouvleivalk

An uncommon, non-breeding migrant from the north, present from October to March and found on areas of open grassland. They feed on small mammals and ground birds as well as insects. They often roost in communal areas along with other harrier species. The plumage is mainly blue/grey above, the wings show a distinctive black bar along the tips of the secondaries and the primary flight feathers are black. The neck and upper breast are grey, merging into white on the lower breast and the belly. In flight the underwings show black barring along the rear edge and chestnut on the coverts. The bill is black, the cere is yellow as are the eyes and the legs and feet. The female lacks the blue/grey colouration of the male and is generally browns streaked with rufous and buff. The female has a whitish face with dark brown patches on the ear coverts and dark brown downward streaks on the paler brown neck.

African Harrier Hawk *Polyboroides typus* Kaalwangvalk

A fairly common resident throughout the area, found in a variety of woodland habitats often known as the Gymnogene. A large agile hawk with a distinctive slow floating flight, seen as the bird searches in tree holes, cavities and in decaying wood for lizards, small birds and rodents. They will also visit birds' nests, particularly weavers, taking eggs and chicks. To aid them in obtaining food, the legs of the Harrier Hawk are extremely flexible, allowing them to gain access into the tightest nooks and crannies. The plumage is predominantly grey with black primary flight feathers. The grey upperwing coverts show some black spots. The tail is black with a broad white band and a thin terminal band of white. The head, neck and breast are grey merging into white on the belly which is heavily barred with black. The small head has a patch of bare yellow skin around the dark eyes, the cere is yellow and the bill is black. The long, thin legs and feet are yellow. The sexes are similar.

Lizard Buzzard *Kaupifalco monogrammicus* Akkedisvalk

A locally common resident in the north and east of our region, found in a variety of woodland habitats, preferring those with long grass ground cover. Usually found singly and almost always perched in tree cover. It is from such perches that they feed on lizards, small mammals, amphibians and large insects. The plumage is slaty grey above with the flight feathers tipped white. The face is pale grey/white and a white patch with a central black streak covers the throat. The neck is grey and the breast and belly are white finely barred with dark brown. The tail is black tipped with white and has a broad white central band. The bill is black, the cere is red as is the orbital eye ring the eyes themselves are dark brown. The legs and feet are red. The sexes are similar.

African Goshawk *Accipiter tachiro* Afrikaanse Sperwer

A locally common resident found in the east and north of our region. They inhabit forests and heavily wooded areas from where they hunt small mammals and birds. They are often difficult to see, having a secretive nature. The plumage is dark slaty grey above, the head is grey and the chin and throat are white finely barred with grey. The breast and belly are white barred with rufous and the primary and secondary flight feathers are dark brown. The tail is blackish with three white patches on the central feathers. The cere is yellow, the bill is dark grey and the eyes are yellow, as are the legs and feet.

Southern Pale Chanting Goshawk *Melierax canorus* Bleeksingvalk

A common species over most of the region, favouring areas of dry thornbush, and open woodlands. They are normally sedentary, living in pairs and can usually be seen perched in elevated positions on dead trees and on man-made structures such as telegraph poles. They feed on lizards and other reptiles as well as small mammals and birds such as doves and francolins. The plumage is similar to that of the Dark Chanting Goshawk, but is much lighter in colour. They have a pure white rump which is usually very distinctive when the bird is seen in flight. The sexes are similar.

Dark Chanting Goshawk *Melierax metabates* Donkersingvalk

A common resident, found in broad-leaved woodlands and areas of more open thornbush country. They hunt from elevated perches, swooping down to take lizards and other reptiles as well as small mammals and insects. Will occasionally associate with Honey Badgers and hornbills in the hope of snapping up disturbed prey items. The plumage is dark slate grey above, the head, neck and throat are grey merging to white on the breast and belly finely barred with dark brown/grey. The primary flight feathers are black. The cere and the base of the bill are red, the bill tip is black, the eyes are brown and the legs and feet are red.

Gabar Goshawk *Micronisus gabar* Kleinsingvalk

A common resident throughout most of the region, in areas of broad-leaved woodlands and dry thornbush country. They hunt both from perches and whilst in flight, taking small birds, lizards and insects. They also raid birds' nests, particularly weavers, taking nestlings. The plumage is grey above with the primary flight feathers dark brown and the rump is white. The head and neck are grey, the breast and belly are white barred with dark brown. The tail is whitish with four dark brown bands. The cere and the base of the bill are red, the bill tip is black. The eyes are dark brown and the legs and feet are red.

Jackal Buzzard *Buteo rufofuscus* Rooiborsjakkalsvoël
A common endemic buzzard found in hill country and mountainous areas. Usually singly or in pairs, they regularly frequent the same area and are often to be seen perched on man-made structures such as telephone poles and pylons. They appear to hunt mainly in the early morning, preying on mammals such as hares and hyrax and small ground birds as well as insects and some road-casualty carrion. The head, nape, back and wings are dark brown/black with white flecking. The tail, both above and below, is bright chestnut. The chin and throat are white with some dark flecking, the breast is bright chestnut and the belly is blackish with white flecking. The primary flight feathers are black and the secondaries are white. In flight the broad wings show a trailing edge of black. The cere is yellow, the bill is black, the eyes are brown and the legs and feet are yellow. The sexes are similar, the female being much larger than the male.

Lesser Spotted Eagle *Aquila pomarina* Gevlekte Arend
An uncommon non-breeding migrant from the north, usually to be found in areas of open woodlands. They survive on a diet of small mammals, mainly rodents, lizards, young birds and road-kill carrion. They will also attend grass fires, seeking out grasshoppers and other insects. The plumage is all dull brown, the tail is brown and lacks any barring. The primary and secondary flight feathers are brown which contrasts with the lighter wing coverts when seen from below. The cere and the eyes are yellow. The bill is black and the legs and feet are a dull yellow. The sexes are similar.

Shikra *Accipiter badius* Gebande Sperwer
A common resident of forests and woodland edges as well as suburban parks and gardens. They move from tree to tree when hunting, spotting prey from perches, taking mainly lizards, which is unique among *accipiter* species, amphibians, small birds and some insects. In areas of high human presence they are very confiding and will often allow a close approach. The head, neck, back and upperwing coverts are plain grey. The throat is white, the breast and belly are white with narrow reddish brown barring. The tail is grey above and white below with 4 grey bands. The cere is yellow, the bill is black and the eyes are a piercing red. The legs and feet are yellow. The sexes are similar, the female being slightly larger and having a browner plumage.

Little Sparrowhawk *Accipiter minullus* Kleinsperwer
An uncommon, solitary resident in northern and eastern parts of Southern Africa, favouring areas of savannah and thornbush country. A small, stocky, short-tailed sparrowhawk, about the size of a dove. Although not shy, they are difficult to see as they spend much of their time in dense cover from where they hunt for small birds, mammals and large insects. The head, neck, back and upperwing coverts are slate grey. The throat is white with faint grey barring. The breast and belly are off-white with brown barring. The tail is blackish above with 2 distinct white central spots, the underside of the tail is whitish with 4 dark bars. The cere is yellow, the bill is black, the eyes are golden yellow and the legs and feet are yellowish. The sexes are similar.

Ovambo Sparrowhawk *Accipiter ovampensis* Ovambosperwer
A locally common bird in the northern parts of our region. Found in areas of open woodland and increasingly in cultivated farmlands and plantations, particularly those of alien species such as eucalyptus. They hunt either from thick cover snatching birds as large as doves, or from open perches attacking weaver flocks and other passing birds. The head, neck, back and wing coverts are slate grey. The chin and throat are grey/rufous barred with brown. The primary and secondary flight feathers are dark brown above and grey below. The tail is grey/brown with 4 dark bars. The cere is reddish, the bill is red at the base with a black tip. The eyes are brown and the legs and feet are dull orange/red.

Tawny Eagle *Aquila rapax* Roofarend

A common resident species found in open grasslands and areas of thornbush throughout much of our region. They do at times appear in areas of cultivated land where man has provided telephone poles and pylons for hunting perches and nesting sites. The plumage is extremely variable, ranging from uniform rufous brown to light brown and buff. The primary flight feathers are black and the tail is brown barred faintly with black. The cere is yellow, the bill is black and the eyes, legs and feet are yellow. This species can easily be confused with the Steppe Eagle, but the plumage is lighter, the bill is larger and the gape line extends to the eye, not beyond as in the Steppe. The sexes are similar, the female being larger.

Steppe Eagle *Aquila nipalensis* Steppe-arend

A locally common non-breeding migrant, found in the north of our region where they arrive in October to depart again in March. When hunting they can often be encountered perched on the ground rather than in an elevated position. They are often to be found in small groups, particularly when there is a termite emergence taking place. They will also eat locusts as well as rodents and small birds. The plumage is a uniform dark brown, the primary flight feathers being almost black. The tail is brown barred with black. The cere is yellow the bill is black, the eyes are brown and the feet are yellow. The legs are heavily feathered brown. They can be easily confused with Tawny Eagles, but the Steppe is bigger, generally darker in plumage and having the gape extending to a point beyond the eye. The sexes are similar.

Wahlberg's Eagle *Aquila wahlbergi* Bruinarend

A common breeding migrant mainly in northern and eastern parts of our range, inhabiting savannah and grasslands as well as woodlands and thornbush country. They usually hunt from perches making low, fast attacks often among trees. They take a wide variety of food items including lizards, small to medium-sized mammals and ground-dwelling birds. A small eagle with long wings and a long tail. The plumage colour varies greatly, there being several colour phases. The normal phase is dark brown with paler areas on the wing coverts. The primary flight feathers are blackish and the tail is dark with faint barring. The cere is yellow, the bill is black, the eyes are brown and the feet are yellow. The pale phase has the head, neck, breast and belly white. The sexes are similar, the female being larger than the male.

Verreaux's Eagle *Aqulia verreauxii* Witkruisarend

A locally common resident in hilly and mountainous regions, in gorges and on steep cliff faces. A very large eagle, usually found in pairs, they maintain a territory throughout the year. Their main source of food is Rock Hyrax and where they are plentiful these eagles will feed on little else. When hyrax are in short supply they turn their attention to mammals as large as Klipspringers and Dik Dik. They very rarely take birds. The plumage is entirely black, with the exception of a white patch on the rump and a white 'V' on the shoulders. The primary flight feathers show paler when the bird is seen in flight. The cere and the eyelids are yellow, the bill is greyish, the eyes are brown and the feet are yellow. The sexes are similar, the female being larger and having more white on the shoulders.

African Hawk Eagle *Aquila spilogaster* Grootjagarend

A locally common resident, found in areas of woodland and dense thornbush country. Usually seen in pairs as they maintain a permanent home range. They hunt both from perches and while on the wing, often using vegetation to cover their approach taking mainly francolins and guineafowls very much by surprise. Often hunts close to waterholes. They will also take small mammals such as hyrax and mongooses should the opportunity arise. The plumage is almost entirely black above with some light flecking on the primary flight feathers. The tail is dark grey with a terminating band of black. The throat, neck, breast and belly are white with bold black streaks. The underside of the wings are mainly white with the trailing edges black tipped. The underwing coverts are black streaked with white. The cere is yellow, the bill is greyish and the eyes are yellow, as are the feet.

Martial Eagle *Polemaetus bellicosus* Breekoparend

An uncommon resident, this is one of the largest eagles in Africa. They are usually found on grassland plains with some woodland or in arid thornbush country. They are usually quite wary of man and can be difficult to locate. They perch on the topmost branches of dead trees from where they launch attacks on prey species. These include a wide variety of birds and mammals from gamebirds such as guineafowl and bustards to ground squirrels and small antelope like Dik Dik. The head, neck, back, wings and upper breast are dark brown. The lower breast, belly and flanks are white spotted with dark brown. The tail is brown barred with black. The cere is yellow, the bill is black, the eyes are golden yellow and the legs are dull yellow/green. The sexes are similar, the female being slightly larger than the male.

Booted Eagle *Aquila pennatus* Dwergarend

A locally common eagle in both woodland and scrubland habitats. The breeding population have their numbers swelled from November to March by the arrival of a migrant population from the north. A small eagle, they hunt on the wing and from perches, swooping on prey with great speed, taking mainly birds, young mammals and reptiles. The head and neck are rufous brown streaked with dark brown. The back and wing coverts are dark brown and the primary and secondary flight feathers are black. The tail is pale brown with darker barring. The chin, throat, breast and belly are white with pale brown streaking. A white arc extends from the breast around the carpal joint of the wing. The cere is yellow, the bill greyish with a black tip, the eyes are brown and the feet are yellow. A dark phase of this species also exists and looks much the same but for the white feathering of the underside being replaced with dark brown feathers streaked with black.

Long-crested Eagle *Lophaetus occipitalis* Langkuifarend

A common resident found in damp woodlands and forest edges. An easy raptor to recognise by its long loosely feathered crest and dark brown plumage. The plumage colour can vary greatly with some individuals being almost black. They have white underwing coverts which are very distinctive in flight and they often show some white on the thighs. They can be generally seen perched on a branch or man-made pole, form where they hunt for small rodents, gamebirds and lizards and insects. The cere is yellow, the bill is black, the eyes are golden yellow, as are the feet, and the legs are white, but quite often brownish in the female.

African Crowned Hawk Eagle *Stephanoaetus coronatus* Kroonarend

An uncommon resident in the northern and eastern parts of our range. They are often difficult to locate being rather shy and wary of man. They are generally found in damp well-established forests and dense woodlands. This large, powerful eagle feeds almost exclusively on mammals, taking forest antelopes, hyrax, mongooses and monkeys. The head is brown with a crest of feathers tipped black. The neck and throat are brown, the breast and belly are white, heavily barred with dark brown/black. The underwing coverts are chestnut. The thighs and upper legs are white finely barred with black. The primary and secondary flight feathers are brown, barred and tipped with black. The long tail is black broadly barred with grey/white. The heavy bill is black, the cere and feet are dull yellow and the eyes are pale yellow/white. The sexes are similar, but the female is significantly larger than the male.

Secretary Bird *Sagittarius serpentarius* Sekretarisvoël

A locally common resident over most of our region. Difficult to mistake this long-legged bird of prey with any other species. They are usually to be encountered walking across open areas of grassland and savannahs searching for snakes, lizards, rodents and insects on which they mainly feed. The forehead, crown, nape, mantle and wing coverts are light grey. The chin, neck and throat are off-white. Long-flowing, black-tipped crest feathers emerge from the nape. A patch of unfeathered skin surrounds the eyes and varies in colour from yellow to bright red. The belly, thighs and flight feathers are black. The grey tail is very long with the central feathers banded black at the tip. The cere is yellow and the bill is greyish, the eyes are brown and the legs and feet are pale pink. The sexes are similar.

Pygmy Falcon *Polihierax semitorquatus* Dwergvalk
A locally common resident in the western part of our region, inhabiting semidesert areas and dry savannahs. The smallest bird of prey in our area, easily mistaken for a shrike from a distance. They are often associated with Sociable Weavers and Red-billed Buffalo Weavers, making their own nest within the communal nest chambers of the weavers. They feed mainly on small rodents, lizards and insects. They normally hunt from a perch, dropping on prey from above, most prey is taken on the ground. The head, back and wing coverts are grey/blue. The rump, face and underparts are white. The flight feathers are black with white spots. The tail is black, having faint grey bands and white spots. The cere is red and the bill is grey, the eyes are dark brown and the legs and feet are orange/red. The sexes differ in plumage, the mantle and back of the male is grey/blue, while in the female they are a rich chestnut.

Lesser Kestrel *Falco naumanni* Kleinrooivalk
A locally common, non-breeding palearctic visitor, quite gregarious and often found in roosting flocks, along with other falcons, in areas of open savannah, grasslands and cultivated farmland. They feed mainly on insects, small mammals and lizards. The head and scapulars are blue/grey, the mantle, back and upperwing coverts are chestnut. The chin and throat are creamy white, the breast and flanks are buff, lightly spotted with black. The underwing coverts are whitish with a wash of rufous. The flight feathers are black. The uppertail is blue/grey tipped with white and has a sub-terminal black band. The cere and the orbital ring are yellow, the eyes are dark brown and the legs and feet are yellow/orange. The female differs from the male in having a whitish forehead with some black streaks, the sides of the head are buff and the undersides are buff streaked with dark brown.

Greater Kestrel *Falco rupicoloides* Grootrooivalk
A common bird in areas of dry open grasslands, acacia woodlands and cultivated farmland. They feed mainly on insects, small rodents and lizards. They hunt from the air, occasionally hovering like other kestrels, but they do most of their hunting from perches. The head and neck are pale rufous finely streaked with black. The mantle, back and scapulars are rufous heavily barred with black. The rump and tail are slaty grey and the tail is tipped white and has a series of black bars. The undersides are pale rufous streaked on the breast and belly with brown and barred on the flanks with dark brown. The primary flight feathers are dark brown/black. The cere and orbital eye ring are yellow. The eyes are pale cream and the legs and feet are yellow. The sexes are similar, the female being slightly larger.

Red-necked Falcon *Falco chicquera* Rooinekvalk
An uncommon resident over much of the northern part of our region. They can be found in dry grassland areas and in open woodlands, favouring areas where *Borassus* palms grow. They hunt on the wing, taking birds throughout the day and bats in the twilight. They will also take lizards and rodents from the ground. A slim, fast-flying falcon with the head, the sides of the neck and the hindneck rufous. They have a black moustachial stripe and eyebrow. The scapulars and upperwing coverts are slate grey with black barring. The sides of the face, the chin, throat and the upper breast are white. The lower breast has a pale rufous band and the remainder of the undersides, including the wing coverts, are white heavily barred with brown/black. The tail is blue/grey above and paler below with a sub-terminal band of black and several other thinner black bars. The cere and the orbital eye ring are yellow, the eyes are pale brown and the legs and feet are yellow. The sexes are similar, the female being slightly larger.

Red-footed Falcon *Falco vespertinus* Westelike Rooipootvalk
A locally common non-breeding palearctic visitor to the northern part of our region. A very gregarious species often seen in large flocks mixed with other falcon species. The male has the head and the whole of the upperside very dark slate grey. The underwing coverts are also dark slate grey, while the throat and breast are a paler slate grey. The lower belly, thighs and undertail coverts are chestnut. The tail is black. The cere, the orbital eye ring and the legs and feet are orange. The eyes are dark brown. The female differs greatly from the male in having the forehead, crown and nape pale chestnut, the mantle and scapulars pale grey and the back, rump and upper tail coverts slate grey barred with black. The female also has a thin black band around the orbital eye ring and a short moustachial stripe.

Sooty Falcon *Falco concolor* Roetvalk

An uncommon, non-breeding visitor, present from November to March and found in woodland and forest edges in the northern and eastern parts of our range. A slim and very active falcon, feeding for the most part on insects and occasionally on bats and small birds. The plumage both above and below is a uniform slate grey, slightly paler on the upperwing coverts, scapulars, rump and upper tail coverts. They show a black patch around the eye, extending down to the bill. The primary and secondary flight feathers are black. The cere and the orbital eye ring are pale yellow. The bill is black, the eyes are dark brown and the legs and feet are orange/yellow.

Dickinson's Kestrel *Falco dickinsoni* Dickinsonse Grysvalk

An uncommon resident in the north and east of our region, frequenting areas of tropical savannah and woodland. They feed on insects, small birds, reptiles and occasionally bats. The entire head is pale grey, with a hint of fine brown streaking. The mantle and back are also greyish and the wings are grey/brown. The tail is pale grey above with six narrow black bars and a broader black sub-terminal band. The chin, throat, breast and belly are pale grey, often with fine black streaking. The bill is black, contrasting sharply with the bright yellow cere and orbital eye ring. The eyes are dark brown and the legs and feet are yellow. The sexes are similar.

Lanner Falcon *Falco biarmicus* Edelvalk

A common resident. The principle large falcon throughout the whole of Southern Africa. As well as a sizeable breeding population the numbers are often increased by migratory birds. They inhabit open grasslands and lightly wooded savannahs as well as cultivated farmland areas, making good use of man-made structures, such as pylons, for nesting in areas where large trees are all but absent. They hunt mainly on the wing, taking birds such as swifts and swallows as well as stooping on ground-dwelling birds like bustards. The forehead is buff white and the crown is rufous. A black moustachial stripe is present and a similar stripe runs from the eye around the sides of the head to the lower nape. The upperparts are grey/brown with darker barring and streaking. The flight feathers are dark brown. The breast and belly are white washed with buff. The tail is grey with brown banding. The cere, the orbital eye ring and the legs and feet are yellow. The eyes are dark brown. The sexes are similar.

Amur Falcon *Falco amurensis* Oostelike Rooipootvalk

A common non-breeding palearctic visitor, undertaking the most extraordinary migration, wintering in Southern Africa but breeding north of the Himalayas. They can be found on dry savannahs and grasslands often roosting in large congregations at favoured sites. They feed mainly on grasshoppers and termites, taking them both in the air and from the ground. The plumage is very similar to that of the Red-footed Falcon *Falco vespertinus*), but the male Amur Falcon has white underwing coverts, not grey. The female has the head, nape, back and upperwing coverts slate grey, the wing coverts being barred with black. The female has a black patch encircling the orange orbital eye ring and a black moustachial stripe. The chin and throat are white. The breast and remainder of the undersides are buff white, heavily barred and spotted with black. The primary and secondary flight feathers are blackish grey. The cere and the legs and feet are orange/red. The bill is pale grey.

Eurasian Hobby *Falco subbuteo* Europese Boomvalk

An uncommon non-breeding visitor, arriving in October and departing in April. They are usually to be found in areas of open woodland in the northern and eastern parts of our region. A graceful, long-winged falcon which, during its time in Southern Africa, feeds mainly on swarming termites which it catches on the wing. They will also take other insects such as dragonflies and beetles. The crown, nape, back and upperwing coverts are black/brown. The cheeks and the sides of the neck are white, contrasting sharply with a black moustachial stripe. The breast and upper belly are buff, heavily streaked and spotted with black; the lower belly, thighs and undertail coverts are rufous. The cere, orbital eye ring and the legs and feet are yellow. The eyes are dark brown. The sexes are similar but the female is usually browner and more heavily streaked below.

Coqui Francolin *Peliperdix coqui* Swempie

A common resident in the north and east of the region, favouring areas of grassland and lightly wooded savannahs. This is the smallest of South African francolins and is usually encountered in pairs or small coveys, often in thick vegetation, feeding on seeds, beetles, ants and other invertebrates. The male has the head and neck ochre, the mantle, breast and belly are white heavily barred with black. The back and wings are a mosaic of rufous, grey, black and buff. The bill is greyish buff, the eyes are mid-brown and the legs and feet are yellow. The female differs from the male in having thin black lines running from above the eye down the sides of the neck and from the gape downward onto and around the throat. The breast is light ochre and has only fine barring.

Crested Francolin *Francolinus sephaena* Bospatrys

A common resident usually found in pairs or in small coveys during the non-breeding season. A bird of thornbush country, areas of scrub and thickets. They are usually encountered scratching around in the leaf litter for insects and larvae, seeds, berries and other plant material. The crown is brown bordered with a black line and the neck is buff finely blotched with dark brown. The breast is white heavily marked with tear-drop blotches of brown, the belly is buff streaked with browns. The back and wing feathers are rufous/grey edged with buff/white. The bill is greyish, the eyes are dark brown and the legs and feet are dull red. The sexes are similar, the female having slightly more cryptic colouring and being slightly smaller than the male.

Shelley's Francolin *Scleroptila shelleyi* Laeveldpatrys

A resident in the northeastern part of our range, where it can be found in areas of tall grasslands and open areas of woodlands as well as on rocky slopes and outcrops. The plumage is a bold mosaic of blacks, browns, buffs and greys. The forehead, crown, nape and hindneck are black. The chin and throat are white, bordered with a narrow band of black and the eyebrow, the cheeks and the sides of the neck are buff ochre. The upper breast and the flanks are grey, heavily blotched with chestnut, the lower breast and belly feathers are white, edged with grey and boldly marked with black. The back, wings and tail feathers are grey edged with white and streaked with black. The sexes are similar.

Red-winged Francolin *Scleroptila levaillantii* Rooivlerkpatrys

A locally common resident to the east of our range, inhabiting areas of high altitude grassland. Usually encountered in pairs or small coveys of about ten birds. They forage among dead leaves and ground vegetation for invertebrates. The male has the forehead, crown and nape dark brown/black. A line of white feathering boldly spotted with black, runs from below the eyes onto the sides of the neck and swings across the throat in the form of a necklace. The chin and throat are white rimmed with ochre. The upper parts are an assortment of buffs and browns presenting a mottled appearance. The breast and belly are buff heavily streaked and blotched with rufous. The bill is greyish black, the eyes are brown and the legs and feet are dull yellow. The sexes are similar.

Cape Spurfowl *Pternistis capensis* Kaapse Fisant

A common endemic resident, found around the Cape region, where they inhabit areas of fynbos and scrub. They feed on bulbs, grain, seed and berries as well as insects such as ants and termites. They occur in pairs and in small coveys. The head and neck are dark brown, but greyer on the ear coverts. The plumage of the upperside is dark brown with irregular barring and streaking in grey and buff. The breast and belly feathers are dark grey/brown edged with white/buff. The bill has the upper mandible dark brown and the lower mandible dull orange. The eyes are brown and the legs and feet are red.

Natal Spurfowl *Pternistis natalensis* Natalse Fisant

A locally common resident found mainly in the eastern part of Southern Africa. They can be located in a wide variety of habitats from wooded savannahs, thickets and forest edges. The crown is dark brown streaked with buff, the remainder of the head and the neck are white with much black spotting and streaking. The breast and belly are white, heavily marked with black chevrons. The upperparts are dark greyish brown with the feathers edged and streaked with buff and black. The bill is pale orange with a flush of green at the base, the eyes are dark brown and the legs and feet are orange/red. The sexes are similar.

Red-billed Spurfowl   *Pternistis adspersus*   Rooibekfisant

Common in the north and west of our region, inhabiting areas of savannah woodland, scrub usually not too far from water. They feed on bulbs, berries, seeds and other plant material as well as on termites, grasshoppers, beetles and other smaller invertebrates. The head and neck are grey brown, finely speckled with buff, the throat, breast and belly are uniformly barred grey and brown/black. The mantle is finely barred with black and white and the wings are dark brown/grey, densely speckled with buff. The tail is greyish/brown speckled with rufous and black. The bill is orange/red, the orbital eye ring is yellow, the eyes are brown and the legs and feet are red. The sexes are similar.

Red-necked Spurfowl   *Pternistis afer*   Rooikeelfisant

A locally common resident in the eastern and northern parts of our range, being found along evergreen forest and woodland edges and in thornbush country. They feed mainly on plant material such as roots, tubers and bulbs as well as seeds and a variety of small invertebrates. They roost at night in dense trees and bushes. The feathers of the head and neck are dark grey edged with white. They have a red bare patch around the eye and on the front of the throat. The breast and belly feathers are dark grey/black heavily streaked with black and white. The mantle, scapulars and upperwing coverts are greyish/brown with some black edging. The bill is red, the eyes are brown and the legs and feet are red. The sexes are similar. There are several races of this species occurring in Southern Africa, all having slightly different plumage characteristics.

Swainson's Spurfowl   *Pternistis swainsonii*   Bosveldfisant

A common bird in the northern and eastern parts of our range, being found in grasslands and savannahs with tall grasses. This species can be confused with the Red-necked Spurfowl, but the black legs and greyish bill of Swainson's separate the two. They feed on seeds, roots and other plant material as well as on spiders, grasshoppers and a whole variety of other invertebrates. The crown and nape are grey/brown finely streaked with black. They have a red patch of bare skin around the eyes and a similar patch on the front of the throat. The mantle, back and wings are greyish, finely streaked with dark brown/black. The tail is grey/brown flecked and streaked with darker tones. The breast and belly are grey/brown edged and flecked with darker browns. The bill is black with a hint of red on the lower mandible. The eyes are dark brown and the legs and feet are dark grey.

Common Quail   *Coturnix coturnix*   Afrikaanse Kwartel

A common breeding migrant throughout Southern Africa. They can be found in areas of grassland and lightly wooded savannahs. They arrive in the region in September and depart in April. Although plentiful, they are difficult to see as they nearly always stay in cover, rarely venturing into open areas. They feed on seeds and other plant material as well as on spiders, flies, termites and other small insects. The forehead, crown and nape are dark brown, bordered by a white stripe running from the base of the upper mandible, above the eye and down the hindneck to the mantle. The scapulars and wings are yellowish brown, each feather having a central streak of white. The chin and throat are black, sometimes with a thin black arc running upwards around the lower face to the ear coverts. The breast is pale chestnut blending into grey on the belly. The bill is blackish, the eyes are brown and the legs and feet are flesh coloured. The female is generally less colourful than the male and lacks the black chin/throat patch.

Harlequin Quail   *Coturnnix delegorguei*   Bontkwartel

Locally common breeding migrant in the northern and eastern sections of our range. Found in areas of grassland and lightly wooded savannahs. They are usually in pairs during breeding times and gather into coveys of around 20 birds during periods of non-breeding. They feed on seed and plant material, but prefer insects such as grasshoppers, termites and ants. The upperparts of the plumage are a varied mixture of browns, black and greys with many of the larger feathers having a central streak of creamy grey. They have a white eyebrow stripe, with the chin, throat and sides of the face white, with a black band extending from the base of the bill to the ear coverts where it joins another black band running across the throat. The breast and belly feathers are rich chestnut with a central streak of black. The bill is greyish, the eyes are brown and the legs and feet are flesh coloured.

Helmeted Guineafowl *Numida meleagris* Gewone Tarentaal

A locally common bird throughout most of Southern Africa. They favour open country and forest and woodland edges as well as areas of cultivated land. They are very gregarious during the non-breeding season and can be seen in flocks of up to 40 birds. They feed on seeds, bulbs and roots during the dry season and take a variety of invertebrates including grasshoppers and harvester termites. The head and the neck are devoid of feathers, the crown has a bony casque buff in colour. The face and neck are powder blue with specks of red on the tips of the gape wattles, along the eyebrow line and at the base of the bill. The remainder of the plumage is dark grey/black with dense white spotting. The bill is red at the base and buff at the tip, the eyes are dark brown and the legs and feet are black. The sexes are similar, the females being slightly smaller.

Crested Guineafowl *Guttera edouardi* Kuifkoptarentaal

A locally common resident in the northeast of our region. They can be found in forests, woodlands and thickets where they feed on a wide variety of plant material and insects. The only guineafowl in Southern Africa to inhabit forests, usually encountered in flocks of up to 50 individuals. The forehead, crown and nape has a short downy crest of black feathers, the remainder of the naked face and neck are bluish grey with a white collar around the neck. The remainder of the plumage is black with a sheen of blue, spotted all over with white. The bill is pale yellow and grey, the eyes are red and the legs and feet are dark grey/black. The sexes are similar.

Grey Crowned Crane *Balearica regulorum* Mahem

A locally common resident in the eastern and north-eastern parts of our range. Usually found in marshes and on floodplains. They are usually to be seen in pairs or family parties and, during non-breeding periods in flocks numbering up to several hundred. They feed on both plant and animal material such as seeds, sedges, millipedes, grasshoppers and amphibians and reptiles. This large slate grey bird is difficult to misidentify, the forehead and forecrown are black. The hindcrown has a stiff crest of yellow feathers, the sides of the face are white, a red wattle is situated on the chin and upper throat, the remainder of the neck and throat are slate grey. The feathering of the lower neck, the breast and the mantle has a loose appearance. The wing coverts are white, the primary and secondary flight feathers are black. The bill is black, the eyes are pale blue and the legs and feet are greyish/black. The sexes are similar, the female has a slightly less well-developed crest.

Blue Crane *Anthropoides paradiseus* Bloukraanvoël

A locally common resident in the eastern part of our range. They are usually to be found on wet grassland and in meadows and pastures. Usually found in pairs or family parties and during non-breeding periods in flocks of a hundred or so. They will feed on grains and the seeds of grasses and sedges as well as on insects such as grasshoppers and locusts. They also take amphibians, fish and some small mammals. The forehead and crown are white, the remainder of the plumage is predominately slate grey. They have loose elongated plumes on the upper breast and the inner secondary feathers are very elongated, sweeping down beyond the tail to the ground. The bill is yellowish pink, the eyes are dark brown and the legs and feet are black. The sexes are similar, the female being slightly smaller.

Wattled Crane *Bugeranus carunculatus* Lelkraanvoël

An uncommon resident, frequenting marshes and wetlands as well as cultivated farmland. They are gregarious during periods of non-breeding when they often flock together in their hundreds. They feed on a wide variety of plant and animal material including roots, grasses and grains as well as amphibians, reptiles and small fish. The crown of the head is slate grey, the remainder of the head, neck and breast is dull white. The belly, thighs, mantle, back and tail are black. The primary and secondary flight feathers are black, the elongated inner secondaries are slate grey and extend beyond the tail curving down to the ground. They have white wattles hanging form the chin and a patch of bare red skin extending from the base of the bill to the eye. The bill is buff, the eyes are pale orange and the legs and feet are black. The sexes are similar.

Red-chested Flufftail *Sarothrura rufa* Rooiborsvleikuiken

A locally common species found in the east and north of our region. Usually encountered in pairs in freshwater marshes, reedbeds and any other thick waterside vegetation. They feed mainly at dawn and dusk, moving through thick vegetation at speed picking up snails, water bugs, flies, termites and seeds of most kinds. A very sedentary species, maintaining a year-round territory. They are under some threat due to the destruction of wetland habitats. The male has the entire head, neck, throat, breast and mantle a rich chestnut, sometimes with a hint of black on the chestnut. The belly is black/brown with streaks of white. The upper plumage is black with streaks of white on the scapulars and wing coverts, the tail is also black but with white spots rather than streaks. The bill is black with a hint of blue/grey, the eyes are dark brown and the legs and feet are grey/black. The female has the entire plumage black, dotted, streaked and barred with buff. The chin, throat, breast and belly are off-white, barred and speckled with black.

Black Crake *Amaurornis flavirostris* Swartriethaan

A common resident over much of Southern Africa, inhabiting swamps, marshes, ponds and rivers where they are active throughout the day but often difficult to see due to their secretive nature. They are normally to be found in pairs, feeding along the edges of reedbeds and other stands of waterside vegetation, picking insects from the surface of the water. They also feed on snails, small fish, worms, seeds and other plant material. They can often be seen scurrying about on lily leaves, their long toes spreading their weight so as not to sink. They can also be seen picking flies and other small insects from the backs of partially submerged hippos. Their movements are rather jerky and they cock their tails almost continuously. The plumage is entirely black, with a hint of brown on the wings. The bill is greenish yellow, the eyes are dark red around which is a red orbital ring. The legs and feet are bright red. The sexes are similar. Immature birds are browner and lack the bill and leg colour of adults.

Baillon's Crake *Porzana pusilla* Kleinriethaan

An uncommon resident in the eastern and northern parts of our range. They inhabit marshes, wetlands and the margins of lakes and ponds. They are quite secretive and skulk in dense waterside vegetation. They are usually in pairs and feed on a variety of aquatic insects as well as on seeds and plant material. They are the smallest crake in Southern Africa. The crown and nape are reddish brown with fine black streaking. The face, neck, throat, breast and upper belly are slaty blue. The lower belly is barred with dark brown and white. The mantle, back, scapulars, wings and tail are all reddish brown with bold black and white streaks. The bill is greenish grey, the eyes are red and the legs and feet are greenish grey. The sexes are similar.

Spotted Crake *Porzana porzana* Gevlekte Riethaan

An uncommon, non-breeding migrant, found in the northern part of our range, where they inhabit marshes, swamps and other areas of shallow water. They are usually found singly or in small groups. They appear to be less secretive than other crakes and will often feed in the open during the day, feeding with and in the manner of waders, wading in the mud and probing for insects. The crown and the centre of the forehead are brown streaked with black, the nape and hindneck are brown covered with fine white spots. The face, throat and upper breast are slate grey with a patch of buff behind the eye. The lower breast is brown/grey with white spots and the belly is off-white barred with dark brown. The upperparts are a greenish brown covered with small white spots and streaks. The bill is greenish with a smudge of red at the base of the upper mandible. The eyes are reddish and the legs and feet are greenish yellow. The sexes are similar, the female being slightly duller in plumage.

Common Moorhen *Gallinula chloropus* Grootwaterhoender

A locally common resident found in bodies of freshwater with margins of aquatic vegetation. They are usually to be seen in pairs or small loose groups feeding on all manner of plant and animal matter. They can occasionally be seen climbing up reeds and into trees and bushes. The forehead has a red frontal shield, the crown and neck are blackish blue. The mantle, breast and belly are slaty blue with a wash of brown. The wing coverts and the primary and secondary flight feathers are brown with some black edging. The tail is black with the undertail coverts a prominent white showing when the tail is flicked upwards in alarm. The bill is red with a yellow tip, the eyes are dark red and the legs and feet are greenish yellow. The sexes are similar, the frontal shield is less well developed in the female.

Allen's Gallinule *Porphyrio alleni* Kleinkoningriethaan

A locally common resident found in the north-eastern portion of our range in wetland habitats with reedbeds and other varieties of aquatic vegetation lining the margins. May well be confused with the African Purple Swamphen but tiny in comparison. They are generally shy, keeping themselves hidden in vegetation, feeding around the margins taking seeds, plant stems and water lilies as well as insects, molluscs and small fish. The forehead has a frontal shield of green/blue. The crown, nape and face are black, becoming deep blue on the throat, neck, breast and belly. The mantle, scapulars and wings are green and the bill is red as are the eyes and the legs and feet. The sexes are similar.

African Purple Swamphen *Porphyrio madagascariensis* Grootkoningriethaan

A locally common resident species over much of the region. They inhabit areas of freshwater swamps, lakes, ponds and rivers with dense vegetation lining the margins. They are generally rather shy, keeping themselves hidden in emergent vegetation for much of the time. They frequently flick their tail up and down to indicate unease, to advertise the approach of a predator or to keep young in contact. They feed mainly on aquatic vegetation, leaves and tubers as well as insects, small fish and some amphibians. The forehead has a frontal shield of red, the head, neck and upper breast are light blue, the lower breast and belly are dark blue/purple. The back, scapulars and wings are iridescent green. The primary and secondary flight feathers are black edged with purple. The heavy bill is red, the eyes too are red as are the legs and feet. The sexes are similar.

Red-knobbed Coot *Fulica cristata* Bleshoender

A very common resident over the majority of Southern Africa. Found in areas of open water such as lakes, ponds and lagoons where they are usually quite confiding and will often gather into large flotillas. They feed mainly on aquatic vegetation as well as water snails and surface-dwelling insects. The entire plumage is black with washes of brown on the rump and the tail. The forehead has a frontal shield of white the apex of which shows two circular red knobs. These knobs are more prominent during the breeding season. The bill is white, the eyes are rich red and the legs and feet are mid-grey. The sexes are similar.

Lesser Moorhen *Gallinula angulata* Kleinwaterhoender

An uncommon species over all but the north of our region where it is an abundant bird. They inhabit a wide range of wetland habitats from swamps, lakes and ponds to floodplains. They are a lot shyer than the Common Moorhen, keeping themselves hidden for much of the time in vegetation. They feed on seeds, flowers and a variety of other plant material as well as on insects such as beetles. The forehead has a red frontal shield and the head is grey black. The mantle, breast and belly are mid-grey and there is a narrow white line on the flank, following the leading edge of the wing. The scapulars and wings are olive brown and the tail is brown / black. The bill is yellow, the eyes are red and the legs and feet are yellowish green. The sexes are similar.

Kori Bustard   *Ardeotis kori*   Gompou
A locally common species throughout the region found in open savannahs, grasslands and lightly wooded areas. Seen singly, in pairs or in small groups, this is the largest bustard south of the Sahara Desert. They feed usually by walking through grasslands snapping up any disturbed insects or reptiles. The crown is black with a short crest extending from the rear. The face and neck are mid grey finely barred with black. The breast and belly are white. The wing coverts are white with a tinge of buff, broadly marked with black. The back and the flight feathers are grey/brown finely marked with greys. The bill is yellowish grey, the eyes are yellow and the legs and feet are greyish yellow. The sexes are similar, the female being slightly smaller.

Ludwig's Bustard   *Neotis ludwigii*   Ludwigse Pou
Locally common in the western regions of Southern Africa, where they inhabit dry areas of savannah and thornbush country. They can usually be seen in pairs or small groups and feed on a wide variety of insects, reptiles and small mammals as well as some vegetable matter. The head is dull brown with white flecking on the chin and the lores. The foreneck is dull brown and the hindneck is greyish white becoming rufous on the lower portion and running on to the mantle. The breast is dull brown and the belly is white. The wings and tail are brown with streaks and fine vermiculations of buff. The bill is greyish, the eyes are light brown and the legs and feet are yellow/green. The sexes are similar.

Black-bellied Bustard   *Lissotis melanogaster*   Langbeenkorhaan
A locally common resident in northern and eastern parts of our range. They frequent savannahs with tall grasses and open wooded areas. They feed on small insects and vegetable matter. The forehead and crown are buff finely speckled with black. The rear portion of the neck is buff speckled with brown, the chin and frontal portion of the neck are black, spreading on to the breast and belly. The mantle, back, rump and wings are tawny buff with dark brown arrow-shaped markings on the centre of the feathers and brown barring on the tail. The bill is greyish yellow, the eyes are brown and the legs and feet are pale greenish yellow.

Northern Black Korhaan   *Afrotis afraoides*   Witvlerkkorhaan
A common and widespread species found in dry savannah and grassland habitats. They feed on a wide variety of insects and vegetable matter. A small bustard with striking plumage. The head, neck, breast and belly are black, with a narrow white line on the sides of the crown, a white patch on the ear coverts and a white collar on the lower hindneck. The mantle, back and wings are closely barred with brown and buff/white. The bill is red, a white orbital ring surrounds the dark brown eyes and the legs and feet are yellow. The sexes are similar.

White-bellied Korhaan   *Eupodotis senegalensis*   Witpenskorhaan
An uncommon resident found in the east of the region in grasslands and savannahs. They feed mainly on invertebrates as well as on seeds, flowers and other vegetable matter. The forehead is black and the crown is bluish grey. The remainder of the head is white with a hint of buff on the cheeks and the throat has a black patch extending on to the sides of the neck. The neck and upper breast are bluish grey, the lower breast and belly are white. The upper parts are a rich brown with darker brown vermiculations. The bill is yellow with a dark tip, the eyes are light brown and the legs and feet are pale yellow. The female lacks the rich head markings and the black throat patch of the male.

Red-crested Korhaan   *Lophotis ruficrista*   Boskorhaan
A common resident species found in areas of light woodland and dry savannah. They feed on a variety of vegetation including fruits and berries as well as taking invertebrates such as grasshoppers, beetles and termites. The forehead and crown are bluish grey. The nape has a distinctive crest of rufous feathers best seen during periods of courtship prior to breeding. The neck and throat are greyish brown, the breast and belly are brown/black. The back, rump and upper tail coverts are brown with dark mottling and the feather edges are bordered with white/buff. The flight feathers are dark brown, spotted with buff and edged with buff/white. The bill is greyish, the eyes are yellow/brown and the legs and feet are greenish yellow.

African Jacana *Actophilornis africanus* Grootlangtoon

A common resident throughout the region in wetland habitats, lakes and river margins. They have extremely long toes, which spreads their weight and stops them from sinking when walking over aquatic vegetation. They are usually to be found in pairs or family parties feeding on small aquatic animals including molluscs, flies and spiders. The crown, nape and hindneck are black, the remainder of the head, the foreneck and the upper breast are white. The forehead has a pale blue frontal shield. The remainder of the plumage is a rich chestnut brown. The bill is blue grey, the eyes are dark brown and the legs and feet are grey blue. The sexes are similar, the female being slightly larger.

Lesser Jacana *Microparra capensis* Dwerglangtoon

An uncommon species mainly to be found in the Okavango Delta in areas with floating vegetation. The smallest of the world's jacana species. The forehead is golden yellow, the crown and hindneck are rufous. They have a white eyebrow line and a black line extends from the base of the bill through the eye. The face, chin, throat, breast and belly are white with a patch of rufous yellow on the sides of the neck and breast. The back is a mixture of brown and buff with dark speckling. The bill is greyish with a black tip, the eyes are dark brown and the long toes and legs are greenish. The sexes are similar.

Greater Painted Snipe *Rostratula benghalensis* Goudsnip

A locally common resident usually to be found on the muddy margins of lakes, ponds and slow-moving rivers. A species that in some respects has evolved a system of role reversal. The male doing all the incubation duties and the raising of the young. Unlike most bird species the females also have the brighter plumage, the males being rather drab by comparison. The female has the forehead and crown dark brown with a thin central stripe extending to the nape. A narrow white line surrounds the eyes and a stripe of white extends from the rear of the eye towards the nape. The chin, throat and neck are dark chestnut becoming darker on the upper breast. A band of white, bordered with black, extends across the lower breast from the shoulders. The belly is white. The upperparts and the wings are green bronze blotched and barred with black. The bill is dull red, the eyes are dark brown and the legs and feet are pale greenish grey. The male has the head and neck grey/buff streaked with brown, the breast is barred with brown and the wings are heavily marked with buffs and browns.

African Black Oystercatcher *Haematopus moquini* Swarttobie

A locally common resident, found around much of the Southern African coastline. They favour areas of rocky coasts and shorelines, where they feed on mussels, limpets, whelks and other shellfish along the inter-tidal strip. They have a specially adapted bill for opening their prey items. The entire plumage is glossy black. The bill is red, and they have orbital eye rings of yellow surrounding the bright red eyes. The legs and feet are also red. The sexes are similar.

Black-winged Stilt *Himantopus himantopus* Rooipootelsie

A common resident and migrant visitor to inland floodplains and marshes as well as to estuaries and coastal lagoons. They feed by wading in shallow water, taking a wide variety of insects, worms, dragonflies, tadpoles and fish. Usually encountered singly or in small groups. The head, neck, breast, belly and mantle are white and the wings are black. The long, straight bill is black, the eyes are red and the extraordinarily long legs and the feet are pinkish

Pied Avocet *Recurvirostra avosetta* Bontelsie

A locally common resident found in wetland areas and shallow water bodies throughout much of the region. They feed in shallow water, sweeping their bills from side to side, locating prey by touch. They seem to prefer small insects such as beetles, and flies as well as worms and small crustaceans. The top portion of the head, the nape and the hindneck are black, the face, mantle, throat, breast and belly are pure white. The scapulars are black, the wing coverts are white at the base with black tips, the secondaries are white and the primary flight feathers are black. The fine, upcurved bill is black, the eyes are brown and the legs and feet are bluish grey. The sexes are similar.

Water Thick-knee *Burhinus vermiculatus* Waterdikkop
A locally common resident around lakes, rivers and swamps, usually singly or in pairs. They are mainly active at night. The crown, hindneck, mantle, back and wing coverts are grey/brown flecked and streaked with dark brown. The wing coverts are black at the base, forming a distinct wing bar. The primary flight feathers are black. The eyebrows, the cheeks and the chin are white. The throat and breast are buff/white, streaked with dark brown. The belly is white. The bill is yellow at the base and tipped with black, the large prominent eyes are yellow and the legs and feet are pale greenish/yellow. The sexes are similar.

Spotted Thick-knee *Burhinus capensis* Gewone Dikkop
A common resident throughout most of Southern Africa, found in a wide variety of habitat types from savannahs and open woodlands to areas of arid scrub, cultivated farmlands and dry riverbeds. Usually to be seen singly or in pairs at dusk and throughout the night. The plumage is pale buff to tawny brown blotched and streaked with dark brown/black. They have a white chin and a white stripe following the line of the eyebrow as well as another line running from the base of the bill below the eye to the ear coverts. The bill is yellow at the base, tipped with black, the large eyes are yellow as are the long legs and the feet. The sexes are similar.

Collared Pratincole *Glareola pratincola* Rooivlerksprinkaanvoël
An uncommon migrant being present in the region from July to February. Mostly found on floodplains and close to large bodies of water. The chin, throat and foreneck are creamy yellow bordered with a band of black. The head, sides of the neck and breast are buff brown merging into white on the lower breast and belly. The wings are mid-brown and the primary and secondary flight feathers are black. The bill is black with a hint of red at the base, a white orbital ring encircles the dark brown eyes and the legs and feet are blackish. The sexes are similar.

Temminck's Courser *Cursorius temminckii* Trekdrawwertjie
A locally common resident found in areas of short grasslands and bush savannah. They are usually seen in pairs or in small flocks of about 20 individuals. They feed on a variety of insects, molluscs and occasionally seeds. The crown is light chestnut. A white eyebrow stripe, bordered below with black, extends from the rear of the eyes to the nape and downwards to the hindneck. The neck, upper breast, mantle and upper parts are grey/brown. The lower breast is chestnut becoming darker on the belly, the remainder of the underparts are white. The secondary flight feathers are grey/brown and the primaries are black. The slightly decurved bill is blackish, the eyes are dark brown and the legs and feet are pale grey. The sexes are similar.

Bronze-winged Courser *Rhinoptilus chalcopterus* Bronsvlerkdrawwertjie
A locally common resident, usually seen singly or in pairs in woodland clearings and areas of thornbush scrub. They are nocturnal in habit, resting by day in the shade of trees and bushes. They are the largest of Africa's coursers having the crown, nape and hindneck mid-brown. A dark brown stripe extends from the rear of the eye to the nape and a broader stripe extends from the base of the bill through the eye to the hindneck. The chin and throat are white and the neck and breast are mid-brown separated from the buff white belly and underparts by a black band. The primaries are black with a sheen of purple and tipped with an iridescent violet. The bill is black, a red orbital ring encircles the dark brown eyes and the legs and feet are pale red. The sexes are similar.

Double-banded Courser *Rhinoptilus africanus* Dubbelbanddrawwertjie
A locally common bird in areas of dry thornbush and bare stony ground. They feed mainly on insects, particularly harvester termites. The crown is pale buff finely streaked with brown/black. A narrow black stripe extends from the base of the bill, through the eye to the nape. The cheeks, chin, throat and neck are buff/white flecked with dark brown. The feathers of the back and wing coverts are sandy brown with dark centres and broadly edged with white/buff. The primary and secondary flight feathers are sandy brown edged with white/buff. The upper breast is buff with a black band encircling the breast and mantle, another black band extends across the lower breast separated from the upper band by a band of sandy buff. The remainder of the underparts are white. The short bill is blackish, the eyes are dark brown and the legs and feet are pale grey.

Long-toed Lapwing *Vanellus crassirostris* Witvlerkkiewiet

An uncommon resident found in the very northern parts of our region, in marshes and floodplains. They are usually to be encountered in pairs or small parties. The forehead, forecrown, face, chin, throat and sides of the neck are white. A broad black band extends from the hindcrown over the nape, hindneck and mantle, where it forms a collar around the lower neck on to the breast. The belly is white. The back and wings are grey/brown. The bill is reddish at the base and black at the tip, the eyes are crimson surrounded by an orbital ring of red. The legs and feet are dull pink/red. The sexes are similar.

Blacksmith Lapwing *Vanellus armatus* Bontkiewiet

A common resident throughout the whole region, found in short grassland areas as well as on the margins of water bodies. They are usually encountered singly or in pairs, but may gather in to flocks of a 100 or more. The forehead and crown are white. The hindcrown, nape, face, chin, neck and breast are black. The hindneck and belly are white. The back and outer scapulars are black, the inner scapulars and the wing coverts are silver/grey. The primary and secondary flight feathers are black, the rump and tail are white, the latter having a terminal band of black. Blacksmith's Lapwings have sharp spurs on the carpal joints of the wings that often protrude through the feathering. These carpal spurs can also be seen on White-crowned Lapwings. The bill is black, the eyes are blood red and the legs and feet are black. The sexes are similar.

Crowned Lapwing *Vanellus coronatus* Kroonkiewiet

A common resident in open grasslands, thornbush country and areas of bare open ground. The forehead is black from which a black stripe extends around the head to the nape. Above this stripe runs a white line which also borders the black crown. The chin is white and the cheeks, neck and upper breast are grey/brown. The lower breast is grey/brown darkening to form a narrow black band which separates the breast from the white belly. The upperparts are grey/brown and the primary and secondary flight feathers are white at the base and black at the tips. The bill is pink/red at the base and black at the tip, the eyes are yellow and the legs and feet are red. The sexes are similar.

African Wattled Lapwing *Vanellus senegallus* Lelkiewiet

A common resident in the north and the east, favouring areas of open grassland in the vicinity of water. A long-legged lapwing with an upright stance. The crown and hindneck are olive brown, flecked with brown/black. The cheeks, throat and foreneck are white heavily streaked with brown. The upperparts are olive brown, the upper throat is black, the breast is buff and the belly is white. At the base of the yellow bill, forward of the yellow eyes, are situated bright red and yellow wattles. The legs and feet are golden yellow. The sexes are similar.

Senegal Lapwing *Vanellus lugubris* Kleinswartvlerkkiewiet

A scarce resident in the north-eastern sector of our region, favouring open areas of savannah, areas of recently burnt grass and dry ground. This species can be confused with the Black-winged Lapwing but the Senegal Lapwing has grey/black not pinkish legs, the black breast band is narrower and they show white trailing edges to the wings when seen in flight. The forehead is white, the remainder of the head is brownish/grey. The upper breast is grey, darkening to form a black band above the white belly. The upperparts and wing coverts are brownish grey, the secondaries are white and the primaries are blackish. The rump and tail are white, the latter tipped with a broad band of brown/black. The bill is black, the eyes are yellow with a narrow red orbital ring and the legs and feet are blackish. The sexes are similar.

White-crowned Lapwing *Vanellus albiceps* Witkopkiewiet

A species restricted to the major river systems in the north and east of our region. They can usually be found on riverbanks and sand bars feeding on molluscs, small fish and frogs as well as insects and larvae. The forehead and crown are white, the remainder of the head and the sides and back of the neck are grey. The centre of the throat, the breast and the belly are white. The mantle, back and the inner portion of the scapulars are buff brown. The outer scapulars are white and the upperwing coverts are black. The primary and secondary flight feathers are white but for the three outer primaries which are black, as is the tail. During the breeding season they have long yellow wattles drooping from the base of the bill, which is yellow at the base with a black tip. The eyes are yellow and the legs and feet are pale lemon. The sexes are similar.

Grey Plover *Pluvialis squatarola* Grysstrandkiewiet

A common non-breeding migrant from the far north, mainly to be found in coastal regions from October to April. They are usually to be seen singly or in pairs or small groups. They feed on shrimps, crabs, prawns, clams and other forms of aquatic life. In non-breeding plumage, the head and chin are greyish white with brown streaking. The throat, breast and belly are pale grey spotted with brown, the spotting fading before merging in to the white belly. The feathers of the upperparts are brown edged with white/buff. The sexes are similar.

Common Ringed Plover *Charadrius hiaticula* Ringnekstrandkiewiet

A locally common migrant from the north, mainly found in coastal habitats such as estuaries and lagoons from September to April. The forehead is white and the forecrown is black, the hindcrown and nape are brown. A white stripe follows the line of the eyebrow. A white collar extends from the lower nape around the neck to the chin and throat. Below this line extends a black/brown collar, which spreads on to and covers the upper breast. The lower breast and the belly are white. The mantle, back and wings are mid-brown. The bill is blackish with a hint of orange at the base. The eyes are dark brown with a narrow orbital ring of yellow and the legs and feet are orange. The sexes are similar.

Kittlitz's Plover *Charadrius pecuarius* Geelborsstrandkiewiet

A locally common resident, found around the edges of lakes, rivers, on tidal mudflats and muddy margins of most wet areas. They feed mainly on small insects. The forehead is white above which is a thin black line running from eye to eye. Above this line is a fine white line, which continues along the line of the eyebrow, around the head to the base of the nape. From the rear of the eyes a broad band of black extends to the side of the neck, upwards to the nape and downwards towards the shoulder, where it merges with the cream/buff of the breast. The chin, throat and belly are white. The crown, nape and wings are brown, the wing feathers being edged with buff. The bill is black, the eyes are dark brown and the legs and feet are black. The sexes are similar.

Three-banded Plover *Charadrius tricollaris* Driebandstrandkiewiet

A common resident throughout the region, found in most wetland habitats from lagoons to the margins of lakes, rivers and swamps. They feed on a variety of small insects. A small plover with striking plumage, the forehead is white from which extends a white band following the line of the eyebrow to the nape. The crown is dark brown, the face is brown merging into white on the chin and throat. A band of white extends from the mantle to and around the lower throat. This band is bordered both on the upperside and the lower with bands of black. The breast and belly are white. The back and wings are olive brown. The bill is red, tipped with black, the eyes are yellow with a red orbital ring and the legs and feet are dull red. The sexes are similar.

White-fronted Plover *Charadrius marginatus* Vaalstrandkiewiet

A common resident in coastal areas throughout the region. Usually occurs in pairs or in small parties, feeding in the inter-tidal zones both during the day and the night. The forehead is white, the forecrown is black and the remainder of the crown and nape are brown. They have a black line extending from the base of the bill through the eye to the ear coverts. A white band follows the line of the eyebrow from the forehead. The lower hindneck has a thin white collar that broadens as it spreads around the neck to cover the chin and throat. A pale rusty brown band extends from the mantle around the sides of the neck to broaden across the upper breast. The belly is white. The back and the wings are brown, some feathers edged buff/white. The bill is black, the eyes are dark brown and the legs and feet are blackish grey. The sexes are similar.

Caspian Plover *Charadrius asiaticus* Asiatiese Strandkiewiet

An uncommon migrant from the far north, to be found only in the northern areas of our region, usually found in flocks in areas of open grassland. They feed almost entirely on insects. The forehead is white. A white eyebrow stripe is quite prominent. The crown, cheeks, neck, throat and upper breast are sandy brown. The belly is white. The wings are sandy brown with the feathers of the scapulars and wing coverts edged with buff. The primary flight feathers are brown/black, the bill is black, the eyes are dark brown and the legs and feet are greyish green. The sexes are similar.

African Snipe   *Gallinago nigripennis*   Afrikaanse Snip
A locally common resident in the eastern parts of our region. They are usually found singly or in scattered groups in areas of swamps, lakes and floodplains. They feed mainly in the evening and through the night, taking aquatic insects and small molluscs. The head is buff with a series of dark brown stripes extending from the base of the bill to the hindneck, these stripes run along the sides of the crown, through the eyes and across the cheeks. The chin, throat and the breast are buff streaked with dark brown. The belly and flanks are white, the flanks having dark brown barring. The wing coverts and flight feathers are dark brown edged and barred with buff and off-white. The extremely long bill is grey with a hint of pink, the eyes are brown and the legs and feet are greenish yellow. The sexes are similar.

Black-tailed Godwit   *Limosa limosa*   Swartstertgriet
A rare migrant visitor from the far north, arriving in October and departing in April. They are usually found on inland bodies of freshwater in the north of our region, in small flocks. They fed on insects, fish, amphibians and molluscs. The head, neck, and breast are grey/brown merging into white on the belly. They have a white bar extending from the base of the bill to the eye, merging with a narrow white orbital eye ring. The upperparts of the plumage are grey/brown, the feathers of the scapulars and wing coverts being edged with light grey/buff. The tail is black. The long straight bill is flesh pink at the base becoming black towards the tip. The eyes are dark brown and the legs and feet are black. The sexes are similar. Could be confused with the Bar-tailed Godwit which is smaller and has an upturned bill.

Common Whimbrel   *Numenius phaeopus*   Kleinwulp
A common non-breeding migrant in coastal areas, estuaries and lagoons, usually present from August to March. They feed on molluscs, shellfish and crustaceans. The forehead and crown have a buff central stripe with a dark brown stripe either side extending to the nape. A pale stripe extends from the base of the bill following the line of the eyebrow to the nape and a dark line runs below this through the eye. The cheeks, neck, chin, throat and breast are whitish buff streaked with dark brown. The belly is white. The wing coverts and the primary and secondary flight feathers are dark brown edged with buff and white. The long decurved bill is black, often with a hint of pink at the base, the eyes are dark brown and the legs and feet are grey/blue.

Common Redshank   *Tringa totanus*   Rooipootruiter
An uncommon migrant usually found on the margins of inland water bodies as well as estuaries and salt marshes during the months of August to January. They are to be found singly or in small parties probing muddy margins or shallow waters for crustaceans and small molluscs. The head and neck are whitish, densely marked with dark brown streaks. A stripe of white extends from the base of the bill through the eye towards the nape. The breast is whitish, heavily streaked and spotted with dark brown. The belly is white. The mantle and scapulars are brown, streaked and barred with dark brown. The flight feathers are dark brown with varying amounts of white edging and spotting. The bill is reddish at the base darkening to black towards the tip. The eyes are brown and the legs and feet are red/orange. The sexes are similar.

Marsh Sandpiper   *Tringa stagnatilis*   Moerasruiter
A common non-breeding migrant from the far north, arriving in October and departing back northwards in March. They are usually to be found on the margins of inland water bodies feeding on small molluscs and aquatic insects. A slender rather delicate sandpiper, resembling a small Greenshank from a distance. The crown, nape, hindneck, mantle and scapulars are pale grey with dark streaking, the face, chin, throat, breast and belly are white. The primary flight feathers are dark brown, the secondaries are grey edged with white. The thin straight bill is black, the eyes are dark brown and the legs and feet are pale greenish yellow.

Common Greenshank   *Tringa nebularia*   Groenpootruiter
A common visitor during the months of August to April. They are to be found on inland waters, estuaries and salt pans. They are normally seen singly feeding on aquatic insects, molluscs, small fish and crustaceans. The head and neck are greyish white heavily streaked with dark brown. The chin, throat, breast and belly are white with the upper breast and flanks being streaked and spotted with dark brown. The primaries are blackish and the secondaries are grey/brown edged with white. The long, slightly upturned bill is black, the eyes are brown and the legs and feet are pale greenish yellow. The sexes are similar.

Green Sandpiper *Tringa ochropus* Witgatruiter

A regular visitor to the north-east of our region during the months of September to May. Found around the margins of lakes, rivers and ponds. They feed mainly on insects and molluscs and usually lead a solitary existence. The forehead, nape, hindneck and mantle are dark olive brown finely streaked with dark brown. A white band extends from the base of the bill to the eye. The chin, throat and breast are white streaked and spotted with dark brown merging on to the white belly. The back and wing coverts are dark olive brown, the primary and secondary flight feathers are blackish brown. The tail is white at the base, being very prominent in flight, with thick blackish bars towards the tip. The bill is blackish, the eyes are dark brown and the legs and feet are greenish grey. The sexes are similar.

Wood Sandpiper *Tringa glareola* Bosruiter

A common non-breeding migrant from the far north, found in a variety of wetland habitats. They are usually encountered singly feeding along the edges of lakes, ponds and muddy creeks taking aquatic insects, molluscs and small fish. Some individuals may stay year-round but most reside from August to April. The forehead, crown, nape and mantle are dark brown with fine white flecking, they have a prominent white band extending from the base of the bill running above the eye to the nape. The foreneck, chin and throat are whitish finely streaked with brown. The breast is white washed with pale brown and streaked and barred with brown. The scapulars and wing coverts are dark brown barred and spotted with pale brown and white. The tail is white with a series of dark brown bars towards the tip. The primary and secondary flight feathers are dark brown. The bill is black with a hint of green towards the base, the eyes are dark brown and the legs and feet are dull yellow. The sexes are similar.

Common Sandpiper *Actitis hypoleucos* Gewone Ruiter

A common non-breeding visitor from the north during the months of September to March. They are usually solitary frequenting all kinds of wetland habitats. They feed mainly along the water's edge, taking insects, spiders, molluscs and snails. The forehead, crown, nape and mantle are olive brown streaked with dark brown, the sides of the neck and upper breast bib are greyish olive streaked with dark brown. The lower breast and belly are white extending as a crescent around the front of the wing. The scapulars and wing coverts are olive brown with dark brown barring and streaking. The primary and secondary flight feathers are dark brown. In flight the upperwings show a white bar. The bill is blackish, the eyes are dark brown and the legs and feet are dull greenish yellow. The sexes are similar.

Curlew Sandpiper *Calidris ferruginea* Krombekstrandloper

A common non-breeding migrant from the far north, arriving in August and departing in March. They are usually found in flocks in coastal areas and on inland wetlands, feeding on worms and insects. The forehead and crown are dark greyish brown, the remainder of the head, neck and breast are white with greyish brown streaking. A rather indistinct narrow band of white extends from the base of the bill over the eye towards the nape. The belly is white. The feathers of the scapulars and the wing coverts are greyish brown edged with white. The primary and secondary flight feathers are blackish brown. The rump is white and the tail is greyish brown. The decurved bill is black, the eyes are dark brown and the legs and feet are black.

White-rumped Sandpiper *Calidris fuscicollis* Witrugstrandloper

A rare non-breeding vagrant favouring coastal mudflats, creeks and lagoons, feeding on insects, molluscs and crustaceans. The forehead and crown are greyish brown with a wash of rufous. The chin and throat are white, the face, neck, mantle and breast are greyish with dark brown streaks and spots. The belly is white. The wing coverts and secondaries are dark brown edged with white and the primary flight feathers are dark brown. At rest the primaries extend beyond the tail. The bill is black, the eyes are dark brown and the legs and feet are blackish grey. The sexes are similar.

Ruddy Turnstone *Arenaria interpres* Steenloper

A common non-breeding migrant from the Arctic regions, arriving from September and departing by April. They can be encountered in coastal habitats throughout the region. The forehead, neck and face are dusky grey/brown. The chin is white, the upper breast has a blackish/brown bib and the lower breast and belly are white. The mantle and scapulars are rufous and dark brown edged with buff. The primary and secondary flight feathers are dark brown edged with buff and rufous. The bill is black, the eyes are dark brown and the legs and feet are dull orange/red. The sexes are similar.

Red Knot *Calidris canutus* Knoet

A locally common visitor from the Arctic regions, arriving in September and departing in April, confined to coastal regions particularly those in the west. They feed on areas of exposed tidal mudflats, taking mainly molluscs and crustaceans. The head and neck are greyish white streaked and spotted with blackish brown. The breast and belly are greyish white with the flanks and breast barred with greyish brown/black. The upperparts are grey, the secondaries being edged with white. The primary flight feathers are black/brown edged with white. During the breeding season the chin, throat, neck and underparts become a rich chestnut. In some cases the semblance of this breeding plumage is visible prior to the birds departing on their northward migration. The bill is black the eyes are brown and the legs and feet are dull grey/green. In non-breeding plumage the sexes are similar.

Sanderling *Calidris alba* Drietoonstrandloper

A common visitor to our coasts during September to April, being confined to coastal regions. They feed along the water's edge and on areas of inter-tidal mudflats, taking mainly molluscs and crustaceans. They are extremely active. The head, neck, mantle and scapulars are grey with some dark streaking. The chin, throat, breast and belly are white. The lesser wing coverts are blackish, giving the impression of a dark shoulder patch. The secondary and primary flight feathers are blackish brown. The bill is black, the eyes are dark brown and the legs and feet are black. In non-breeding plumage the sexes are similar.

Little Stint *Calidris minuta* Kleinstrandloper

A common, non-breeding migrant from the north, arriving in October and departing in April. They are to be found on coastal lagoons and marshes, salt pans and estuaries as well as on inland lakes and floodplains. They are usually in small groups and are frequently seen in the company of Curlew Sandpipers. They are very active feeders, picking insects, molluscs and crustaceans from the water surface and from exposed areas of wet mud. The head, neck, mantle and scapulars are greyish brown with dark central streaks to the feathers. The chin, throat, breast and belly are white with fine streaking on the sides of the upper breast. The primary flight feathers are blackish with white outer edges. The bill is black, the eyes are dark brown and the legs and feet are black. The sexes are similar.

Ruff *Philomachus pugnax* Kemphaan

A common non-breeding migrant from the north, arriving in September and departing in February. They frequent areas of marshland, inland water bodies and floodplains. They feed on worms and aquatic insects as well as on seeds. The head and the sides of the neck are brown with dark streaking. The throat, breast and belly are white with some mottling on the sides of the breast and flanks. The mantle and scapulars are darkish brown with a hint of tawny, the wing coverts are greyish brown edged with buff and the flight feathers are dark brown/black. The slightly curved bill is black, the eyes are brown and the legs and feet are orange. The sexes are similar in non-breeding plumage.

Red Phalarope *Phalaropus fulicarius* Grysfraiingpoot

A locally common visitor from the north during the period November to March. They are usually to be found in small groups in areas of the open ocean but can also be found inland during periods of extreme weather. They feed by spinning in tight circles as well as by upending. The crown, nape, hindneck, mantle and back are plain grey. The forehead, cheeks, neck, breast and belly are white. A small area to the rear of the eye appears as a smudge of black. The primary and secondary flight feathers are dark grey with some white edging. The bill is blackish, the eyes are dark brown and the legs and feet are grey. The sexes are alike in non-breeding plumage.

Subantarctic Skua *Catharacta antarctica* Bruinroofmeeu

A fairly common species found around the south and west coasts throughout the year but more commonly during the winter months. A large, well built skua with broad wings and a relatively short tail. They spend much of their time resting on the surface of the ocean, singly or in very small groups. They are often associated with trawlers, feeding on offal, fish, crustaceans and other scraps. They will also harass other seabirds, particularly shearwaters and petrels, grabbing them by the wings or tail and forcing them to regurgitate their last meal. At a distance they look uniform dark brown in colour with distinctive white patches on both the upper and lower surfaces of the primary flight feathers. A closer view will show the plumage to be mottled with light flecking on the upperparts. The bill is blackish, the eyes are brown and the legs and feet are brownish black. The sexes are similar.

Pomarine Jaeger *Stercorarius pomarinus* Knopstertroofmeeu

A fairly common summer visitor to coastal regions, particularly along the coast of northern Namibia, where they can be found singly or in small groups. They can also be found in larger groups when scavenging from fishing vessels. They also feed by harassing other seabirds, forcing them to disgorge their last meal. They will also take and eat other seabirds such as small gulls and terns. The blunt, spatulate shaped central tail feathers are a diagnostic feature when present. There are two colour phases, the light phase has the forehead, crown, nape and upper section of the face dark brown and often showing buff on the sides of the upper neck. The lower neck has a faint band of grey/brown extending around the upper breast. The belly is whitish with dark barring along the flanks. The upper plumage is brown/grey. The dark phase has the upper body plumage black/brown. In flight the primary feathers show white at the base. The bill is greyish black, the eyes are dark brown and the legs and feet are greyish black. The sexes are similar.

Parasitic Jaeger *Stercorarius parasiticus* Arktieseroofmeeu

A fairly common visitor to the west and south coasts from September to April. Mainly to be found on areas of inshore coastal waters, where they feed by harassing other seabirds into disgorging their latest meal or by snatching fish and other food items from small gulls and terns. They also scavenge from the refuse created by fishing vessels. The plumage varies tremendously, with light phase birds, dark phase and intermediates. The light phase plumage has the forehead, crown and the upper portion of the face dark brown, becoming paler and buffer on the sides of the neck. The chin and throat are pale buff and a faint greyish collar extends from the mantle across the upper breast. The scapulars and wing coverts are brown and the secondary and primary flight feathers are dark brown/black with a pale area at the base of the primaries, which can be seen in flight. The dark phase birds are brown/black with the exception of the white bases of the primaries, the black forehead and crown and slightly paler underparts. The bill is black, the eyes are dark brown and the legs and feet are black. The sexes are similar.

Long-tailed Jaeger *Stercorarius longicaudus* Langstertroofmeeu

A fairly common non-breeding visitor during the period of September to April. They are usually to be found in oceanic waters with inland records being rare, The smallest of the jaegers, they have an easy, buoyant flight and are usually encountered singly or in small groups of 6 or so birds. They can, however, be found in larger groups at migration times. Less piratical than other jaegers, they feed from scraps jettisoned by fishing vessels and by taking small fish and carrion from the water surface. Although plumage variation is less obvious than with other jaeger species, there are light, dark and intermediate phases. The light phase has the forehead, crown and upper portion of the face dark brown/black, the rest of the head and the neck are white. The chin, throat, breast and belly are white, often with a hint of a grey band across the breast and with some faint grey barring on the flanks. The upperparts are greyish and the tail is grey at the base becoming darker towards the tip. The dark phase is a uniform dark slate grey all over, with the exception of the dark brown/black crown and pale throat and breast. The bill is black, the eyes are dark brown and the legs and feet are black. The sexes are similar.

Kelp Gull *Larus dominicanus* Kelpmeeu

A very common species present throughout the year. They inhabit coastal regions, where they feed on fish, crustaceans and other marine creatures as well as eggs, chicks and adults of other bird species. They may also follow fishing vessels in the hope of scraps and have been recorded doing so up to 150 km from land. They are colonial nesters, with up to four pairs breeding within a square metre, usually on off-shore islands or on mainland cliffs. The head, throat, neck, breast and belly are white, while the mantle, back and most of the upperwings are slaty black. The trailing edge of the wings are white and the outer primary feathers are black with prominent white spots or mirrors. The large, heavy bill is yellow with an orange spot towards the tip of the lower mandible, the eyes are brown and have a red orbital ring. The legs and feet are olive/yellow. The sexes are similar, with the female being slightly smaller.

Lesser Black-backed Gull *Larus fuscus* Kleinswartrugmeeu

An uncommon visitor to the northern parts of our region. Found mainly in Botswana, northern Namibia and northern parts of Zimbabwe. They are mainly to be found in the vicinity of inland water bodies such as lakes, dams, rivers and marshes, but also frequent coastal estuaries and rocky shorelines. They feed on a wide variety of foodstuffs, including other birds and their young, small rodents, beetles, marine creatures, grains and seaweeds. They also occasionally scavenge on human rubbish tips. In many ways the plumage is similar to that of the Kelp Gull, but the build is much slimmer and the bill much smaller. The head, neck, breast and belly are white, the wings and back are black with white tips to the secondaries. The black primaries show small white mirrors or spots. The bill is yellow with a reddish spot towards the tip of the lower mandible, the eyes are lemon yellow with a narrow red orbital ring and the legs and feet are yellow. Apart from the female being a little smaller than the male the sexes are similar.

Hartlaub's Gull *Larus hartlaubii* Hartlaubse Meeu

A common species in coastal areas and off-shore islands in the west of our region. As well as feeding on a wide variety of marine creatures, they regularly scavenge on humane rubbish tips. They can easily be mistaken for Grey-headed Gull, but they are smaller with a finer bill and have dark brown eyes. The head, neck, throat, breast and belly are white, the head having a flush of lavender forming a hood. The mantle, back and wing coverts are grey, the primary flight feathers are black with a series of white spots or mirrors towards the tips. The bill is red to black, the eyes are dark brown with a maroon orbital ring and the legs and feet are black with a hint of red. The sexes are similar.

Grey-headed Gull *Larus cirrocephalus* Gryskopmeeu

A very common gregarious gull, inhabiting both coastal areas and inland wetlands and rivers. They feed on fish, molluscs, insects and will readily scavenge from human rubbish tips and snatch unguarded eggs and chicks from the nests of seabird colonies. The crown, face and chin are a soft grey with a thin darker line bordering the rear edge of this hood. The neck, breast and belly are white. The mantle, back and wing coverts are grey, the primary flight feathers are white at the base becoming black towards the tips with small spots or mirrors. The thin bill is red, the eyes are lemon yellow with a red orbital ring and the legs and feet are red. The sexes are similar.

Sabine's Gull *Larus sabini* Mikstertmeeu

A regular visitor to coastal areas and off-shore waters in the west of our region from September to May. They feed singly or in small flocks, taking fish, offal from fishing vessels and marine invertebrates. A small slender built gull with a buoyant, tern-like flight and a slight fork in the tail. The head, neck, throat, breast and belly are white, with a smudge of grey on the nape. The mantle, back, wing coverts and secondaries are grey, the latter tipped with white. The primary flight feathers are black with white tips and edges. The fine bill is black tipped with yellow, the eyes are dark brown with a red orbital ring and the legs and feet are dark grey/black. The sexes are similar.

Caspian Tern *Sterna caspia* Reusesterretjie

An uncommon and local breeding resident, found in coastal regions and estuaries as well as occasionally on inland water bodies. They feed on small fish which they usually take by hovering before diving head first in to the water. The captured prey is swallowed on the wing. A very large tern, with the forehead, crown, nape and upper portion of the face black. The lower face, neck, breast and belly are white. The mantle, wing coverts and secondary flight feathers are ash grey, while the rump and tail are white. The primary feathers are a darker grey, the heavy bill is bright red, the eyes are dark brown and the legs and feet are black. The sexes are similar.

Lesser Crested Tern *Sterna bengalensis* Kuifkopsterretjie

An uncommon but regular visitor to the eastern coastal regions of Southern Africa, frequenting estuaries and lagoons where they feed mainly on fish and crustaceans. Most of their fish prey is caught by vertical plunge diving, often completely submerging. The captured fish are quickly swallowed on the wing to avoid the attention of predators. The forehead, crown and nape are black, the neck, breast and belly are white and the mantle, scapulars and wing coverts are bluish grey. The primary flight feathers are grey with silver edging. The bill is bright orange/yellow, the eyes are dark brown and the legs and feet are black. The sexes are similar.

Sandwich Tern *Sterna sandvicensis* Grootsterretjie

A common, non-breeding visitor to coastal regions from September to May, feeding mainly on fish which they obtain by a method of plunge diving, from heights of up to 10 m, often submerging completely. In non-breeding plumage the hindcrown and upper nape are black with some white speckling, the forehead, forecrown, neck, breast and belly are white. The back, scapulars and wing coverts are ash grey and the secondary and primary flight feathers are grey edged with white. The bill is black with a yellow tip, the eyes are dark brown and the legs and feet are black with yellow soles. The sexes are similar.

Swift Tern *Sterna bergii* Geelbeksterretjie

A common breeding resident, found in coastal regions throughout Southern Africa. Distinguished from other tern species of the region by its all yellow bill. They feed almost exclusively on fish, which they catch by a method of plunge diving. They feed singly or in small flocks often with other tern species. They breed in dense colonies on offshore islands or on inland pans. The crown and elongated crest feathers of the nape are black while the remainder of the head, the neck, breast and belly are white. The mantle, back, rump and wing coverts are light blue/grey and the primary and secondary flight feathers are grey edged with white. The eyes are dark brown and the legs and feet are black. The sexes are similar.

Common Tern *Sterna hirundo* Gewone Sterretjie

A very common non-breeding migrant from the north, arriving in September and departing in April. They are present in coastal regions, rarely venturing far inland. They feed mainly on fish but also take crustaceans. They often feed far out to sea in large flocks, scavenging offal from fishing vessels. In non-breeding plumage the forehead, forecrown, neck, breast and belly are white, the hindcrown and nape are black. The mantle, back, rump and wing coverts are grey, the primary flight feathers are dark grey/black edged with white. The bill can be red or black, the eyes are dark brown and the legs and feet are brownish red. The sexes are similar.

Antarctic Tern *Sterna vittata* Grysborssterrejie

A common non-breeding visitor from the south, arriving in May and departing in September, usually found along southern coastal areas of our region. They breed in the Antarctic and on sub-antarctic islands. They feed on small fish, usually in small parties, and often follow ships in the hope of picking up scraps. In non-breeding plumage the forehead, neck, breast and belly are white. The hindcrown and the nape are black. The mantle, back and wing coverts are blue/grey, the secondaries are grey tipped and edged with white. The primary flight feathers are dark grey with white edging. The bill is dull red/black, the eyes are dark brown and the legs and feet are brownish. The sexes are similar.

Little Tern *Sterna albifrons* Kleinsterretjie

A common non-breeding visitor from the north, arriving in August and departing in March. They can be found in coastal lagoons and estuaries around the western and southern coasts of our region. They often feed along side other tern species and adopt a method of plunge diving to take small fish, they also feed on marine invertebrates, which they pluck from the water surface. The crown, nape and upper head to a line below the eye, is brown/black flecked with white, the remainder of the head, neck, breast and belly is white. The back and wing coverts are blue/grey and the primary flight feathers are blackish grey. The bill is yellow or black, the eyes are dark brown and the legs and feet are dull yellow.

Sooty Tern *Sterna fuscata* Roetsterretjie

A common non-breeding summer visitor to the coastal waters to the west of our region. They are usually found in large flocks feeding out to sea, with nearly half of their diet consisting of squid, the remainder being small fish and marine invertebrates. The forehead is white, the crown and nape are black with a black stripe extending from the crown through the eye to the base of the bill. The remainder of the head, neck, breast and belly are white. The upperparts are brown/black. The bill is black, the eyes are dark brown and the legs and feet are black. The sexes are similar.

Whiskered Tern *Chlidonias hybrida* Witbaardsterretjie

A common breeding resident over much of the region, favouring coastal estuaries as well as inland water bodies. They feed on small fish, invertebrates and occasionally amphibians. During the breeding season, the forehead, crown and nape are black. The chin is pale grey becoming darker on the breast and darker still, almost black, on the belly and flanks, the vent area is white. The mantle, back, wing coverts and secondary flight feathers are grey. The primary flight feathers are dark grey edged and tipped with lighter grey. The bill is dull red, becoming black towards the tip, the eyes are dark brown and the legs and feet are red. During non-breeding periods the plumage is generally paler. The sexes are similar.

White-winged Tern *Chlidonias leucopterus* Witvlerksterretjie

A common non-breeding migrant from the far north, arriving in September and departing in March. They can be found on inland water bodies, marshes and other wetland areas, where they feed on fish, invertebrates and very occasionally amphibians. In non-breeding plumage the forehead and forecrown are white, with a smudge of grey/brown on the hindcrown and the ear coverts. A dark spot is also present in front of the eye. The remainder of the head, the neck, breast and belly are white. The upperparts are slaty grey, the bill is black, the eyes are dark brown and the legs and feet are blackish with a hint of red. The sexes are similar.

Black Tern *Chlidonias niger* Swartsterretjie

A non-breeding migrant from the far north being present from September to April. Common along the Namibian coast, less common elsewhere. They feed on fish, crustaceans and invertebrates. In non-breeding plumage the crown, nape and ear coverts are blackish with a similar blackish spot in front of the eye. The remainder of the head, neck, breast and belly is white. The mantle is slate grey extending in a half collar around the sides of the neck. The remainder of the upperparts are slate grey, becoming darker on the primary flight feathers and around the shoulder of the wing. The bill is black, the eyes are dark brown and the legs and feet are black. In breeding plumage the head, neck, breast and belly are entirely black. The sexes are similar.

African Skimmer *Rynchops flavirostris* Waterploeër

A species sparsely distributed through the region, inhabiting lakes and large rivers, favouring those with exposed sandbars on which they can nest. They feed on fish in a most unusual manner. Flying low over the water they slice the surface with their elongated lower mandible, which snaps shut when making contact with a food item. They have a very slow, buoyant flight. The crown, including the eye, nape, hindneck and wings are black, with the secondary flight feathers being edged and tipped with white. The tail is forked. The forehead, cheeks, side of neck, breast and belly are white. The bill is orange/red with the lower mandible being significantly longer than that of the lower mandible, this elongated section is yellow. The eyes are dark brown and the legs and feet are orange/red.

Yellow-throated Sandgrouse *Pterocles gutturalis* Geelkeelsandpatrys

An uncommon resident in areas of short grasslands and cultivated fields. They are usually to be found in pairs or small groups feeding on a wide variety of seeds. They gather each morning, shortly after sunrise, into large flocks as they fly off to the nearest waterhole to drink. After drinking they again break up into small groups, returning to their favoured feeding grounds. The male has the forehead, crown and nape olive grey merging into buff olive on the neck and breast. The chin and throat are creamy, yellow buff, the throat being bordered below by a dark brown/black band, which extends to the sides of the neck. A thin dark brown stripe extends from the base of the bill through the eye to the ear coverts. The belly is chestnut brown. The mantle, back, scapulars and wing coverts are greyish yellow, the latter with smudges of grey/brown. The primary and secondary flight feathers are blackish brown. The female has a plain creamy buff chin and throat. The remainder of the upper and lower plumage is a mixture of rich buffs, browns, ochre's and greys affording excellent camouflage. The bill is greyish, the eyes are dark brown and the legs and feet are reddish brown.

Double-banded Sandgrouse *Pterocles bicinctus* Dubbelbandsandpatrys

A locally common species in the northern parts of our region, inhabiting areas of wooded savannah, particularly those of acacia and mopane. They are most active at dawn and towards dusk and on moonlit nights will forage throughout the night, in pairs or in small groups. During the daytime they will rest in the shade of bushes, trees and rocks. They come to water to drink well after sunset, often having to find their way in total darkness. The male is a most attractive bird, with the forehead and forecrown white, separated by a prominent black band. The hindcrown and nape are olive buff speckled with black. The chin, throat, neck and breast are olive buff, the breast being bordered with a white and black band. The belly is buff and is heavily barred with blackish brown. The mantle, scapulars and wing coverts are rufous and olive buff with white tips to many of the feathers. The primary and secondary flight feathers are dark brown with pale tips and edges. The female is light rufous/buff in colour, barred, streaked and spotted with browns, blacks and buffs acting as excellent camouflage. The bill is yellow at the base and red at the tip, the eyes are dark brown and the legs and feet are dull brown.

Namaqua Sandgrouse *Pterocles namaqua* Kelkiewyn

A bird of dry semidesert habitats, gathering in to large flocks, particularly when flying to water, as they do just after sunrise. They are mainly restricted to the western part of our region, feeding almost exclusively on small seeds. The only Sandgrouse in the region with long central tail feathers. The adult male has the crown, nape, sides of the neck and breast buff olive, the chin and throat are rusty orange. The breast is bordered below by an upper band of white and a lower band of dark brown. The belly is chestnut grading to greyish, rusty red towards the postural area. The tail is olive brown, tipped with white and has elongated central feathers. The plumage of the back, scapulars and wing coverts are a mosaic of rich browns, buffs and ochres. The adult female is mottled above with barring and streaking on the breast and belly. The face and throat are yellowish. The bill is grey, the eyes are dark brown and the legs and feet are greyish buff.

Burchell's Sandgrouse *Pterocles burchelli* Gevlekte Sandpatrys

A bird of arid savannahs, locally common. They are to be found singly, in pairs or in very small groups of 4 or 5 birds. A very secretive species best seen as they arrive at waterholes in the morning for their daily drink. They feed on seeds. They are solitary breeders, making a shallow scrape in soil near to a grass clump. On hatching both parents tend to the chicks as they forage together as a family party. The parents will often fly up to 40 km to fetch water for the chicks which they do by soaking their belly feathers, allowing the chicks to obtain moisture on their return to the breeding site. The forehead and crown are olive/buff finely speckled with brown, the face, ear coverts and sides of the neck are buff streaked finely with brown. The chin and the throat are blue/grey. The breast is a pale rufous/ochre with white spotting and grey banding. The belly is rufous grey with white spots and smudges. The feathers of the mantle and scapulars are olive/yellow with white spots. The primary and secondary feathers are darkish brown edged and tipped with white. The bill is black, the eyes are dark brown and the legs and feet are yellowish. The sexes are similar, the female having the chin and throat yellow, not blue/grey as the male.

Rock Pigeon   *Columba livia*   Tuinduif

A common, introduced species covering most of the region, favouring urban areas, city parks, industrial complexes and cultivated farmland. They feed on seeds and earthworms. The plumage of this species is extremely variable, normally the forehead and face are grey, the crown and nape are blue/grey and the neck and upper breast are a mixture of reflective metallic greens and purples. The lower breast and belly are light, slaty grey. The mantle and scapulars are slaty grey and the rump is white. The wing coverts are ash grey and the greater coverts have a broad black sub-terminal bar. A similar black bar extends across the width of the secondary flight feathers. The primaries are mid grey with darker grey tips. The bill is grey with a white cere, the eyes are red and the legs and feet are orange. The sexes are similar.

Speckled Pigeon   *Columba guinea*   Kransduif

A common resident, inhabiting areas of farmland, mountains, cliffs and gorges as well as towns and cities. They feed on seeds and cultivated crops, doing considerable damage to yield levels, and are regarded as pests by farming communities. They also feed on small fruits. A very handsome bird with the head, neck, breast and belly grey, with stiff divided feathers of chestnut tipped with white on the upper breast and neck. The scapulars and wing coverts are chestnut and the greater wing coverts are chestnut with prominent white tips. The tail is black with a broad grey sub-terminal band. The primary flight feathers are black edged with grey. The bill is dark grey with a light grey cere, the eyes are yellow with a bare red orbital patch, and the legs and feet are yellow/orange. The sexes are similar.

African Olive Pigeon   *Columba arquatrix*   Geelbekbosduif

A common resident in the eastern and southern parts of our range, found in mountain forests and plantations, where they feed on fruits, seed and some insects. The forehead and cheeks are light purple, the crown, nape and chin are blue/grey. The sides of the neck and the breast are mauve grading to dark maroon on the belly which also is spotted with white The mantle feathers are dark brown with mauve edges. The back, rump and tail are brown/black. The scapulars are dark maroon with white spots, the wing coverts and the flight feathers are dark maroon/brown. The bill is yellow, the eyes are yellowish surrounded by a bare area of bright yellow skin and the legs and feet are also yellow.

African Green Pigeon   *Treron calvus*   Papegaaiduif

A common resident found mainly in woodlands and evergreen forests, where they feed almost exclusively on fruits, particularly figs. The head, throat, neck, breast and belly are a bright yellow/green. The mantle, back and rump are rich olive green, the upper mantle being tinged with grey. The primary and secondary flight feathers are grey/brown edged with yellow. The wing coverts are grey/brown with broad yellow edges forming a conspicuous wing bar and they have a mauve patch on the shoulder of the wing. The bill is grey at the tip and red at the base, the eyes are pale blue/grey and the legs and feet are yellow. The sexes are similar.

African Mourning Dove   *Streptopelia decipiens*   Rooioogtortelduif

Locally common in the north of our region, found in savannah woodlands and areas of scrub. They usually feed alone or in small parties, taking seeds and small fruits. The forehead, crown and face are ash grey, the neck, throat and breast are pale mauve and a prominent black half collar sits at the base of the hindneck. The belly is pale grey with a wash of mauve/pink. The mantle, scapulars, back and wing coverts are mid-grey/brown, the primary and secondary flight feathers are brown edged with pale grey. The bill is dark grey, the eyes are yellow with a red orbital ring, the legs are feathered yellow and the feet are red. The sexes are similar.

Lemon Dove   *Aplopelia larvata*   Kaneelduifie

A locally common resident, favouring areas of lowland evergreen forests and wooded parks and gardens. They feed mainly on the ground, usually in pairs, taking seeds and fallen fruits as well as some small insects. The forehead, forecrown and face are white, the hindcrown, nape and mantle are iridescent green. The chin and throat are greyish white and the breast is pale rufous merging to iridescent green on the sides of the breast and to cinnamon on the lower breast and belly. The back, wing coverts and rump are mauve/brown with a hint of iridescent green and the flight feathers are dark brown. The bill is black, the eyes are brown with a red/purple orbital ring and the legs and feet are dull red. The sexes are similar.

Red-eyed Dove *Streptopelia semitorquata* Grootringduif
A fairly common resident found in a variety of woodland habitats and forest edges. They feed for the most part on seeds and berries. The forehead is white merging into grey on the crown and nape. The neck, throat, breast and belly are pinkish/grey. A prominent black half collar sits at the base of the nape. The mantle, scapulars and wing coverts are grey/brown and the primary and secondary flight feathers are brown edged with pale grey. The bill is black and the eyes are red surrounded by an area of bare orange/red skin, the legs and feet are red. The sexes are similar.

Cape Turtle Dove *Streptopelia capicola* Gewone Tortelduif
A very common resident found in a wide variety of habitat types from savannahs to parks, gardens and woodlands. They also eat a wide variety of foods including seeds, fruits, insects and the leaves of some plants. The forehead is pale bluish grey, becoming slightly darker on the crown. The nape and neck are pale grey with a wash of pink. A black half collar sits at the base of the nape. The breast and belly are pale mauve/pink. The mantle, back and wing coverts are mid-brown, the primary flight feathers are dark brown with narrow white edging and the secondaries are greyish/brown edged with pale grey. The bill is black, the eyes are dark brown and the legs and feet are pale red. The sexes are similar.

Laughing Dove *Streptopelia senegalensis* Rooiborsduifie
A very common resident over most of our region, found in a wide array of habitat types including woodlands, parks and gardens in towns and cities and cultivated farmland. They forage on the ground for seeds, fruits and insects. The forehead, face and chin are pale grey/pink. The throat and upper breast has the appearance of a broad half collar of rufous/pink, speckled with black. The lower breast is rufous/pink merging to white on the belly. The mantle and scapulars are pale brown, the back and rump are blue/grey as are the outermost wing coverts. The inner secondaries are dark brown and the outermost are blue/grey. The primary flight feathers are dark brown. The bill is black, the eyes are dark brown and the legs and feet are dull red.

Emerald-spotted Wood Dove *Turtur chalcospilos* Groenvlekduifie
A locally common resident in northern and western regions, frequenting woodland habitats of many types. They forage singly or in pairs on the ground feeding on seeds, grasses and small invertebrates. The forehead is pale grey, merging to bluish/grey on the crown and nape. The neck, throat and breast are pinkish/grey becoming peach on the belly. The mantle, back and rump are tawny brown, the rump having two to four conspicuous black bars running across it. The greater wing coverts are brown with bright metallic green patches. The inner primaries are brown the outer feathers are dark grey/black. The bill is blackish, the eyes are brown and the legs and feet are dull red. The sexes are similar.

Tambourine Dove *Turtur tympanistria* Witborsduifie
A locally common species in the northern and eastern parts of our region. They are to be found in mountain and lowland forests and in well-wooded parks and gardens. They feed on the forest floor usually singly or in pairs, taking seeds small fruits and some insects. The forehead and the face are white with a narrow black line running from the base of the bill to the eye and a broader black bar extending from the lower rear of the eye to the ear coverts. The throat and upper breast are grey merging to white over the lower breast and belly. The mantle, back and wing coverts are dark brown, the coverts carrying two black spots. The primary and secondary flight feathers are mostly chestnut brown, very little of which shows until the bird becomes airborne when all is revealed. The bill is black, the eyes are dark brown and the legs and feet are red. The sexes are similar.

Namaqua Dove *Oena capensis* Namakwaduifie
A very common and widespread resident to be found in a variety of habitat types, including savannah, woodland and parks and gardens. The smallest of Africa's doves, they are extremely fast fliers. The male has the forehead, face, throat and central breast black, the remainder of the head, neck and sides of the breast are pale grey merging into white on the belly. The hindcrown, nape and mantle are mid-brown. The tail is very long with the dark grey central feathers being nearly twice as long as the black outer ones. The primaries and secondaries are mainly rufous, the wing coverts are grey with a series of dark blue spots. The bill is orange the eyes are dark brown and the legs and feet are dull red. The female lacks the black facial mask and bib of the male, having grey/brown feathering instead.

Rosy-faced Lovebird *Agapornis roseicollis* Rooiwangparkiet

A bird of dry woodlands and scrub in the north-west of the region where they are locally common. They are usually to be found in small flocks rarely far from water, as they need to drink several times a day. The forehead are red, the face, chin and throat are pink. The remainder of the head, breast and belly are yellow/green. The mantle, back and wing coverts are green/yellow and the rump is bright blue. The tail is a deep green and the primary flight feathers are dark green edged with white. The bill is pale yellow, the eyes are dark brown and the legs and feet are greyish/green. The sexes are similar.

Meyer's Parrot *Poicephalus meyeri* Bosveldpapegaai

A locally common parrot, resident in dry savannah woodlands, usually encountered singly, in pairs or small flocks in the northern parts of our region. They feed on seeds, nuts and fruits. The head, face, chin, throat, upper breast and upperparts are dark brown, with a broken band of yellow across the forecrown. The lower breast and belly are green. The shoulder of the wing, from the carpal area to the primaries is yellow, the remaining wing coverts and the primary and secondary flight feathers are dark brown. The bill is black, the eyes are blood red and the legs and feet are black. The sexes are similar.

Brown-headed Parrot *Poicephalus cryptoxanthus* Bruinkoppapegaai

An uncommon resident of open woodlands in the Kruger, KwaZulu-Natal and surrounding areas in the east. They are usually to be found in small flocks feeding on seeds, fruits and young shots as well as cultivated grains. The entire head, including the nape, chin and throat is greyish olive/brown. The breast and belly are yellow/green. The mantle is brown with green margins. The wing coverts are yellow. The upper mandible is slaty black, the lower mandible is pale yellow, the eyes are yellow with a grey orbital ring and the legs and feet are slaty black. The sexes are similar.

Livingstone's Turaco *Tauraco livingstonii* Mozambiekloerie

A common resident in coastal forests in the northeast and in evergreen forests in Zimbabwe. They are usually to be found in pairs or small parties feeding in the upper storeys of forest trees, taking a wide variety of fruits. The head, neck, mantle and breast are bright yellow/green with a white stripe extending from the base of the bill to the top of the eye. Another white line extends from the gape, below the eye to the ear coverts. A black line separates these two white lines. The feathers of the hindcrown are elongated in the form of a crest and are tipped with white. The belly is green/brown, the back, rump, tail, scapulars and wing coverts are dark green. The primary and secondary flight feathers are rich red with blackish tips. The bill is red, the eyes are dark brown with a red orbital ring and the legs and feet are black. The sexes are similar.

Knysna Turaco *Tauraco corythaix* Knysnaloerie

A common endemic along an eastern strip, inhabiting areas of evergreen forest singly or in pairs. They feed on a variety of fruits as well as taking some insects. The head, neck, mantle and breast are bright yellow/green, with a white stripe curving from the base of the bill to the top of the eye, and another similar stripe extends from the gape, below the eye to the ear coverts. The feathers of the hindcrown are elongated in the form of a crest and are tipped with white. The belly is dull grey/brown. The wing coverts and the tail are violet blue and the primary and secondary flight feathers are crimson which provide a brilliant burst of colour as the bird flies. The bill is red, the eyes are brown surrounded by a red orbital ring and the legs and feet are grey/black. The sexes are similar.

Purple-crested Turaco *Tauraco porphyreolophus* Bloukuifloerie

A common resident in the north-eastern part of our range, inhabiting dense forests and plantations. They usually occur singly or in pairs and feed on a wide variety of fruits. The forehead and upper cheeks are glossy emerald green, the crown has a rounded crest of purple feathers merging into violet/black on the nape. The lower face and throat are olive green, the mantle and breast are dull orange and the belly is slaty blue. The wing coverts and tail are blue/black with a wash of iridescent green. The primary and secondary flight feathers are crimson edged with black. The bill is black, the eyes are dark brown surrounded by a red orbital ring and the legs and feet are blackish/grey. The sexes are similar.

Grey Go-away-bird *Corythaixoides concolor* Kwêvoël

A common resident in the northern parts of our range in areas of acacia woodland as well as in parks and gardens, usually in the vicinity of water. They feed on a wide variety of fruits, will take nectar from flowers and occasionally will feed on termites. A rather noisy bird usually seen in pairs or small flocks. The whole of the plumage is a soft warm grey with slightly lighter patches on the ear coverts, the throat and the sides of the breast. The feathers of the crown are elongated and form a crest, warm grey at the base becoming white at the tips. The long tail is grey at the base terminating with a broad brown band. The bill is black, the eyes are brown with a pale grey orbital ring and the legs and feet are black. The sexes are similar.

Jacobin Cuckoo *Clamator jacobinus* Bontnuwejaarsvoël

A common migrant breeder, arriving in October and departing in April. They are mainly to be found in dry acacia savannah and are usually in pairs. They are parasitic breeders, their principle hosts being bulbuls. They feed mainly on insects, being particularly fond of hairy caterpillars as well as termites. The upper portion of the head is black, with the elongated feathers of the crown forming a crest. The lower part of the head and the chin, throat, neck, breast and belly are off-white with some fine streaking. The wings and tail are black with a bluish/green sheen, the feathers of the tail are tipped white. The primary flight feathers are white at the base, which forms a prominent wingbar when the bird is at rest. There is considerable variation in plumage as a dark phase (having no white on the underside) also occurs. The bill is black, the eyes are brown and the legs and feet are dark grey. The sexes are similar.

Great Spotted Cuckoo *Clamator glandarius* Gevlekte Koekoek

A reasonably common breeding migrant, arriving in August and departing in April, found in areas of open acacia bush where they feed on hairy caterpillars, termites and grasshoppers. A brood parasite, using the nests of Pied Crows and Cape Rooks, among others, in which to lay their eggs. The forehead and crown are silver grey, the latter having elongated feathers which form into a crest. A dark grey band extends from the base of the bill to the nape. The sides of the neck and the throat are creamy buff, which merges into white over the breast and belly. The scapulars, wing coverts and flight feathers are an olive/brown many of the feathers being tipped with white which produce a series of white wingbars when the bird is seen at rest. The bill is blackish, the eyes are dark brown and the legs and feet are grey. The sexes are similar.

Red-chested Cuckoo *Cuculus solitarius* Piet-my-vrou

A common breeding migrant, arriving in September and departing in March, they can be found in wooded areas in the east of our region, feeding mainly on hairy caterpillars. They are brood parasites and select mainly robins and thrushes as foster parents for their young. The head, nape and mantle are mid-grey, the breast is rufous red and the belly is creamy white with heavy dark brown barring. The wing coverts, the tail and the primary and secondary flight feathers are charcoal grey, the tail having irregular white spots and bars. The bill is black, the eyes are dark brown surrounded by a yellow orbital ring and the legs and feet are yellow. The female is similar to the male but has barring on the breast and the sides of the neck. Immature, as illustrated, lacks rufous breast and is generally darker.

African Cuckoo *Cuculus gularis* Afrikaanse Koekoek

A fairly common breeding migrant present from August through to April. They are usually to be found in areas of open woodland and scrub in the northern parts of our region. They feed on all types of caterpillars, as well as on termites and beetles. They are brood parasites, laying their eggs in the nests of Fork-tailed Drongos. Very similar to the Common Cuckoo, which occurs in the same locations and habitats, the African Cuckoo having more yellow on the bill and the outer tail feathers are barred not spotted as in the Common Cuckoo. The head, neck, throat, breast, mantle and wing coverts are slaty grey. The belly is off-white with prominent dark grey barring. The primary and secondary flight feathers are dark grey barred on the inner edges with white. The bill is yellow at the base and for much of its length, the tip is black. The eyes are yellow surrounded by a yellow orbital ring and the legs and feet are also yellow.

Diderick Cuckoo *Chrysococcyx caprius* Diederikkie

A common breeding migrant being present from September to March, found in damp woodlands, gardens and savannah scrub. They are brood parasites, usually laying their eggs in the nests of weavers. They feed on a wide variety of insects including caterpillars, beetles, termites, grasshoppers and butterflies. The forehead, crown and ear coverts are metallic green and a white stripe extends along the line of the eyebrow. The sides of the neck, the chin, the throat and the breast and belly are white with faint green barring on the flanks and the thighs. The back and rump are green with a wash of coppery bronze. The wing coverts and the primary and secondary flight feathers are green with a varying amount of white barring and spotting. The bill is greyish black, the eyes are red and the legs and feet are grey/green. The plumage of the female is duller than that of the male and has a greater amount of barring on the undersides.

Klaas's Cuckoo *Chrysococcyx klaas* Meitjie

A reasonably common migrant being present in the region from September through to April, favouring woodland habitats, parks and gardens. They feed on a variety of insects including caterpillars and bugs, as well as on some fruits. They are brood parasitic, laying their eggs in the nests of small passerine species particularly those of warblers and sunbirds. The head and all upperparts are metallic green with a wash of copper. The ear coverts are metallic green and they have a short white line extending from the rear of the eye to the ear coverts. The outer tail feathers are white, barred and spotted with dark green towards the tips. The sides of the neck are metallic green and form a half collar onto the sides of the breast. The remainder of the undersides, from the chin to the belly, are white with some faint green streaks on the flanks. The bill is olive green, the eyes are dark brown and the legs and feet are greyish green. The female differs greatly from the male in plumage colour, the upperparts being bronze/brown and the white underparts being barred extensively on the flanks with browns.

White-browed Coucal *Centropus superciliosus* Gestreepte Vleiloerie

A common resident in the far north of our region, favouring areas of woodland and vegetation near to watercourses. A bird that spends much of its time skulking in thick vegetation searching out a wide array of food items including grasshoppers, lizards, frogs, nestling birds and small rodents. The forehead, crown and ear coverts are dark olive brown. They have a white stripe which extends from the base of the bill following the line of the eyebrow. The sides of the neck, the mantle and the scapulars are brown with numerous creamy/white streaks. The underparts are buff/white with light brown streaking. The bill is black, the eyes are red and the legs and feet are blackish/grey.

Senegal Coucal *Centropus senegalensis* Senegalvleiloerie

An uncommon resident in the northern part of our region in damp woodlands and scrub and tall cultivated crops. A shy bird that spends much of its time skulking in dense vegetation. They feed on large insects such as grasshoppers and crickets, small rodents and birds, eggs and chicks of other species. The upper portion of the head, the hindneck and the nape and mantle are deep blue/black. The chin, throat, breast and belly are cream/white. The wing coverts and the primary and secondary flight feathers are rich chestnut red and the tail is black with a wash of metallic green. The bill is black, the eyes are red and the legs and feet are greenish/grey. The sexes are similar.

Coppery-tailed Coucal *Centropus cupreicaudus* Grootvleiloerie

A locally common resident in the north of the region, in areas with thick papyrus and other waterside vegetation. The upper portion of the head, the nape and the hindneck are black with a wash of violet. The mantle is black and the back is rufous. The tail is very dark brown with a wash of copper and the wings are rufous brown. The chin, throat, breast and belly are white. The bill is black, the eyes are red and the legs and feet are blackish. The sexes are similar.

Southern White-faced Owl *Ptilopsis granti* Witwanguil

An inhabitant of woodlands throughout much of our region, favouring those with meagre ground cover. They are nocturnal and will emerge from their roosting places at twilight, taking up positions on perches overlooking favourite hunting grounds. Here they will take a wide variety of invertebrates, small mammals and roosting birds. One of the most beautiful of Africa's owls, the facial disk is white, finely vermiculated with greys and surrounded by a broad black border. The eyebrows are white and the 'ear tufts' are grey finely streaked with black. The remainder of the underparts have grey/buff feathers with dark central streaks. The mantle, back and tail are grey/brown with darker barring. The upper plumage is predominately grey/brown, streaked, barred and flecked with browns and black. The bill is grey, the eyes are golden yellow and the legs and feet are pale grey/brown. The sexes are similar.

Cape Eagle Owl *Bubo capensis* Kaapse Ooruil

An uncommon resident in areas of rocky cliffs, gorges and mountainous terrain. A very large owl, measuring up to 50 cm in length, they are predominantly nocturnal but will occasionally hunt during daylight hours. They feed on a wide variety of insects, medium-sized mammals such as hyraxes, hares and squirrels as well as taking other bird species. The facial disk is not as pronounced as in some other owl species, being dull white streaked and blotched with dark brown and edged with a dark brown/black border. The throat is white, the upper breast is buff with heavy dark brown blotches, the lower breast and the belly are white barred and blotched with browns. The head, neck, mantle and back are dark brown with buff blotches, the 'ear tufts' are dark brown and buff. The remainder of the upper plumage is dark brown blotched and spotted with buff, white and black. The bill is pale grey, the eyes are orange and the legs and feet are buff/brown. The sexes are similar.

Spotted Eagle Owl *Bubo africanus* Gevlekte Ooruil

A common owl throughout the region which may be found in a variety of habitat types from rocky gorges and cliffs, to open woodlands. They are nocturnal in habits, stirring from their roosts at twilight, taking up positions on favoured perches above areas with thin ground cover where they hunt for small mammals and birds as well as insects and some reptiles. The facial disk is off-white barred with grey and surrounded with a black border. The head, neck and mantle are mid-grey/brown spotted with buff and white. The breast is pale grey merging to white on the belly, both being heavily blotched and barred with dark grey, the belly showing a hint of buff. The upper plumage is a montage of greys, browns and buffs. The bill is black, the eyes are yellow and the legs and feet are blackish. The sexes are similar.

African Scops Owl *Otus senegalensis* Skopsuil

A common breeding resident in the northern parts of our region, favouring areas of dry savannah thornbush and scrub as well as parks and gardens. They roost throughout the day in foliage or on a branch tucked in next to the trunk. They are purely nocturnal, hunting through the night for grasshoppers and other large insects, small rodents, frogs and small roosting birds. A small owl, only 16 cm in total length, the plumage is a mosaic of browns, buffs, greys, blacks and whites. The facial disk is off-white finely but densely vermiculated with dark grey and edged with a dark brown/black border. The outer edges of the scapulars and of the primary flight feathers are edged with white. The entire plumage provides fantastic camouflage and even at very close range this owl can be very difficult to see. The bill is black, the eyes are yellow and the legs and feet are pale dusty brown. The sexes are similar.

Barn Owl *Tyto alba* Nonnetjie-uil

Found throughout the whole region in most habitats other than forests, commonly found in towns and villages and makes good use of many man-made structures for both roosting and breeding. They are best seen at dawn, dusk and throughout the night when they are engaged in hunting for small rodents, bats, other bird species and large insects. Almost unmistakeable with the white facial disk surrounded by feathering of golden buff and greys on the forehead, crown and sides of the head. The throat, breast and belly are white with variable amounts of grey and black streaks. The nape, back, scapulars and wing coverts are a mixture of gold, buff and grey spots and streaks. The primary and secondary flight feathers and the tail are golden buff with a series of broad mid-brown bars. The bill is pale grey, the eyes are dark brown/black and the legs and feet are greyish. The sexes are similar.

Verreaux's Eagle Owl *Bubo lacteus* Reuse-Ooruil

A reasonably common resident in all but the most southern and western parts of our range, where they can be found in wooded savannahs and in small patches of mature open forests. A large owl, measuring around 62 cm in length, they are active throughout the night, hunting for medium-sized mammals like hares and monkeys as well as large insects, reptiles and roosting birds. The facial disk is off-white with fine streaking and is bordered by a band of black. The entire upper plumage is grey/brown with fine black vermiculations and white tips to the wing coverts. The underparts are buff/grey on the breast, merging to white on the belly and the whole being heavily streaked and spotted with dark greys and blacks. The bill is pale grey, the eyes are dark brown with very distinctive pink eyelids and the feet are pale grey, the talons being black. The sexes are similar, the female being larger than the male.

African Wood Owl *Strix woodfordii* Bosuil

A comparatively common resident of dense woodlands and evergreen forests mainly in the north and east of our region. They are strictly nocturnal, roosting during the daylight hours in thick vegetation and foliage high in the treetops. They hunt from a perch, watching for the movement of prey below, taking grasshoppers, cockroaches, and cicadas as well as frogs, snakes and roosting birds. The facial disk is white with mid-brown patches surrounding the eyes and with fine barring of mid-brown to the sides of the disk. The head and neck are mid-brown with the feather tips white resulting in a stippled effect. The throat, breast and belly are white with russet and brown barring, this barring being densest on the breast and diminishing on the belly. The upperparts are rufous brown with very fine white streaking. The scapulars are rufous brown with white bars on the outer portion forming a line down the shoulder. There is a certain degree of variation in plumage colour within the species, with some individuals tending to show more rufous. The bill is pale yellow, the eyes are dark brown and the feet are dull yellow.

Pearl-spotted Owlet *Glaucidium perlatum* Witkoluil

The commonest small owl in the region, found in acacia woodland and scrub with little ground cover beneath. They are active during the day as well as through the night, particularly when they have the added pressure of young to feed. They hunt from perches, watching the ground below for movement indicating a possible prey item. They will feed on a wide variety of insects, lizards and small birds and mammals. The head is rich brown finely speckled with white, the nape has two dark brown patches edged with rufous and give an impression of 'false eyes'. The facial disk is off-white edged with rufous brown. The throat, breast and belly are white broadly streaked with rufous. The upper plumage of the back, wings and tail is rufous spotted with white. The bill is pale yellow, the eyes are yellow and the feet are yellow/brown. The sexes are similar.

African Barred Owlet *Glaucidium capense* Gebande Uil

A locally common resident in the north and east of our region in areas of open woodland and forest edges. Although they are most active from twilight to dawn, they can regularly be seen during the daytime, hunting for small mammals, reptiles and a variety of insects. At first glance they resemble the Pearl-spotted Owlet but the head is far larger, they have rufous spotting on the breast and belly, not streaks, they lack the 'false eyes' of the nape and the mantle, back and wing coverts lack the fine white speckling of the Pearl-spotted. The tail is rufous with dark brown bands, not spots as in the Pearl-spotted. The bill is pale yellow, the eyes are bright yellow and the feet are yellow. The sexes are similar.

Marsh Owl *Asio capensis* Vlei-uil

An owl of grasslands and marshes, a locally common resident species. Mainly crepuscular in habits although they can be seen during the daytime usually when hungry young need to be fed. They feed mainly on small rodents, birds and insects. The facial disk is light brown with darker brown rings around the eyes and bordered around the rim with dark brown and buff. The breast is mid-brown merging to buff on the belly, the whole of the underparts being barred with browns and buffs. The mantle, back and wing coverts are brown, the latter having white tips. The primary flight feathers are tawny buff and the secondary flight feathers are mid-brown edged with pale buff. The bill is blackish grey, the eyes are dark brown and the feet are brown. The sexes are similar, the male often being paler than the female.

Fiery-necked Nightjar *Caprimulgus pectoralis* Afrikaanse Naguil

A common resident, favouring areas of deciduous woodland and acacia scrub. The crown is black, speckled with silver grey. They have a silver grey stripe which follows the line of the eyebrow, as well as a black eye stripe. They have a tawny/buff half collar on the nape and the sides of the neck. They have a white triangular patch on the throat, the breast is dark rufous merging into pale buff on the belly with faint dark barring. The mantle, back and rump are brown, the scapulars are grey and black, the primary and secondary flight feathers are black barred with rufous. The bill is black, the eyes are dark brown and the feet are black. The sexes are similar.

Swamp Nightjar *Caprimulgus natalensis* Natalse Naguil

Also known as the Natal Nightjar this species is an uncommon resident in the central north and central eastern parts of our range, favouring areas of grasslands and swamps. The plumage is a cryptic mixture of browns and greys, often with a white eyebrow line, which extends to the sides of the nape and a moustachial stripe, which curves around the ear coverts. The male has white outer tail feathers, the same feathers being buff on the female. They are active throughout the night, feeding on airborne insects, especially beetles. The sexes are similar.

Pel's Fishing Owl *Scotopelia peli* Visuil

A bird of forests and woodlands along riverbanks and the margins of swamps and lakes, mainly in the north-eastern part of our region. As its name suggests, they feed principally on small fish but they have also been recorded taking reptiles and amphibians. They usually hunt over areas of shallow water, detecting fish by observing the ripples caused by their movement. They are usually located in the daytime roosting high in the canopy of a large tree. The entire plumage is a rich rufous, liberally marked with black lines, bars and spots. The bill is blackish, the large eyes are dark brown and the legs are grey and unfeathered. The sexes are similar.

Speckled Mousebird *Colius striatus* Gevlekte Muisvoël

A common bird in acacia woodlands, forests, gardens and parks. They are often to be seen in family parties, moving from tree to tree searching out fruits of many kinds. They are quite easy to recognise in flight, with short wings and a very long tail. The forehead is black and the remainder of the head is ashy grey with longer feathers on the crown forming a crest. The breast is greyish brown merging into tawny buff on the belly and tail. The mantle, back and rump are brown with fine vermiculations and the flight feathers are dark brown. The lower mandible is white and the upper is black, the eyes are dark brown and the legs and feet are dull red. The sexes are similar.

Red-faced Mousebird *Urocolius indicus* Rooiwangmuisvoël

A very common and widespread bird of savannahs, woodlands, gardens and fruit orchards. The forehead and crown are warm grey, the feathers of the crown are elongated forming a crest. The base of the bill and a patch of bare skin around the eyes are bright red. The throat is buff, becoming paler on the lower breast and the belly. The mantle, back and wing coverts are grey, the uppertail coverts are bluish and the long tail is dark grey as are the primary and secondary flight feathers. The bill is black with a bright red section at the base of the upper mandible, the eyes are brown and the legs and feet are dull red. The sexes are similar.

Narina Trogon *Apaloderma narina* Bosloerie

A bird of damp forests, woodlands and well-wooded parks and gardens, mainly to be found in the eastern part of our region. The head, neck and upper breast are metallic green. The lower breast and belly are bright crimson. They have and blue patch of bare skin around the eye. The mantle and back are metallic green with a slight blue sheen and the primary flight feathers are blackish with narrow white edges. The long tail is dark blue above and blue/black below with some white edges. The bill is yellow, the eyes are dark red and the legs and feet are reddish. The sexes are quite similar but the plumage colours of the female are much subdued compared to those of the male.

African Palm Swift *Cypsiurus parvus* Palmwindswael
A common resident in wooded regions, particularly those areas that have mature palm trees. A very sleek, slender swift with a deeply forked tail and long narrow wings. They build their nests from feathers and plant material, which they gather on the wing and glue with saliva onto the side of a palm frond. The eggs, usually two, are also glued into the nest with saliva. The plumage of the upperparts is a uniform greyish brown, with a slightly darker crown and nape. The primary flight feathers are also dark grey/brown. The undersides are grey/brown, lighter on the chin and throat. The bill is black, the eyes are dark brown and the legs and feet are black. The sexes are similar.

Alpine Swift *Tachymarptis melba* Witpenswindswael
A fairly common resident in most areas but favours grasslands in montane regions. The largest of Africa's swifts, they are very fast fliers and cover great distances, up to 1000 km a day, in search of airborne insects such as winged termites, bees and beetles which form the bulk of their diet. The upperparts are greyish brown, the forehead is light grey and a thin white line extends from the forehead around the upper portion of the eye. The tail and the primary flight feathers are dark greyish brown. The chin and throat are white and the remainder of the undersides are greyish brown except for the belly which is also white. The bill is black, the eyes are dark brown and the legs and feet are flesh pink. The sexes are similar.

Common Swift *Apus apus* Europese Windswael
A common migrant visitor, arriving in October and departing in March, they can be encountered over a wide variety of habitats throughout our range. They fly with rapid wing beats, seeking food at a height of around 100 metres, taking airborne insects such as winged termites, flies and beetles. The entire plumage is blackish brown with lighter areas appearing on the crown, forehead and the lores. The chin and throat also appear lighter. The bill is black, the eyes are dark brown and the legs and feet are greyish black. The sexes are similar.

African Black Swift *Apus barbatus* Swartwindswael
A locally common resident whose numbers are swelled by migratory birds which arrive in August and depart in May. They can be encountered over a range of differing habitats, particularly in the non-breeding season. They feed on a wide variety of flying insects including termites, beetles and bees. The plumage is mainly dark blackish brown, lighter on the forehead, crown and lores. The chin and throat are whitish grey. The bill is black, the eyes are dark brown and the legs and feet are brown. The sexes are similar. It can be extremely difficult to distinguish this species from the Common Swift even at very close range.

Little Swift *Apus affinis* Kleinwindswael
A common resident found over a variety of habitats throughout the region. They are the commonest swift in towns and villages and are extremely gregarious and very noisy at their breeding and roosting sites. They feed on airborne insects such as termites, flies and beetles. The upperparts are grey/brown, being paler on the forehead and the lores. The rump is white and the tail is dark grey/brown above and pale grey below. The chin and the throat are white and the breast and belly are dark brownish/black. The bill is black, the eyes are dark brown and the legs and feet are blackish/red. The sexes are similar.

White-rumped Swift *Apus caffer* Witkruiswindswael
A common migrant visitor from August to May, usually to be found hawking for insects over areas of savannah, farmland and towns and villages. A slim swift with a pale face and a long deeply forked tail, at first glance they can resemble the Little Swift. Almost the entire plumage is brown/black, darker on the crown and paler on the forehead. The mantle, back and scapulars are almost black. They have a thin grey/white stripe extending from the base of the bill following the line of the eyebrow. The upper rump bears a distinctive white crescent mark, the chin and throat are white and the breast and belly are black/brown. The bill is black, the eyes are dark brown and the feet are brown/black. The sexes are similar.

Malachite Kingfisher *Alcedo cristata* Kuifkopvisvanger
A common resident, mainly to be found in the eastern part of our range, almost anywhere that there is water. They feed on small fish, aquatic insects and dragonflies. The forehead is red, the crown and nape are blue/black with fine azure blue barring. They have a white patch to the rear of the ear coverts and the lower portion of the head and the neck are deep orange merging to pale rufous on the lower breast and belly. The mantle, back and tail are rich purple/blue, the wing coverts are deep blue with lighter blue speckling. The primary and secondary flight feathers are blue/black. The bill is bright red, the eyes are dark brown and the legs and feet are red. The sexes are similar.

African Pygmy Kingfisher *Ispidina picta* Dwergvisvanger
A reasonably common bird in areas of damp forests, lush glades and the banks of rivers and streams. One of the smallest kingfishers to be found in Africa, they feed mainly on insects. The centre of the forehead, the crown and the nape are black with blue barring. They have an orange stripe extending from the sides of the forehead following the line of the eyebrow to the lower nape. The sides of the face and the hindneck are violet and they have a white patch to the rear of the ear coverts. The chin and throat are white, the breast and belly are orange. The mantle, back and rump are a bright blue and the tail is dark blue. The bill is red, the eyes are dark brown and the legs and feet are orange red. The sexes are similar.

Grey-headed Kingfisher *Halcyon leucocephala* Gryskopvisvanger
A locally common species found only in the far north of our region, where they inhabit wooded areas and scrubby grasslands as well as cultivated areas and parks and gardens. They feed mainly on grasshoppers and a variety of other large insects and occasionally lizards. The head, neck, chin, throat and breast bib are pale greyish/white, slightly darker on the crown. The sides of the breast and the belly are a rich chestnut. The scapulars, wing coverts and primary flight feathers are black, the latter being broadly edged with bright azure blue. The rump and the tail are also azure blue. The bill is red, the eyes are dark brown and the legs and feet are red. The sexes are similar.

Woodland Kingfisher *Halcyon senegalensis* Bosveldvisvanger
A fairly common kingfisher to be found in the north-eastern section of our range in areas of wooded savannah, scrubby grasslands and parklands and gardens. The forehead, crown and nape are greyish/white, the sides of the face, the neck, chin, throat, breast and belly are white, the throat and upper breast showing a wash of pale blue. A black stripe extends from the base of the upper mandible to the eye. The wing coverts are black, the scapulars and the back are azure blue and the primary flight feathers are black edged with azure, the secondaries are azure with black tips. The upper mandible is red, the lower mandible is black, the eyes are dark brown and the legs and feet are black. The sexes are similar.

Brown-hooded Kingfisher *Halcyon albiventris* Bruinkopvisvanger
A fairly common resident species found in most types of wooded habitats. They feed mainly on large insects. The forehead, crown and nape are brownish/buff with dark streaking. A broad white collar encircles the neck merging with the white of the sides of the neck and the throat. The breast and belly are buff/brown, the entire undersides are streaked with dark brown/black. The mantle, scapulars and wing coverts are black, the secondaries are turquoise blue with brown inner webs and the primaries are brown/black finely edged with turquoise. The bill is red, the eyes are dark brown and the legs and feet are pale orange. The sexes are similar.

Striped Kingfisher *Halcyon chelicuti* Gestreepte Visvanger
A locally common resident of woodlands, grasslands and thornbush country. They feed for the most part on insects. Rather a dull-looking kingfisher with the forehead, crown and nape tawny brown with dark streaks. A white collar extends from the base of the nape widening on the sides of the neck and face and merging with the white chin. The breast is whitish with a wash of buff and is streaked with dark brown. The mantle and wing coverts are brown, the latter with some white tips to the feathers. The back and rump are turquoise blue, the tail is a duller shade of grey/blue. The secondaries are brown on the inner webs and azure blue on the outer webs, the primaries are dark brown edged with azure. The bill is red at the base and black towards the tip, the eyes are dark brown and the legs and feet are red. The sexes are similar.

Giant Kingfisher *Megaceryle maxima* Reusevisvanger

The largest kingfisher in Africa and a common resident in our region, they are to be found almost anywhere there is water. They spend much of their time perched on an overhanging branch from where they make shallow dives in pursuit of fish. The feathers of the forehead, crown and nape are slaty black streaked with white. Those of the crown and nape are elongated in the form of a shaggy crest. The chin, throat and sides of the neck are white with black streaking. In the male the breast is rufous and the belly is white with some black streaks; in the female the breast is white with dark streaks and the belly is rufous. The plumage of the upperparts is slaty black with small white spots. The bill is blackish, the eyes are brown and the legs and feet are greyish black.

Pied Kingfisher *Ceryle rudis* Bontvisvanger

The commonest kingfisher in Southern Africa, found throughout much of the region in habitats that hold water. It is the only all black and white kingfisher in Africa. They feed mainly on fish, from a perch or by hovering above the water surface and plunge diving onto prey. The forehead, crown and the centre of the hindneck are black with some fine white streaking. They have a broad white irregular band extending from the base of the bill following the line of the eyebrow to the nape. The chin, throat, breast and belly are white, with a double black breast band on the male and a single band on the female, which is broken in the centre. The upperparts are black with white streaking and spotting. The bill is black, the eyes are dark grey and the legs and feet are greyish black.

European Roller *Coracias garrulus* Europese Troupant

A common migrant from the north during the period from October to March, in areas of open woodlands and on telephone and power poles and lines. They feed mainly on large insects. The head and neck are light powder blue, the chin, throat, breast and belly are also powder blue with some faint white streaking. The mantle, back and scapulars are rufous, the rump is deep blue and the tail is blue/brown in the centre and has azure blue outer feathers. The bill is black, the eyes are dark brown and the legs and feet are brownish black. The sexes are similar.

Lilac-breasted Roller *Coracias caudatus* Gewone Troupant

A common resident of dry open woodlands, grassland savannahs and parklands. They feed on insects of all kinds as well as on small reptiles. They are probably the most colourful of all the rollers in our region. The forehead and eyebrow stripe are white merging with the green of the crown and the nape. The ear coverts are lilac/brown, the chin is white and the breast is lilac finely streaked with white. The belly and the underside of the tail are azure blue. The mantle and back are brown and the scapulars and rump are dark blue, the primary coverts are a bright azure. The tail is blue with the outermost feathers forming into long streamers during the breeding season. The bill is black, the eyes are brown and the legs and feet are greenish. The sexes are similar.

Purple Roller *Coracias naevia* Groottroupant

An uncommon resident over much of the region in dry woodlands and savannahs. A large, robust roller with the forehead and eyebrow stripe white, the crown, nape, sides of the neck and ear coverts are rufous/red. The chin is white and the breast and belly are rufous/red heavily streaked with white and the undertail coverts are lilac/blue. The mantle and scapulars are olive green, the back and rump are deep lilac and the tail is blue/green. The wing coverts are lilac and purple and the primary and secondary flight feathers are deep blue. The bill is black, the eyes are brown and the legs and feet are yellowish. The sexes are similar.

Broad-billed Roller *Eurystomus glaucurus* Geelbektroupant

A fairly common small roller found only in the north-eastern parts of our range in lowland forest edges, clearings and river valleys. They feed mainly on insects, particularly species of flying ants and termites. The head, mantle, back, scapulars and upperwing coverts are a rich cinnamon red. The shallow forked tail is azure blue with a dark blue tip. The ear coverts, throat, breast and belly are lilac. The bill is yellow, the eyes are dark brown and the legs and feet are brownish. The sexes are similar.

White-fronted Bee-eater *Merops bullockoides* Rooikeelbyvreter

A locally common breeding resident, usually found close to water bodies, where they can be seen hawking for insects from a favoured perch. They feed on a variety of airborne insects, mainly honey bees. The forehead is white merging to buff then rufous on the crown and the nape. A black band extends from the base of the bill, through the eye to the ear coverts and a white band runs underneath the black band to include the chin. The throat is scarlet red, the breast and belly are orange/buff and the undertail coverts are blue. The upperparts, including the wings and tail, are green/blue. The bill is black, the eyes are dark brown and the legs and feet are greyish black. The sexes are similar.

Little Bee-eater *Merops pusillus* Kleinbyvreter

A locally common resident found in dry woodlands quite often near to water bodies. They are usually to be seen in pairs or small groups and are the commonest and smallest bee-eater in the region. They feed on a variety of airborne insects, which they catch from a favoured perch. The forehead, crown and upperparts are a rich leaf green. A black band extends form the gape through the eye to the ear coverts. A metallic ultramarine band follows the line of the eyebrow. The chin and throat are yellow and a black band is present across the upper breast, the remainder of the breast being rufous becoming paler on the belly. The tail is slightly forked with green central feathers and rufous outer feathers with black tips. The bill is black, the eyes are deep red and the legs and feet are black. The sexes are similar.

Swallow-tailed Bee-eater *Merops hirundineus* Swaelstertbyvreter

A locally common resident found in dry woodlands and scrubby savannah areas. The forehead, crown, nape, mantle and wing coverts are green. The deeply forked tail has green central feathers and blue outer feathers tipped with black. The chin and throat are bright yellow. A black band extends from the gape of the bill through the eye to the ear coverts with a pale blue band below merging into a bright blue collar across the upper breast. The remainder of the breast is green and the belly is blue. The bill is black, the eyes are deep red and the legs and feet are reddish black. The sexes are similar.

Blue-cheeked Bee-eater *Merops persicus* Blouwangbyvreter

A common non-breeding migrant from the north found in damp open woodlands. The forehead is white merging to green on the crown, nape, sides of the neck, breast, belly and the mantle. The chin is yellow merging to red on the throat. A black band extends from the bill through the eye to the ear coverts, this band being bordered both above and below by a band of blue. The wings are dark green, the tail is green and has elongated central feathers helping to give the bird its sleek, slender appearance. The bill is black, the eyes are red and the legs and feet are a dull greyish yellow. The sexes are similar.

Southern Carmine Bee-eater *Merops nubicoides* Rooiborsbyvreter

A bird of open woodlands and savannah areas, reasonably common in the northern parts of our region. An easy bee-eater to recognise with its bright carmine red plumage. The forehead and crown are iridescent blue/green. A black band extends from the gape through the eye to the ear coverts. The nape, mantle, neck, chin, throat, breast and belly are carmine red. The undertail coverts are green/blue. The scapulars and wing coverts are reddish/pink, the wings are carmine red, the primary and secondary flight feathers being tipped and edged with black. The tail is carmine red with elongated central feathers being black towards the tips. The bill is black, the eyes are red and the legs and feet are grey. The sexes are similar.

European Bee-eater *Merops apiaster* Europese Byvreter

A common bird of the area, most individuals being migrants from the north, arriving in October and departing again in March. A bird of open woodlands, cultivated land and the margins of water bodies. The forehead is white merging into chestnut on the crown, nape and mantle. A black band extends from the gape across the ear coverts and crosses the throat as a narrow collar. The chin and the throat are pale yellow. The breast is green/blue becoming paler on the belly and undertail coverts. The scapulars, back and rump are golden yellow. The wing coverts are green and chestnut, the tail is green and the primary flight feathers are blue/green tipped with black. The bill is black, the eyes are red and the legs and feet are blackish brown. The sexes are similar.

African Hoopoe *Upupa africana* Hoephoep
A common resident in areas of open woodland, cultivated farmlands and orchards. They feed on the ground, foraging amongst the leaf litter for insect larvae, beetles, locusts, ants and the occasional lizard. Difficult to confuse with any other species. The head, neck, mantle, breast and belly are bright rufous. The feathers of the forehead and the crown form a crest which, when erect, is fan shaped, these crest feathers are tipped with black. The wing coverts are black with broad white bands and the primary and secondary flight feathers are black with a white band towards the tips. The tail is black with a broad white band across the centre. The decurved bill is black, the eyes are dark brown and the legs and feet are grey/black. The sexes are similar, the female being slightly duller in plumage and a little smaller than the male.

Green Wood-hoopoe *Phoeniculus purpureus* Rooibekkakelaar
A common resident over most of the region, favouring areas of woodlands and forests where they feed on a wide variety of items including, caterpillars, beetles, millipedes some small lizards and fruits in season. They are usually found to be in small groups of around 6 to 12 birds, noisily working their way through the trees in search of food. A slender bird with a very long tail, the bulk of the plumage is dark green/blue with an iridescent sheen showing purple and blue. The primary and secondary flight feathers are deep blue/black with white flashes, the long slender tail is blue with white markings on the outer feathers. The decurved bill is red, the eyes are dark brown and the legs and feet are red. The sexes are similar, the female being slightly smaller.

Common Scimitarbill *Rhinopomastus cyanomelas* Swartbekkakelaar
A common bird throughout the region in areas of open woodland and dry thornbush country. They are usually to be found in small parties foraging through the trees and bushes searching out food. Their main diet consists of insects such as flying ants, caterpillars, pupae, seeds and some fruits. The plumage is almost entirely dark iridescent black with the crown and face showing a hint of blue. The nape, mantle, scapulars and uppertail coverts show a hint of violet. The chin, throat, breast and belly are dark black with a wash of violet. The primary flight feathers are deep blue/black washed with violet and have white bars on the inner portions, the wing coverts are dark blue, occasionally tinged with violet. The bill is black, the eyes are dark brown and the legs and feet are black. The sexes are similar.

Greater Honeyguide *Indicator indicator* Grootheuningwyser
An uncommon species found in open woodlands, thornbush country and forest edges as well as pinewoods and stands of eucalyptus. They are known to guide humans and Honey Badgers to the nests of bees by fluttering their way through the trees to the hive. They then wait until the hive is opened to secure a portion of the contents for themselves. They also feed on ants, termites and other insects. They are a nest parasite species when it comes to breeding, laying their eggs in the nests of other unwitting species. They use a very wide range of host species, mainly using species that nest in tree holes or holes in riverbanks. The forehead, crown, nape, hindneck, chin and throat are blackish brown, the ear coverts are off-white. The upper breast is grey, sometimes with a wash of yellow and the lower breast and belly are white, darkening on the latter with some streaking. The wing feathers are brown/black, the primary and secondary flight feathers are edged with light greyish brown. The bill is whitish/ pink, the eyes are dark brown and the legs and feet are grey.

Lesser Honeyguide *Indicator minor* Kleinheuningwyser
A common resident in areas of dry thornbush country, small forest clumps and forest edges. They feed on beeswax as well as on adult bees, wasps and other insects. They are a nest parasite species using the nests of a variety on species into which it lays their own eggs. The forehead, crown and nape are grey/green and they have a dark grey moustachial stripe. The chin is white, becoming greyer on the throat, and the breast and belly are off-white with grey/ brown streaking. The back is olive green/grey becoming greener on the rump with some dark streaking. The wing feathers are brownish black with some green edges and tips. The bill is blackish with the lower mandible lighter than the upper, the eyes are dark brown and the legs and feet are greyish. The sexes are similar.

Red-billed Hornbill   *Tockus erythrorhynchus*   Rooibekneushoringvoël

A common resident hornbill in the north and east of our region, usually found in wooded savannahs and areas of scrub with limited ground cover. They feed on insects, particularly dung beetles, as well as grasshoppers and termites. The crown and nape are grey/black and a broad white band follows the line of the eyebrow to the ear coverts, which are white heavily streaked with dark grey. The chin, breast and belly are white. The wing coverts are black with large white spots and edging. The decurved bill is red, the eyes are yellow and the legs and feet are greyish/black. The sexes are similar.

Crowned Hornbill   *Tockus alboterminatus*   Gekroonde Neushoringvoël

A locally common bird in the eastern and northern parts of our range, usually to be found in most wooded habitats. They live in pairs or in small parties, foraging among the trees for insects and fruits. The head, neck, wings, back and tail are brown/black, the chin throat and breast are dark brown/black and the belly is white with some grey streaking. The large bill has a casque ridge along the top mandible and is red in colour. At the base of both upper and lower mandibles there is a pale yellow patch. The eyes are yellow and the legs and feet are black.

Southern Yellow-billed Hornbill   *Tockus leucomelas*   Geelbekneushoringvoël

A very common resident in the northern part of our range, occupying a wide range of habitat types. They are usually found in pairs or in small parties, feeding on the ground taking mainly small insects. The crown and nape are dark grey/black and a broad white band extends from the base of the upper mandible above the eye to the ear coverts, which, like the sides of the neck and the chin, throat and breast are white with dark grey flecking. The wing coverts are black with large spots of white towards the tips. The primary and secondary flight feathers are black with white spots in the centre and broadly edged with white. The tail is black above and off-white below. The heavy decurved bill is bright yellow, the eyes are yellow surrounded with a patch of bare pink skin and the legs and feet are black.

African Grey Hornbill   *Tockus nasutus*   Grysneushoringvoël

A locally common resident in all types of woodland habitats they forage amongst the trees for grasshoppers, beetles, fruits and reptiles and amphibians. The head and neck are dark grey with a band of white extending from the side of the forehead along the line of the eyebrow to the sides of the nape. The throat and the breast are dark black merging to light grey on the belly. The wings and the coverts are brown/grey edged with white and buff. The tail is blackish brown, the outermost feathers being tipped with white. The bill is black with a white patch at the base of the upper mandible, which also shows a small casque. A series of white lines are present across the base of the lower mandible. The eyes are dull red and the legs and feet are blackish. The sexes are similar with the female having the bill dark red at the tip and pale yellow at the base of the upper mandible.

Trumpeter Hornbill   *Bycanistes bucinator*   Gewone Boskraai

A locally common resident of lowland forests and woodlands. They are usually in pairs but at roost sites and favourable feeding areas flocks of several hundred have been seen. They feed mainly on fruits. The head, neck, back, throat and upper breast are black with some grey flecking on the sides of the face. The lower breast and belly are white. The wings are black with some white tips on the primary and secondary flight feathers. The tail is black with white tips to the outermost feathers. The bill is grey/black and has a large casque, the eyes are brown and the legs and feet are black. The sexes are similar, the female having a smaller casque.

Southern Ground Hornbill   *Bucorvus leadbeateri*   Bromvoël

A bird of open woodlands and grasslands in the north and east of the region. They are usually found in pairs or small family parties foraging on the ground, taking large insects, reptiles and amphibians as well as mammal as large as hares, squirrels and rodents. A very large bird, not likely to be confused with any other species. The entire plumage is black with the exception of the primary flight feathers, which are white. They have a bright red patch of bare skin covering an area around the eyes and on the throat where it resembles a deflated sac. The large bill is black with a casque ridge, the eyes are yellow and the legs and feet are black. The sexes differ in the colour of the throat skin, the females having violet blue patches and the immatures having pale yellow facial skin.

Red-fronted Tinkerbird *Pogoniulus pusillus* Rooiblestinker

A common resident species in the eastern part of our region, usually in damp woodland areas, forest edges, gardens and scrublands. They are usually found singly, only coming together during the breeding season. They nest in tree holes, which they excavate for themselves on the underside of dead branches. The lower forehead is black, the upper forehead and the crown is bright red. The sides of the crown and the nape are black with pale yellow streaks. The eyebrow is pale yellow. They have a band of black extending from the sides of the forehead to the nape, another band of black runs from the forehead through the eye and across the ear coverts and yet another black band stretches from the gape across the cheek to the hindneck. The chin and throat are pale yellow and the breast and belly are off-white with a wash of yellow. The wing coverts and the primary and secondary flight feathers are black broadly edged with yellow/white. The bill is black, the eyes are dark brown and the legs and feet are greyish brown. The sexes are similar.

Acacia Pied Barbet *Tricholaema leucomelas* Bonthoutkapper

Found singly or in pairs in areas of dry savannah and acacia scrubland. For the most part they feed on fruits but will also take insects as well as nectar from aloes and other nectar-rich plants. The lower forehead is black, the upper forehead and the crown are bright red. The eyebrow is yellow becoming white as it extends to the hindneck. The remainder of the head is black with the exception of the cheeks, which are white. The chin, throat and upper breast are black, the lower breast and belly are white merging to grey. The back is black boldly spotted with yellow, the rump is yellow and the tail is blackish brown with yellow edged on the outer feathers. The wing coverts are black with yellow spotting and the primary and secondary flight feathers are blackish brown with yellow/white edges and tips. The bill is black, the eyes are dark brown and the legs and feet are greyish. The sexes are similar.

Black-collared Barbet *Lybius torquatus* Rooikophoutkapper

A common resident species in the east, favouring areas with fruit-bearing trees, particularly figs. They will feed singly or in pairs and as well as taking fruits will readily feed on termites, bees, beetles and other insects. They can be extremely vocal and very aggressive to other species in good feeding areas. They excavate nesting chambers in dead tree stumps and branches in the manner of woodpeckers, both birds taking turns. The forehead, crown, area to the rear of the eyes, the cheeks, chin and throat are red. A glossy black collar extends from the hindneck around the sides of the head and on to the upper breast. The lower breast and belly are pale yellow, streaked with flecks of grey/brown. The back, mantle and wing coverts are brownish black with fine vermiculations of yellow. The tail is black with yellow edging to the outer feathers. The primary and secondary flight feathers are black with yellow edges. The large toothed bill is black, the eyes are red and the legs and feet are black. The sexes are similar.

Crested Barbet *Trachyphonus vaillantii* Kuifkophoutkapper

A common resident in the eastern part of our range favouring habitats of dry acacia woodlands and parks and gardens. They feed on a wide range of food items including fruits, worms, beetles, grasshoppers and locusts. They forage singly or in pairs, spending a good deal of time on the ground. The forehead is red, the crown and nape are black with slightly elongated feathers forming a crest. The remainder of the head is yellow with red flecking, the chin and throat are plain yellow. The mantle and wings are black with bold white barring and spotting. From the base of the nape a black collar with white spots extends around the neck and across the upper breast. The lower breast and the belly are yellow. The back is black, the rump is yellow and the uppertail coverts are black broadly tipped with red. The long tail is black, boldly spotted with white. The bill is pale yellow with a dark tip, the eyes are red and the legs and feet are brown/grey. The sexes are similar, the female is usually duller.

Bennett's Woodpecker *Campethera bennettii* Bennettse Speg

A locally common species found in the north and eastern sections of our range in deciduous woodlands. The forehead, crown and nape are red with some black streaking on the forehead. They also have a red moustachial stripe and the cheeks and ear coverts are white. The sides of the neck are white, heavily spotted with black. The chin and throat are white, merging in to pale yellow on the breast and belly, which are spotted with blackish markings. The race of this species that occurs in Namibia has little or no spotting on the breast and belly. The mantle is dull yellow/green with white barring. The flight feathers are greenish brown with white spots. The stiff tail is yellowish green with yellow spots. The bill is greyish black, the eyes are red and the legs and feet are greyish green. The female differs from the male in having the forehead and forecrown black with white spots and the chin and throat brown.

Golden-tailed Woodpecker *Campethera abingoni* Goudstertspeg

A common resident found in woodland habitats over much of the region. They are usually encountered singly or in pairs feeding on ants, termites and other insects. The forehead and the crown are black with red speckling and the nape is red. The edges of the forehead and crown are bordered with a thin black line. They have a red moustachial stripe. The ear coverts, cheeks, chin and throat are white with black streaks. The breast and the belly are pale yellow with bold brown/black spotting. The mantle and back are olive brown/green with yellow barring. The stiff tail is brownish yellow with greenish yellow bars. The flight feathers are olive brown edged and barred with yellow/white. The bill is greyish black, the eyes are red and the legs and feet are greyish green. The sexes are similar, the female having the forehead and forecrown black with white spots.

Cardinal Woodpecker *Dendropicos fuscescens* Kardinaalspeg

A common resident throughout most of the region. They feed on the larvae and pupae of moths, beetles and other insects. The forehead and forecrown are grey/brown, the hindcrown and nape are red. The ear coverts and the cheeks are white with grey smudges and streaks. The chin and throat are black, the sides of the neck, the breast and the belly are white with heavy black streaks, and the belly has a wash of yellow. The mantle and back are olive green barred with yellow/white. The flight feathers are brown with white barring. The bill is grey/black, the eyes are deep red and the legs and feet are greyish brown. The sexes are similar but the female has a black crown and nape as against the red of the male.

Bearded Woodpecker *Dendropicos namaquus* Baardspeg

A common bird found in the northern parts of our region in deciduous woodlands, usually in pairs. They feed on the larvae and pupae of wood-boring beetles and other insects. The forehead is black with white spots, the crown is bright red and the nape is black. The face is white with a broad black stripe extending from the rear of the eye across the ear coverts. The chin and throat are black and the breast and belly are white with olive brown barring. The wing coverts are brownish green with white bars and the primary and secondary flight feathers are brown edged with white. The bill is grey, the eyes are red and the legs and feet are olive/black. The sexes are similar, but the female has black not red on the crown, which is finely spotted with white.

Monotonous Lark *Mirafra passerina* Bosveldlewerik

A locally common bird of open woodlands, scrub and stony ground where they feed on seeds and a wide variety of insects. The feathers of the upperparts are brown with pale edges and dark centres particularly on the wing coverts. They have a rather indistinct white eyebrow and a very prominent white chin and throat. The breast is buff with dark streaks merging in to plain white on the belly. The flight feathers are dark brown edged with buff. The bill is greyish pink, the eyes are brown and the legs and feet are pinkish grey. The sexes are similar.

Rufous-naped Lark *Mirafra africana* Rooineklewerik

A common resident over much of the region, favouring areas of grassland. The forehead, crown and nape are pale rufous. The hindneck and mantle are rufous brown streaked with black and the flight feathers are brown broadly edged with rufous. The face, chin and throat are white, the cheeks and ear coverts being smudged with grey/brown. The upper breast is pale rufous with some brown streaking and merges with the plain off-white of the lower breast and belly. The bill is yellow/grey, the eyes are brown and the legs and feet are flesh pink. The sexes are similar.

Cape Clapper Lark   *Mirafra apiata*   Kaapse Klappertjie

A common bird in the south and west of our region, usually to be found in areas of scrub, grasslands and rocky hillsides. They can be encountered singly or in pairs foraging on the ground, where they feed on ants, termites and other insects as well as seeds. The forehead, crown and nape are dull rufous with some dark streaking. The mantle is pale rufous/grey. The sides of the neck are buff streaked with dark brown and the cheeks and ear coverts are buff/grey with darker streaks. The chin and throat are pale grey and the breast is rufous with dark brown spots, the belly is rufous becoming paler towards the undertail coverts. The primary and secondary flight feathers are brown with buff and grey margins. The bill is pale grey, the eyes are light brown and the legs and feet are flesh pink. The sexes are similar.

Fawn-coloured Lark   *Calendulauda africanoides*   Vaalbruinlewerik

Fairly common throughout the region, well away from the coasts, they favour areas of grassland and savannah and are usually found singly or in pairs foraging on the ground for invertebrates of all kinds as well as for seeds. The crown, nape, mantle and back are pale rufous finely streaked with brown. They have a white stripe extending from the base of the upper mandible following the line of the eyebrow to the top of the ear coverts. This stripe joins another white line, which encircles the eye. The chin and throat are white, the upper breast is buff streaked with brown and merges with the plain white of the belly. The wing coverts and the primary and secondary flight feathers are fawn brown edged with rufous. The bill is yellowish grey, the eyes are light brown and the legs and feet are flesh pink.

Karoo Lark   *Calendulauda albescens*   Karoolewerik

A common species in the south-west, favouring areas of scrub, open thornbush country and sand dunes. They forage on the ground singly or in pairs, taking ants, termites and other invertebrates. The forehead, crown, nape and mantle are grey/brown streaked and spotted with dark grey/black. They have a white ring around the eye merging into a white stripe, which extends from the top of the upper mandible and follows the line of the eyebrow to the ear coverts. They also have a white moustachial stripe bordered below with black. The breast and belly are white, the former being heavily streaked with brown/black. The flight feathers are dark brown with buff edges. The bill is black, the eyes are light brown and the legs and feet are pale grey. The sexes are similar.

Chestnut-backed Sparrowlark   *Eremopterix leucotis*   Rooiruglewerik

A locally common resident found in dry grasslands and savannahs where they feed on seeds and a variety of insects. The male has the crown, face, sides of the neck, chin, throat, breast and belly dark brown/black. They have a white patches on the nape and on the ear coverts. The feathers of the mantle, back and scapulars are rich mid-brown edged with white. The bill is pale grey, the eyes are brown and the legs and feet are flesh pink/grey. The female lacks the bold plumage of the male, having the crown and ear coverts brownish grey. She has a pale grey nape, the grey extending around the neck as a collar and merging in to the grey of the chin, throat and breast. The belly is dark brown/black.

Red-capped Lark   *Calandrella cinerea*   Rooikoplewerik

A common resident throughout the region in areas of grasslands, scrub and cultivated farmland. They have a rufous crown and a rufous patch on the side of the breast. A white stripe extends from the forehead following the line of the eyebrow to the ear coverts, which are rufous/grey. The chin and throat are white, the upper breast has a wash of pale rufous and the lower breast and belly are white. The feathers of the mantle, back and scapulars are brown/grey finely streaked and marked with blackish brown. The flight feathers are dark brown edged with buff. The bill is black, the eyes are light brown and the legs and feet are brown/black. The sexes are similar.

Large-billed Lark   *Galerida magnirostris*   Dikbeklewerik

A locally common resident in the southern parts of our region, inhabiting areas of dry grasslands, coastal scrub and fallow farmlands. They forage on the ground feeding on a wide variety of insects and seeds. The upperparts of the plumage are a uniform light brown streaked with dark brown/black. A whitish stripe extends from the forehead follows the line of the eyebrow and circles the ear coverts to merge with the whitish chin and throat. The breast and belly are off-white with heavy dark streaks on the breast. The bill is dark grey with some yellow towards the base. The eyes are brown and the legs and feet are flesh pink/brown. The sexes are similar.

Sand Martin *Riparia riparia* Europese Oewerswael

A locally common, non-breeding migrant from the north, arriving in September and departing in March. They are to be found almost anywhere there are airborne insects, particularly in marshes and around other bodies of water. A very gregarious species, particularly at night-time roosts when thousands of birds gather together in reedbeds along with other related species. They feed on the wing, taking midges, mosquitoes and flies among other insects. The upperparts of the plumage from the forehead to the tail are dusky brown. The chin, throat and sides of the neck are white finely streaked with dusky brown. The breast is also dusky brown becoming white on the belly with dusky brown streaking. The bill is black, the eyes are dark brown and the legs and feet are black. The sexes are similar.

Banded Martin *Riparia cincta* Gebande Oewerswael

A fairly common species usually found singly, in pairs or in small flocks. They feed on the wing taking all kinds of flying insects usually in the vicinity of water. They also can be found darting low over pastures, taking insects disturbed by grazing cattle. They are usually solitary riverside nesters, excavating a tunnel up to 90 cm in length. The entire plumage of the upperparts from forehead to tail is a uniform dusky brown. They have a prominent white stripe, which extends from the base of the upper mandible and follows the line of the eyebrow. The chin and throat are white and a dusky brown band arcs across the upper breast. The lower breast and belly are white. The primary and secondary flight feathers are black edged with buff/grey. The bill is black, the eyes are dark brown and the legs and feet are brownish black.

Rock Martin *Hirundo fuligula* Kransswael

A common resident over most of our region in mountainous areas with craggy cliffs, ravines and gorges. They build their mud nests on overhanging rock faces, in loose colonies. In areas where rock faces are not available the birds will make use of man-made brick structures. Both the male and the female are involved in nest building and the pair are faithful to a particular nesting site, often using it for many years. The plumage of the upperparts is a uniform dark brown with a wash of grey. The slightly forked tail has a series of white spots towards the tip, which are only visible when the tail is spread. The chin and throat are pale cinnamon, the breast and belly are dark brown. The bill is black, the eyes are dark brown and the legs and feet are reddish brown. The sexes are similar.

Common House Martin *Delichon urbicum* Huisswael

A locally common species, they migrate from the north, arriving in September and departing again in April. They are to be found flying over most open types of habitat, taking numerous types of airborne insects; they are becoming increasingly common in cities. The forehead, crown, nape, mantle, back, scapulars and wing coverts are blue/black. The rump is pure white and very prominent when the bird is in flight. The slightly forked tail is black/brown above and below. The lores and upper ear coverts are black, the lower coverts and the cheeks, chin, throat, breast and belly are white. The bill is black, the eyes are dark brown and the legs and feet are feathered white. The sexes are similar.

Barn Swallow   *Hirundo rustica*   Europese Swael

A very common non-breeding migrant, arriving in the region in September and departing by May. They can be found in most habitats wherever there is an abundance of airborne insects, which form the bulk of their diet. They gather in huge flocks at favoured roosting sites performing an aerial ballet before plunging into the chosen site, usually reedbeds, for the night. The forehead is chestnut red, the crown, nape, mantle, back, wing coverts and tail are blue/black. The outermost feathers of the tail form into streamers towards the onset of the breeding season giving the effect of a deeply forked tail. The chin and throat are chestnut red bordered below by a band of blue/black across the upper breast. The lower breast and belly are white. The bill is black, the eyes are dark brown and the legs and feet are brown/black. The sexes are similar.

Wire-tailed Swallow   *Hirundo smithii*   Draadstertswael

A locally common bird in the eastern part of our range. They can be found in open country, usually in the vicinity of water and in towns and villages. They feed in pairs or small groups, hawking for airborne insects with other related species. The forehead and crown are chestnut red, the nape, mantle, back and wing coverts are blue. The tail is black edged with purple and the outermost feathers are elongated into thin wire-like streamers; these streamers are longer in the male than the female. The primary and secondary flight feathers are brown/black. The feathering around the eyes is black. The chin, throat, breast and belly are white and a band of blue/black extends down the flanks at the base of the undertail coverts. The bill is black, the eyes are dark brown and the legs and feet are blackish. The sexes are similar.

White-throated Swallow   *Hirundo albigularis*   Witkeelswael

A fairly common bird throughout our region encountered in a variety of differing habitat types, but with a particular liking for open grasslands, usually near to water, where there is an abundant supply of airborne insects on which to feed. The forehead is chestnut red. The crown, nape, mantle, back, wing coverts and tail are blue/black, the outermost feathers of the tail being elongated. The chin and the throat are white, bordered below with a band of blue/black across the upper breast, this band is narrower towards the centre. The lower breast and belly are white. The bill is black, the eyes are brown and the legs and feet are black. The sexes are similar.

Lesser Striped Swallow   *Hirundo abyssinica*   Kleinstreepswael

A common swallow in the north and east of our range. They prefer areas of open grasslands and savannahs, often near water, they also occur in towns, villages and farms where they often feed on the insects disturbed by grazing cattle. One of the most attractive of all the swallows, with the forehead, crown, nape, neck and ear coverts chestnut red. The chin, throat, breast and belly are white with heavy, bold streaks of black. The mantle and back are blue/black and the rump is chestnut red. The tail is brownish black and the outermost feathers are elongated in the form of streamers, these are shorter in the female than the male. The primary and secondary flight feathers are brown/black. The bill is black, the eyes are dark brown and the legs and feet are blackish. The sexes are similar.

Mosque Swallow   *Hirundo senegalensis*   Moskeeswael

The largest of Africa's swallows occurring in the northern most parts of our range. They can be found in a variety of habitat types from tall well-matured woodlands, grasslands and savannahs to villages and cultivated farmland. They are usually seen singly or in pairs but can gather in to larger flocks when feeding conditions are favourable, such as near to grass fires or when a hatch of flying insects occurs. The forehead, crown, nape, mantle and back are blue, the rump is rufous and the primary and secondary flight feathers are black. The tail is black with the outermost feathers elongated to form streamers. The ear coverts are rufous, becoming paler on the cheeks and the throat and chin. The upper breast is pale rufous becoming darker on the lower breast and the belly. The bill is black, the eyes are dark brown and the legs and feet are blackish. The sexes are similar.

African Pied Wagtail   *Motacilla aguimp*   Bontkwikkie

A common resident throughout much of the region, usually to be found in areas reasonably close to water as well as in parks and gardens and on cultivated farmland. They are usually seen singly or in pairs, feeding on insects including moths and butterflies, dragonflies, flies and grasshoppers. The crown, nape, mantle and back are black. A white stripe extends from the sides of the forehead, at the base of the upper mandible, and follows the line of the eyebrow to the side of the nape. A square patch of white is present on the sides of the neck below the ear coverts, the chin and throat are white, and a black band extends from the black ear coverts down the sides of the neck and across the upper breast. The lower breast and belly are white. The wing coverts are black with broad white outer edges and the primary and secondary flight feathers are black edged with white. The central tail feathers are black, the outer most feathers are white. The bill is black, the eyes are dark brown and the legs and feet are blackish. The sexes are similar.

Cape Wagtail   *Motacilla capensis*   Gewone Kwikkie

A very common resident throughout the region found in a variety of habitats but usually close to water. Parks and gardens with areas of close-cropped lawns and farmland pastures are particularly favoured. They are also very much at home in towns and villages, usually in pairs or in family parties. They eat mainly insects, taking dragonflies, moths, beetles, termites, ants and mosquito larvae, plus a host of other small creatures. While feeding they constantly flick their tail up and down. They often forage at the feet of livestock, feasting on the insects disturbed by the hooves of the grazing animals. The forehead, crown, nape, sides of the neck, ear coverts, mantle and back are dark grey. The chin and throat are white. A band of grey extends across the upper breast joining with the grey of the sides of the neck. The lower breast and belly are white with the sides of the breast and the flanks having a wash of grey. The central tail feathers are dark brown/black contrasting with the outer most feathers, which are white. The bill is black, the eyes are dark brown and the legs and feet are dark grey/black. The sexes are similar.

Yellow-throated Longclaw   *Macronyx croceus*   Geelkeelkalkoentjie

A common resident in the eastern part of our range found in areas of short grassland and savannah and thornbush country. They are usually encountered in pairs or in small family parties, foraging on the ground in search of insects and their larvae and nymphs. They will often feed at the feet of livestock, feasting on the insects disturbed by the movement of the grazing animals. The forehead, crown, nape and the sides of the neck are greyish brown. A stripe of bright yellow extends from the base of the upper mandible following the line of the eyebrow to the rear of the ear coverts. The chin and throat are bright yellow bordered below by a black necklace extending around the upper breast from the gape of the bill. The lower breast and belly are bright yellow with some dark flecking on the sides of the breast. The upperwing coverts are dark brown edged with buff and the underwing coverts are brown edged with white. The tail is olive brown with some buff/yellow edges. The bill is blackish with a hint of grey/blue at the base, the eyes are dark brown and the legs and feet are flesh pink/brown. The sexes are similar; the female is usually duller than the male.

Cape Longclaw   *Macronyx capensis*   Oranjekeelkalkoentjie

A locally common species in the eastern part of our region, found in short grassland areas, in fynbos and in damp marshes in pairs or small flocks. They feed on an array of insects and their larvae with a special liking for grasshoppers; they will also take seeds. The forehead, crown and nape are olive brown. The sides of the neck and the ear coverts are greyish. A yellow stripe extends from the base of the upper mandible to the ear coverts, encircling the eye. A black line extends from the gape of the bill, around the sides of the throat and across the upper breast in the form of a necklace, becoming wider in the centre. The chin and throat are bright orange, the lower breast and the belly are yellow/orange. The upperwing coverts are brown edged with buff and the primary and secondary flight feathers are dark brown edged with buff and yellow. The bill is blackish, the eyes are dark brown and the legs and feet are flesh pink. The sexes are similar, the female being duller than the male.

Rosy-throated Longclaw *Macronyx ameliae* Rooskeelkalkoentjie

An uncommon resident in the northern parts of our region, found in damp grasslands and around the margins of inland water bodies. They are usually to be found in pairs or in family parties, foraging on the ground taking insects including grasshoppers, termites and locusts also the occasional amphibian. Compared to other Longclaw species the Rosy-throated has a slender appearance and a longer tail. The forehead, crown, nape, mantle and wing coverts are warm brown with black streaking, many of the feathers being edged with buff and rufous. They have an indistinct stripe extending from the side of the forehead following the line of the eyebrow and circling the ear coverts to the throat. The chin and throat are a deep rich pink bordered below with a broad black necklace. The sides of the neck are buff heavily streaked with black. The lower breast is pink merging to buff on the belly. The primary and secondary flight feathers are warm brown edged with buff. The bill is greyish yellow, the eyes are dark brown and the legs and feet are flesh pink. The sexes are similar, but the plumage of the female is generally duller.

Plain-backed Pipit *Anthus leucophrys* Donkerkoester

A locally common resident in the north and east of our region, found in areas of short grasslands and savannahs, bare scrubby hillsides and well-grazed areas of cultivated land. They are usually to be seen singly or in pairs, foraging on the ground for insects of many types as well as for seeds. During the course of foraging they occasionally stop and wag their tail up and down in the manner of a wagtail. As their name suggests, the plumage of the back and upperparts is a plain uniform olive brown in colour. The head has some faint streaking. They have a strong white stripe extending from the base of the upper mandible following the line of the eyebrow to the ear coverts. They also have a thin black molar stripe bordered with white above and below. The chin and throat are white/buff, the breast is brown/buff becoming paler on the belly. The primary and secondary flight feathers are blackish brown broadly edged with buff. The bill is blackish with a hint of yellow at the base of the lower mandible, the eyes are dark brown and the legs and feet are pinkish brown. The sexes are similar.

African Pipit *Anthus cinnamomeus* Gewone Koester

The most abundant pipit in Southern Africa, found throughout the region in a wide variety of habitats but favouring those of short grasslands and savannahs. A very upright long-legged pipit, which is often encountered in flocks during periods of non-breeding. They forage on the ground on bare earth or on short vegetation, seeking out a wide variety of insects on which they feed. They will also take some seeds. The forehead, crown and nape are buff brown with fine dark brown streaking. The mantle and back are greyish brown, the tail is dark brown with the outer webs of the outermost feathers edged with white. They have a white stripe extending from the base of the upper mandible following the line of the eyebrow and circling the ear coverts. The chin and throat are white broken by a thin black molar stripe. The breast is buff/brown heavily streaked with dark brown and merging to buff/grey on the belly. The bill is blackish with a hint of yellow at the base of the lower mandible, the eyes are dark brown and the legs and feet are pinkish yellow.

Long-billed Pipit *Anthus similis* Nicholsonse koester

A common species of grassland and savannah habitats over much of the region. They can be encountered singly, in pairs or small parties, foraging on the ground, with an upright posture, seeking out insects of all shapes and sizes, They seem to favour grasshoppers, crickets and termites. When flushed they show a strong undulating flight usually flying some distance before alighting again. The forehead, crown, nape and mantle are brown with dark streaking. The tail is dark brown with the outermost feathers showing buff white on the outer webs. They have a white/buff stripe extending from the base of the upper mandible, following the line of the eyebrow to the rear of the ear coverts, which are brown. The chin and throat are whitish merging in to the buff of the breast. The breast is heavily streaked with dark brown, this streaking extending on to the flanks. The belly is buff/white. The wing coverts are brown with warm buff edges and tips. The bill is dark grey with a flush of yellow, the eyes are dark brown and the legs and feet are flesh pink. The sexes are similar.

Dark-capped Bulbul *Pycnonotus tricolor* Swartoogtiptol

Usually encountered in pairs or small parties, they inhabit areas of woodland of varying types as well as parkland and gardens. They are a very common species in the eastern section of our range. They feed on fruits and seeds as well as nectar from flowers and some insects. They can do considerable damage to cultivated fruit crops. The forehead and crown are dark brown with the feathers of the hindcrown being elongated to form a short crest. The nape and mantle are warm brown and the face, chin and throat are dark brown. The breast is warm brown merging in to grey/white on the belly and having bright yellow undertail coverts and a dark brown tail. The primary and secondary flight feathers are brown edged with buff/white. The bill is black, the eyes are dark brown and the legs and feet are blackish. The sexes are similar, the females being slightly smaller than the males.

African Red-eyed Bulbul *Pycnonotus nigricans* Rooioogtiptol

Very common throughout the whole region, found in dry woodlands, acacia savannahs, parks and gardens and cultivated farmlands. Although they prefer dry habitats, they are dependent on a regular water supply. They are usually in pairs or small parties and can be seen foraging in trees and bushes feeding on fruits such as figs as well as on a wide variety of insects which they occasionally take by 'hawking' from a favoured perch. The forehead, crown, nape, chin and throat are dark brown/black, the feathers of the crown and nape being slightly elongated forming a short crest. The mantle and wing feathers are dull brown with pale edging and the tail is dark brown. The sides of the neck and the breast are brown merging to white on the belly, with bright yellow undertail coverts. The bill is black, the eyes are red surrounded by a prominent orange red orbital ring and the legs and feet are black. The sexes are similar, the female being slightly smaller than the male.

Cape Bulbul *Pyconontus capensis* Kaapse Tiptol

A fairly common species in the Cape region usually found in pairs in areas with mature shrubs, fynbos, on cultivated farmland and in parks and gardens. They feed on a range of seasonal fruits as well as taking a variety of insects often by 'hawking' from a perch. They come regularly to bird feeders. The forehead, crown, nape and mantle are ashy brown with the feathers of the crown and nape being elongated and forming a crest. The lores and cheeks are dark brown/black. The breast is ashy brown becoming paler as it merges with the belly, the undertail coverts are bright lemon yellow. The tail is dark brown. The primary and secondary flight feathers are brown with fine cream/white edges. The bill is black, the eyes are dark brown, surrounded by a prominent white orbital ring, and the legs and feet are black. The sexes are similar.

Sombre Greenbul *Andropadus importunus* Gewone Willie

A common resident in the eastern part of our range, usually found in dense vegetation, in thickets and scrub, singly, in pairs or in flocks during non-breeding periods. A very shy bird which is seldom caught sight of but which is constantly to be heard singing as it skulks in deep cover. They feed on a variety of insects as well as wild berries and fruits. The forehead, crown, nape, mantle, wing coverts and back are olive green. The tail is a slightly darker green, the outermost feathers being finely edged with white and green. The chin, throat, breast and belly are olive grey/green. The bill is dark grey/black, the eyes are pale yellow/white and the legs and feet are blackish. The sexes are similar, the females being slightly smaller than the males.

Yellow-bellied Greenbul *Chlorocichla flaviventris* Geelborswillie

A common resident found in forests with substantial ground cover, thickets and dense bush, usually in pairs or in small non-breeding flocks. They feed on a wide range of insects as well as on fruits, flowers and seeds. They will often forage with other species and will 'hawk' for insects in flight. They have also been recorded grooming antelope species, in the manner of oxpeckers, in search of parasites. A rather shy bird, remaining for the most part in thick vegetation when approached. The forehead, crown and nape are olive brown/green, the mantle, wing coverts, back and tail are olive green. The face is olive brown and the chin and throat are pale yellow. The breast and belly are yellow with a wash of brown across the upper portion of the breast. The bill is greyish black, the eyes are dull red surrounded by a white orbital ring and the legs and feet are blackish. The sexes are similar, the males being slightly larger than the females.

Cape Rock Thrush *Monticola rupestris* Kaapse Kliplyster

A common resident to be found on mountain slopes, in gorges and on cliffs and rocky hillsides. Usually encountered in pairs or in small flocks during non-breeding periods. Pairs often maintain a breeding territory throughout the year. They forage on the ground, taking insects of all kinds, small frogs, seeds, fruits and molluscs. The entire head is blue/grey, slightly lighter on the forehead, chin and throat. The blue of the head is sharply separated from the rich rufous of the mantle, the neck, breast and belly. The tail is rufous the outermost feathers being edged with black. The wing coverts are brown edged with rufous, and the primary and secondary flight feathers are dark brown edged with buff. The bill is black, the eyes are dark brown and the legs and feet are blackish. The female has the head greyish brown, not blue as on the male.

Groundscraper Thrush *Psophocichla litsitpsirupa* Gevlekte Lyster

A locally common resident throughout much of the region in areas of open woodlands, cultivated farmlands, parks, gardens and human habitations. A sturdy, robust thrush with bold plumage markings making for easy identification. They are usually encountered in pairs or in small parties, searching the ground for insects, earthworms and occasionally small reptiles. The entire upperparts, from the forehead to the rump, are slaty grey. The tail is grey/brown. The ear coverts, cheeks and lores are white with a black stripe extending from the side of the crown, through the eye and on to the base of the ear coverts. They have another black stripe, which runs from the rear of the eye and follows a line around the rear of the ear coverts. The chin is white, the throat, breast and belly are white with heavy black spots. The sexes are similar.

Short-toed Rock Thrush *Monticola brevipes* Korttoonkliplyster

A reasonably common resident, found on escarpments, rocky outcrops and ruined buildings usually in pairs but can be solitary. They forage on the ground, among rocks and stones, seeking an array of insects, as well as scorpions and seeds of many kinds. The forehead and forecrown are greyish white, darkening on the hind crown, the nape, mantle, back and scapulars to a blue/grey. They are blue/black on the ear coverts merging to a lighter blue/grey on the sides of the neck and on the chin and the throat. A sharp edge separates the blue/grey of the throat from the rich orange/red of the breast and belly. The primary flight feathers are brownish black edged narrowly with grey. The bill is black, the eyes are dark brown and the legs and feet are blackish. The female lacks the blue/grey plumage of the male, having ashy brown upperparts.

Kurrichane Thrush *Turdus libonyana* Rooibeklyster

A locally common resident, inhabiting woodlands, rocky hillsides, parks and gardens. They are usually found singly or in pairs and forage on the ground, seeking out insects, caterpillars, earthworms and locusts. The forehead, crown, nape and mantle are brown/grey. The ear coverts and the cheeks are brown/grey. The chin and upper throat are white with a black molar stripe. The lower throat and the upper breast are slate grey, the lower breast and the belly are grey/white through the centre, merging with the rufous orange of the flanks. The primary and secondary flight feathers are brown/grey. The bill is orange, the eyes are dark brown surrounded by an orange orbital ring and the legs and feet are yellow/orange. The sexes are similar.

Olive Thrush *Turdus olivaceus* Olyflyster

A common resident in the south and east of our region, inhabiting all types of forests as well as parks and gardens. They can be encountered singly, in pairs or in small flocks during periods of non-breeding, or on rich feeding grounds. They feed on a wide variety of insects, grubs, caterpillars and grasshoppers, as well as on seasonal fruits, which can bring them into conflict with local growers, as they can do significant damage to the crop. The forehead, crown, nape and mantle are olive brown, the back and the tail are a warm brown. The chin and the throat are white with dense black/brown streaking. The sides of the throat and the centre of the upper breast are greyish brown, while the lower breast and the belly and flanks are dull orange. The primary and secondary flight feathers are brown. The bill is yellow/orange, the eyes are dark brown and the legs and feet are dull yellow. The sexes are similar.

Rattling Cisticola   *Cisticola chiniana*   Bosveldtinktinkie

A very common resident in areas of savannah with light scrub, dry woodland and overgrown farmland. They feed in short grasses, in bushes and on the ground, seeking out insects such as termites, ants and flies; they will also feed on the nectar of flowers. The forehead, crown and nape are warm brown with dark brown streaking. The mantle, scapulars and wing coverts are greyish brown with whitish edges to the feathers. The chin, throat, breast and belly are off-white, sometimes with a wash of buff. The primary and secondary flight feathers are brown edged with buff/white. The tail feathers are brown/grey with white tips. The bill is greyish with a black tip, the eyes are dull red and the legs and feet are flesh pink. The sexes are similar.

Rufous-winged Cisticola   *Cisticola galactotes*   Swartrugtinktinkie

A locally common resident in the north-eastern parts of Southern Africa. They are to be found in damp grasslands in and around marshes and in most types of waterside vegetation. They usually forage in vegetation, taking a wide array of insects including grasshoppers, crickets, caterpillars and damselflies. They build their nests among grass and reed stems and are frequently parasitised by Pin-tailed Whydahs. The forehead, crown and nape are dull rufous finely streaked with dark brown, the ear coverts are pale grey/brown and the chin, throat, breast and belly are pale buff merging with grey on the flanks. The mantle, back and wing coverts are brown/grey and the tail is brown/grey tipped with buff/white. The primary and secondary flight feathers are dark brown, the secondaries having the broad outer edges of the feathers rufous which shows as a distinct wing patch when the wing is folded. The bill is greyish brown, the eyes are brown and the legs and feet are flesh pink/brown. The sexes are similar.

Tinkling Cisticola   *Cisticola rufilatus*   Rooitinktinkie

A common resident in damp grasslands, savannahs and marshes and often near to human habitations. They are usually in pairs and forage in vegetation for insects such as grasshoppers and crickets. A slender cisticola with a long tail, which it often jerks from side to side when disturbed. The forehead, crown and nape are rufous brown and a conspicuous white stripe extends from the base of the bill following the line of the eyebrow. The ear coverts are light rufous brown and the chin, throat, breast and belly are pale buff/grey. The mantle and back are dark brown, the tail is dark brown with the central feathers tipped buff and the outer feathers tipped with white. The primary and secondary flight feathers are dark brown edged with buff and rufous. The bill is greyish black, the eyes are brown and the legs and feet are flesh pink/brown. The sexes are similar.

Desert Cisticola   *Cisticola aridulus*   Woestynklopkloppie

A locally common bird throughout the region in dry, arid habitats, particularly areas of grassland with tall vegetation. They are usually found singly, in pairs or in small flocks during periods of non-breeding. They feed on an assortment of small insects. Although they build their nests deep in grassy tufts and well out of sight, they are occasionally still parasitised by the Cuckoo Finch. The forehead, crow, nape, mantle and wing coverts are dark brown with buff streaks, the primary and secondary feathers are pale brown with buff/white edges. The tail is a uniform dark brown with a narrow white tip. The chin, throat, breast and belly are white, with a wash of buff on the flanks and across the upper breast. The bill is blackish, the eyes are light brown and the legs and feet are flesh pink/brown. The sexes are similar.

Zitting Cisticola   *Cisticola juncidis*   Landeryklopkloppie

A very common resident over most of the region, to be found in a wide variety of habitat types from both wet and dry grasslands, marshes, floodplains and woodland edges. They usually forage in pairs, taking grasshoppers, spiders, moths, crickets and various other small creatures. The forehead is black, the crown is dark brown heavily streaked with black and the nape and neck are brown with a wash of buff. An indistinct stripe extends from the base of the bill following the line of the eyebrow and circling the grey/brown ear coverts. The chin and throat are white, the breast and belly are buff with a wash of pink on the latter. The rump is warm brown, the short tail is dark brown edged with buff and each feather has a broad white tip. The primary and secondary feathers are dark brown edged with buff. The bill is blackish, the eyes are brown and the legs and feet are flesh pink. The sexes are similar.

Tawny-flanked Prinia *Prinia subflava* Bruinsylangstertjie

A common resident to be found mainly in the eastern part of our range, in areas of scrub and thornbush in close proximity to water. They are usually found in pairs or in small family parties foraging together in vegetation, seeking out insects. The commonest and most widely distributed prinia in Southern Africa, they are parasitised by several cuckoo species. The forehead, crown, nape and ear coverts are greyish brown, they have a white eyebrow stripe and the sides of the neck are grey/brown with a wash of buff. The chin and throat are white and the breast and belly are whitish with a wash of buff. The flanks and undertail coverts are pale rufous/buff. The mantle and back are grey/brown and the rump and tail are rufous. The primary and secondary flight feathers are dark brown with rufous edges. The bill is black, the eyes are red and the legs and feet are flesh pink. The sexes are similar.

Karoo Prinia *Prinia maculosa* Karoolangstertjie

Found in the southern part of our region, this prinia is common in areas of fynbos, scrub, coastal dunes and thickets, usually in pairs, foraging in vegetation taking insects of many kinds, caterpillars and mantids. They often defend a territory throughout the year, the male spends much time engaged in vigorous singing at peak breeding time. The forehead, crown, nape, ear coverts, mantle and back are olive brown and they have a faint white eyebrow stripe. The chin, throat and breast are yellow/white heavily streaked with brown/black. The belly and undertail coverts are buff/white with dark brown streaks on the coverts and on the flanks. The tail feathers are grey/brown with a dark subterminal bar and faint white tips. The wings are brown, the outer edges of the primaries and secondaries are buff. The bill is black, the eyes are brown and the legs and feet are flesh pink/brown. The sexes are similar.

Yellow-breasted Apilis *Apilis flavida* Geelborskleinjantjie

A common resident, usually in pairs or small family parties in a range of habitats, particularly woodland and forest edges. They are very busy feeders, constantly searching bushes, dense thickets and trees for insects, caterpillars and fruits. They will maintain a territory throughout the year. The forehead, crown, upper nape and ear coverts are pale grey. The lower nape, mantle, back, rump and tail are pale green. The tail feathers are pale green tipped with yellow. The chin and throat are white. The breast is yellow bordered below by a black band. The belly is white and the undertail coverts are white with a wash of yellow. The wing coverts are pale green and the primary and secondary flight feathers are black edged with green. The bill is blackish/grey, the eyes are bright red and the legs and feet are flesh pink. The sexes are similar; the female lacks the black breast band.

Grey-backed Camaroptera *Camaroptera brevicaudata* Grysrugkwêkwêvoël

A common resident in the northern parts of our region, inhabiting forests, damp savannah woodlands and suburban gardens and parklands. They feed on a variety of small insects, spiders and termite larvae, usually in pairs or in small family parties. They can be extremely shy and secretive, often staying concealed in bushes and scrub. When foraging through the undergrowth they often cock the tail high over the back. The whole of the upperparts from the forehead to the tip of the tail are grey/brown. The chin, throat, breast, belly and flanks are grey/white, the latter having a wash of buff. The primary and secondary flight feathers are brown edged with green. The bill is blackish, the eyes are light brown and the legs and feet are flesh pink. The sexes are similar.

Cape Grassbird *Sphenoeacus afer* Grasvoël

A common resident in the southern and eastern parts of our range in grasslands, in rank grasses along the edges of water bodies and in fynbos. They are usually seen singly or in pairs, feeding on the ground, seeking out insects of many kinds as well as fruits and seeds. They remain hidden in deep vegetation for much of the time being rather secretive by nature, but will often sing from an open perch at daybreak. The forehead, crown, nape and ear coverts are rufous with some dark streaking on the nape. The chin and upper throat are white with a black molar stripe. The lower throat, breast and belly are pale rufous/buff with heavy streaks of blackish brown. The feathers of the mantle and wing coverts are dark brown broadly edged with buff. The longish tail is rufous brown, the central feathers being longer than the outer feathers. The bill is blackish, the eyes are brown and the legs and feet are brownish black. The sexes are similar.

Sedge Warbler *Acrocephalus schoenobaenus* Europese Vleisanger

A common non-breeding migrant arriving from the north in October and departing in March. They are to be found throughout most of our region in damp waterside habitats with reeds and sedges. They forage in reedbeds and similar areas, taking insects from plant stems and leaves, catching midges and by gathering worms from surrounding muddy margins. The forehead, crown and ear coverts are olive brown with dark streaking, the nape is olive brown and the mantle and scapulars are olive brown with dark heavy streaking. They have a broad creamy white stripe extending from the base of the bill following the line of the eyebrow to the rear of the crown. The chin, throat and the centre of the belly are white and the breast, the sides of the belly and the undertail coverts are buff. The flight feathers are dark brown edged with buff. The bill is black, the eyes are brown and the legs and feet are pinkish brown. The sexes are similar.

Great Reed Warbler *Acrocephalus arundinaceus* Grootreitsanger

Quite a common non-breeding migrant from the north, arriving in October and departing in March. They are to be found in reedbeds in tall grasses and in cultivated crops. They feed on insects, snails and occasionally small amphibians. The forehead, crown, nape, mantle, back and wings are warm brown. They have a white eyebrow stripe and the ear coverts are warm brown. The chin, throat and the centre of the breast and belly are white while the sides of the breast and belly and the flanks are buff. The flight feathers are dark brown thinly edged with white/buff. The bill is brown/black, the eyes are brown and the legs and feet are brownish. The sexes are similar.

Willow Warbler *Phylloscopus trochilus* Hofsanger

A very common non-breeding migrant from the north, arriving in October and departing in March. They can be found in a range of woodland habitats and in parks and gardens. They feed on a wide variety of insects. The forehead, crown, nape, ear coverts and mantle are olive green with a wash of brown. They have a stripe of yellow/white, which extends from the base of the bill, following the line of the eyebrow, to the side of the nape. The chin, throat, breast and belly are whitish, the breast having a wash of yellow. The primary and secondary flight feathers are brown edged with olive green. The bill is greyish yellow, the eyes are dark brown and the legs and feet are flesh pink. The sexes are similar.

Garden Warbler *Sylvia borin* Tuinsanger

A fairly common non-breeding migrant from the far north, arriving in October and departing in March. They can be found in woodlands, thickets and areas of dense scrub in small loose flocks, feeding on a variety of insect life as well as on caterpillars, berries and fruits. The forehead, crown, nape and mantle are greyish brown, the chin and throat are white. The breast and belly are off-white with a wash of buff. The primary and secondary flight feathers are dark brown edged with olive brown. The bill is brown/black, the eyes are dark brown and the legs and feet are slaty grey. The sexes are similar.

Long-billed Crombec *Sylvietta rufescens* Bosveldstompstert

A very common resident seen in pairs or small family parties foraging through dense thickets, dry acacia scrub and bushes, feeding on very small insects and small caterpillars. Like other crombecs, the Long-billed has a tailless appearance. The upperparts are warm grey, the chin, throat and face are buff/white with fine grey streaking. They have an indistinct white eyebrow. The breast, belly and flanks are buff. The bill is blackish, the eyes are light brown and the legs and feet are flesh pink. The sexes are similar.

Chestnut-vented Tit Babbler *Parisoma subcaeruleum* Bosveldtjeriktik

A common bird throughout the region found in dry woodlands and in areas of scrub, bush and thickets. They are usually seen singly or in pairs, foraging through the bush, taking insects from branches and twigs; they also feed on fruits. The forehead, crown, nape, mantle, scapulars and wing coverts are grey with a wash of brown. The chin and throat are white/grey, with blackish streaks, the breast and belly are grey becoming paler in the centre and the undertail coverts are chestnut. The tail is black with white outer edges and the primary and secondary flight feathers are dark brown with grey edges. The bill is black, the eyes are white and the legs and feet are dark grey. The sexes are similar.

Southern Black Flycatcher *Melaenornis pammelaina* Swartvlieevanger
A very common resident of open woodlands of most types, as well as in forest clearings, plantations and in parks and gardens. From a low perch they scan the surrounding area and hop quickly to the floor to capture any insect that betrays its presence. The plumage is a uniform black with a sheen of blue on the head and body feathers when strong light reflects at certain angles. The flight feathers are brown/black and the black tail is broad ended and slightly forked. The bill is black, the eyes are brown and the legs and feet are blackish. The sexes are similar.

Marico Flycatcher *Bradornis mariquensis* Maricovlieevanger
A common resident over much of the region, encountered in acacia savannah and mixed acacia woodlands. They are usually found singly or in pairs perched on the outermost branches of trees and bushes, from where they scan the ground below for insects. They feed on termites, ants, caterpillars and will occasionally feast on fruits. The forehead, crown, nape, sides and back of the neck, ear coverts, mantle, back and rump are mid sandy brown. The tail is dark brown/grey. They have a buff orbital ring of feathers surrounding the eye. The entire underside is white. The primaries and secondaries are dark brown edged with buff. The bill is black, the eyes are dark brown and the legs and feet are greyish black. The sexes are similar.

Pale Flycatcher *Bradornis pallidus* Muiskleurvlieevanger
A locally common resident in the north-east of our region, found in dry savannahs and in various types of woodlands. They are usually in pairs or in small family parties. They have rather drab plumage, the head, sides of the neck, mantle, scapulars and upper tail coverts are brown/grey. The chin and throat are off-white with a wash of yellow, the breast and belly are white with a wash of buff and the flanks are buff/brown. The primary and secondary flight feathers and the tail are dark buff/brown edged with off-white. The bill is black with a hint of yellow at the base of the lower mandible, the eyes are chestnut and the legs and feet are greyish black. The sexes are similar.

Fiscal Flycatcher *Sigelus silens* Fiskaalvlieevanger
A common bird of open woodlands, thickets and parks and gardens. They are usually seen singly or in pairs and will sit on a favoured perch scanning the ground below for insect prey. They will also hawk for insects in flight and will feed on seasonal soft fruits. The forehead, crown, sides of the neck, nape, mantle, scapulars and back are black, often with a bluish sheen. The tail is blackish brown, the outermost tail feathers having white edges. The chin and throat are white. The breast and belly are white with a wash of grey on the former. The wings are black with a white stripe visible on the lower wing and another white patch midway along the secondaries. The bill is black, the eyes are dark brown and the legs and feet are blackish grey. The female is similar to the male but has more brown in the plumage on the upperside.

Spotted Flycatcher *Muscicapa striata* Europese Vlieevanger
A common non-breeding migrant arriving in October and departing in April. They will usually be encountered in open woodlands, in plantations and in parks and gardens. They feed on insects, taking many of them by hawking to and from a favoured perch. The forehead, crown, nape, neck and mantle are warm grey/brown, with faint streaking on the forehead and crown. The chin, throat and upper breast are white with fine streaking; the lower breast and belly are off-white with a wash of greyish buff. The tail is dark brown as are the primary and secondary flight feathers. The bill is brown/black, the eyes are dark brown and the legs and feet are brown/black. The sexes are similar.

African Dusky Flycatcher *Muscicapa adusta* Donkervlieevanger
A bird of the eastern part of our range where they may be found in most woodland habitats, plantations, parks and gardens. They feed on winged insects by catching them in flight, departing and returning to and from a favoured open perch. The forehead, crown, nape, ear coverts, and mantle are all grey/brown, they have a white eyebrow stripe and the chin and throat are whitish with broad brown/grey streaks down the sides. The breast and belly are greyish with grey/brown streaks as the throat. The bill is grey/black with a hint of yellow at the base of the lower mandible, the eyes are dark brown and the legs and feet are grey/brown. The sexes are similar.

White-browed Robin-chat *Cossypha heuglini* Heuglinse Janfrederik

A common resident usually to be found in dense cover along the sides of watercourses, in parks and in gardens, singly or in pairs. Generally they are rather shy and spend much time skulking in thick undergrowth, but in urban situations can become very tame. The forehead, crown and nape are black and a white stripe extends from the base of the upper mandible following the line of the eyebrow to the base of the nape. The face and ear coverts are black. The chin, lower cheeks, throat, neck, breast and belly are orange/red. The mantle, back and scapulars are olive brown and the wing coverts and primary and secondary flight feathers are slaty brown. The central tail feathers are olive brown and the outer feathers are dull orange/red. The bill is black, the eyes are dark brown and the legs and feet are blackish brown. The sexes are similar, but the female is often browner on the mantle and the back.

Cape Robin-chat *Cossypha caffra* Gewone Janfrederik

A resident in areas of scrub and thickets, woodland and forest edges and parks and gardens, particularly in the southern and eastern sectors of our range. They are usually encountered singly or in pairs, foraging on the ground in search of earthworms, insects, molluscs, the occasional small lizard and fruits. They also regularly attend garden bird tables taking scraps. They are easily identified from other robin-chats by being the only ones to have a grey belly. The forehead, crown, nape, mantle and scapulars are brown. They have a white stripe extending from the base of the upper mandible following the line of the eyebrow to the ear coverts. The chin, throat and centre of the breast are orange, the outer breast and the belly are grey, the undertail coverts are buff with a hint of orange. They have a moustachial stripe of white below which is a molar stripe of black. The bill is black, the eyes are dark brown and the legs and feet are blackish. The sexes are similar.

White-throated Robin-chat *Cossypha humeralis* Witkeeljanfrederik

A locally common species found in the north-eastern part of our range. They are most likely to be found in acacia scrub and open woodland, alongside watercourses and in suburban parks and gardens. They are usually in pairs and forage mainly on the ground, taking beetles, ants and termites, caterpillars, spiders and moths as well as fruits. They also occasionally feed by hawking for insects, often towards the end of the day. The forehead, crown, nape, mantle and back are slaty grey. The face and sides of the neck and breast are black. The chin, throat and remainder of the breast are white, the belly is buff/orange. They have a white band extending from the base of the upper mandible following the line of the eyebrow to the side of the nape. The tail has the central feathers blackish and the outer feathers orange/red. The wing coverts and the primary and secondary flight feathers are black, the coverts being broadly edged with white, and the flight feathers with grey. The bill is black, the eyes are dark brown and the legs and feet are blackish. The sexes are similar, the females being slightly duller.

White-browed Scrub-robin *Cercotrichas leucophrys* Gestreepte Wipstert

A common resident over much of the eastern and eastern parts of our range, found in woodland habitats of most kinds, in scrub and overgrown areas. They feed mainly on the ground, searching among the leaf litter for termites, beetles, crickets and other insects; they will also take fruits. The forehead, crown, nape, mantle, back and scapulars are greyish brown. They have a stripe extending from the base of the upper mandible following the line of the eyebrow to the ear coverts, which are buff/brown. The chin and throat are white with a faint molar stripe of brown. The breast and the sides of the neck are off-white streaked with dark grey/brown. The flanks are buff and the belly is white. The primary and secondary flight feathers are dark brown edged with white forming a conspicuous wing bar. The bill is black, the eyes are brown and the legs and feet are brownish grey. The sexes are similar.

Kalahari Scrub-robin *Cercotrichas paean* Kalahariwipstert

A common resident over much of our central and northern areas. The forehead, crown and nape are warm grey, the mantle and back are sandy and the rump is orange. The tail, which is often held in an erect position, is orange with black towards the tip and edged with white. The primary and secondary flight feathers are dark brown edged with warm buff. They have a broad, prominent white stripe following the line of the eyebrow, bordered above and below with a narrow stripe of black. The chin and throat are white and the breast and belly are pale sandy grey. The bill is black, the eyes are brown and the legs and feet are grey. The sexes are similar.

African Stonechat   *Saxicola torquata*   Gewone Bontrokkie
A very common resident in the eastern parts of our range, inhabiting areas of open country with scrub and bushes, also grassy slopes, marshes and cultivated farmland. They take insects, spiders, caterpillars and earthworms. The head, nape, mantle, chin and throat are black and the centre of the breast is a rich chestnut. The sides of the neck and the sides of the breast are white, as are the belly and undertail coverts. The wing coverts are black edged with white forming a distinctive wing bar when perched. The primary and secondary flight feathers are black. The bill is black, the eyes are dark brown and the legs and feet are blackish. The female is much duller and browner than the male.

Mountain Wheatear   *Oenanthe monticola*   Bergwagter
A locally common resident found over much of the region, on rocky hillsides, mountain slopes and in areas of semidesert. They are usually seen singly or in breeding pairs, foraging on the ground for insects, which form the bulk of their diet. The plumage varies greatly as there are colour phases within the species. The black phase has the entire body plumage black, while the grey phase has pale warm grey feathering. In the black phase the crown and nape vary from black to grey or even white. They have a prominent white wing bar on the shoulder and the upper and undertail coverts are white. The central tail feathers are black and the outermost feathers are white. The bill and the legs and feet are black, the eyes are dark brown. The female has the entire plumage blackish brown with the exception of the tail which matches the male.

Capped Wheatear   *Oenanthe pileata*   Hoeveldskaapwagter
A locally common bird over most of the region in areas of dry grassland, particularly overgrazed areas, and ploughed farmland. They are usually solitary, in pairs or small family parties foraging on the ground for insects such as ants, beetles, caterpillars, spiders and flies. The forehead is white, joined with a stripe following the line of the eyebrow. The crown is black merging into chocolate brown on the nape, mantle, back and wing coverts. The cheeks and the sides of the neck are black joining with a black breast bib. The chin, throat and belly are white, with a wash of buff on the flanks. The primary and secondary flight feathers are dark brown/black edged with buff. The rump is white and the tail is black with white at the base. The bill is black, the eyes are dark brown and the legs and feet are blackish grey. The sexes are similar.

Familiar Chat   *Cercomela familiaris*   Gewone Spekvreter
A common resident over most of the region inhabiting open woodlands, scrub, rocky outcrops and dry riverbeds. Usually encountered in pairs, foraging on the ground for insects from a low perch. They regularly flick their wings and raise their tails when foraging. The forehead, crown, nape, sides of the neck, mantle and scapulars are warm grey/brown, merging to rufous on the rump and tail. The ear coverts are brown, the chin, throat, breast, belly and flanks are grey/buff. The primary and secondary flight feathers are dark brown edged with buff. The bill is black, the eyes are dark brown and the legs and feet are blackish. The sexes are similar.

Ant-eating Chat   *Myrmecocichla formicivora*   Swartpiek
A common bird over most of Southern Africa, found on open grasslands, along the sides of tracks and in areas of semidesert. They are usually encountered in pairs or family parties of around six individuals, feeding mainly on the ground and, as its name suggests, eat ants and termites along with other insects as well as some seasonal fruits. The entire plumage is brownish black, the only exception being the primary flight feathers, which are white at the base, showing as a very conspicuous wing bar in flight. The bill is black, the eyes are dark brown and the legs and feet are blackish. The sexes are similar.

Mocking Cliff-chat   *Thamnolaea cinnamomeiventris*   Dassievoël
A locally common species found on cliffs, escarpment edges and rocky hillsides. They are usually seen in pairs, foraging in trees and bushes as well as on the ground. They feed on a variety of insects and spiders and, when available, figs. The head, chin, throat, breast and mantle are black. A narrow white band separates the black breast from the rich orange/red of the belly and undertail coverts. The wings are black, the coverts are white showing as a conspicuous wing patch. The bill is black, the eyes are dark brown and the legs and feet are blackish. The female has the head, mantle, chin, throat and breast dark slate grey and, unlike the male, shows no white wing patch.

White-tailed Shrike *Lanioturdus torquatus* Kortstertlaksman
A common bird in areas of Namibia and Angola, frequenting woodlands of several types and rocky outcrops. They are usually encountered singly, in pairs or, in non-breeding times, small flocks of around a dozen individuals. They forage mainly on the ground and have an upright posture and a short, stumpy tail. They feed for the most part on insects such as beetles, grasshoppers, mantids and butterflies. The forehead is white while the crown, nape, lores and ear coverts are black. The chin, throat and sides of the neck are white. The upper breast has a black bib below which the lower breast is grey/blue to the sides and white in the centre, this pattern is continued on the belly. The mantle, scapulars, back and tail are grey/blue. The wing coverts are black with white tips and the primary and secondary flight feathers are black with white bases and tips. The bill is black, the eyes are pale yellow and the legs and feet are blackish. The sexes are similar.

Chinspot Batis *Batis molitor* Witliesbosbontrokkie
A common resident in the north and east of our region, inhabiting areas of dry savannah woodlands, open scrub, forest edges and parks and gardens. They are very active feeders, constantly on the move as they hop through the canopy in search of insects and small caterpillars. The forehead, crown and nape are slate grey and a white stripe extends from the base of the upper mandible following the line of the eyebrow to the rear of the ear coverts. The lores, ear coverts and sides of the hindneck are black, while the mantle, scapulars, back and rump are slaty blue/grey. The tail is black. The chin and throat are white and a broad band of black extends across the upper breast. The lower breast and belly are white. The bill is black, the eyes are pale yellow and the legs and feet are blackish. The female differs from the male in having the breast band chestnut and a triangular chin/throat patch of the same colour.

African Paradise Flycatcher *Terpsiphone viridis* Paradysvlieevanger
A common species over much of the region with both resident and migratory populations occurring. They are found in most non-arid areas including savannah woodlands, thickets, mature parks and gardens and evergreen forests. They are usually to be found in pairs, hawking for insects from open perches or collecting food by searching the leaf canopy. The entire head, neck, chin and throat are blue/black, the feathers of the crown being elongated to form a crest. The breast, and belly are slaty grey and the undertail coverts are rufous. The mantle, scapulars, back and tail are rufous, the central tail feathers being very elongated. The bill is blue/grey, the eyes are dark brown surrounded by a blue/grey orbital ring and the legs and feet are blackish grey. The female differs from the male in lacking the long, flowing central tail feathers.

Arrow-marked Babbler *Turdoides jardineii* Pylvlekkatlagter
A locally common resident in the north-eastern part of our range, found in open woodlands, scrub, swamp edges and dense undergrowth. They are usually encountered in small but noisy flocks, foraging from bush to bush feeding on a wide range of insects, fruits, seeds and small reptiles. The feathers of the head and neck are dark brown edged with buff/white and the lores are blackish. The chin, throat, breast and belly are grey/brown, all but the latter having the feathers tipped with white in the shape of arrowheads. The central tail feathers and the primary flight feathers are dark brown, the remainder of the tail and wings are ashy brown. The bill is black, the eyes are yellow/orange and the legs and feet are grey. The sexes are similar.

Bare-cheeked Babbler *Turdoides gymnogenys* Kaalwangkatlagter
A locally common resident in a few areas in the north-west. They can be found around dry riverbeds, in thickets and dry woodlands and scrub. They feed mainly on insects, usually foraging in small parties. The forehead, crown and cheeks are white with some grey mottling. They have small areas of black skin visible below and behind the eyes. The nape is rufous, the mantle and wing coverts are earth brown. The chin, throat and central portion of the breast are pale grey, the sides of the breast and the belly are white and a smudge of rufous appears on the thighs. The wings and tail are brown. The bill is black, the eyes are yellow and the legs and feet are blackish. The sexes are similar.

Orange-breasted Sunbird *Anthobaphes violacea* Oranjeborssuikerbekkie
A common resident in the Cape region, can be found singly, in pairs or in loose flocks in areas of fynbos and in flower-rich gardens and parks. The forehead, crown, nape, mantle and upper scapulars are metallic green, the remainder of the upper plumage being dull green. The tail is brown with the centre feathers elongated to around twice the length of the outer feathers. The lores are black, the chin and throat are iridescent green merging into a violet band, which extends across the upper breast. The lower breast is orange/red, with a yellow tuft at the point where the wing joins the body. The belly is yellow. The primary and secondary flight feathers are dark brown edged with olive green. The bill is black, the eyes are dark brown and the legs and feet are blackish. The female lacks the colour of the male, having the upperparts olive grey/brown and the underparts olive yellow with a wash of buff. The crown of the head is mottled brown.

Amethyst Sunbird *Chalcomitra amethystina* Swartsuikerbekkie
A common resident throughout the region with the exception of central and western areas. Inhabiting open woodlands and scrub, gardens, parks and forest edges. They feed on small insects and the nectar of a wide variety of flowering plants. The forehead and the crown are metallic green, the remainder of the upper plumage being black. The chin and throat are reddish/metallic purple and the breast and belly are black. The wing coverts show metallic purple. The bill is black, the eyes are dark brown and the legs and feet are blackish. The female lacks the colour of the male, with the upperparts being olive yellow and the underparts olive green with faint dark mottling.

Scarlet-chested Sunbird *Chalcomitra senegalensis* Rooiborssuikerbekkie
A common resident in the north and east of our region, in open woodlands, in scrubby areas and in parks and gardens. The forehead and the crown are bright metallic green, the sides of the head and the remainder of the upperside plumage is a dense black. The tail is black but shows some brown. The chin and throat are metallic green and the upper breast is bright red, the lower breast and belly are black. The bill is black, the eyes are dark brown and the legs and feet are blackish. The female lacks the colour of the male, the upperparts along with the chin and throat, being dark brown. The underparts are olive yellow, streaked with dark brown.

Malachite Sunbird *Nectarinia famosa* Jangroentjie
A common resident found in fynbos, in open mountain grasslands and along forest edges either singly, in pairs or in small family parties. They feed on some insects but mainly survive on nectar taken from a wide range of flowering species, proteas being a particular favourite. The head, neck, mantle, back and scapulars are rich green, the tail is black with the central feathers elongated to a length almost equal to that of the bird's body. The lores are black and the underparts are a mixture of greens. They have a yellow patch at the shoulder of the wing. The bill is black, the eyes are dark brown and the legs and feet are blackish. The female differs from the male, having the upperparts grey/brown, the chin and throat and the upper breast mottled greyish brown and the lower breast and belly grey/yellow.

White-bellied Sunbird *Nectarinia talatala* Witpenssuikerbekkie
A common resident in areas of dry acacia savannah, thornbush country and dense scrub. The head, neck and upperparts are metallic green, becoming black on the tail. The chin is blue and a broad band of purple crosses the upper breast. The lower breast and the belly are white. The wing coverts are metallic green and the primary and secondary flight feathers are brown edged with buff. The bill is black, the eyes are dark brown and the legs and feet are blackish. The female differs from the male in having the upperparts grey/brown and the underparts whitish.

Southern Double-collared Sunbird *Cinnyris chalybeus*
Klein-rooibandsuikerbekkie
Commonly found in the southern parts of our range in fynbos, eroded hillsides, dry riverbeds and parks and gardens. The head, neck, mantle and scapulars are rich metallic green, the tail is brown/black. The chin and throat are metallic green and a narrow band of blue above a broad band of bright red extends across the upper breast. The lower breast and belly are mid-grey. The bill is black, the eyes are dark brown and the legs and feet are blackish. The female differs from the male in having the upperparts grey/brown and the underparts warm brown.

Greater Double-collared Sunbird *Cinnyris afer* Grootrooibandsuikerbekkie
A common resident in the eastern and southern parts of our range, in open savannahs and bushlands, in coastal scrub and protea-rich parks and gardens. They are usually seen singly or in pairs and feed on small insects and nectar. The entire head, neck, mantle, scapulars and back are rich metallic green. The chin and throat are metallic green and a metallic blue band extends across the upper breast, the remainder of the breast is bright red with yellow tufts at the sides. The belly is olive grey. The bill is black, the eyes are dark brown and the legs and feet are blackish. The female lacks the bright colouration of the male, having the upperparts greyish brown and the underparts pale grey/buff with a wash of yellow.

Dusky Sunbird *Cinnyris fuscus* Namakwasuikerbekkie
A common resident in the western section of our range, found in dry semidesert areas with scattered trees and bushes. They catch small insects in flight by hawking from a favoured perch as well as taking nectar from aloes and other flowering plants. The head, neck, mantle and back are brown/black with iridescent reflections of green and purple. The tail is blackish with a wash of blue. The chin, throat and upper breast are black with green/purple reflections and orange/red feather tufts appear at the point where the wing meets the body. The lower breast is brownish merging to white on the belly. The bill is black, the eyes are dark brown and the legs and feet are blackish. The female is paler than the male, the upperparts being grey/brown, the chin, breast and flanks are grey becoming white on the belly.

Marico Sunbird *Cinnyris mariquensis* Maricosuikerbekkie
A reasonably common resident in areas of acacia savannah, open bushlands and acacia woodlands. They have a particular liking for aloes and will take small insects. The head, neck, mantle, scapulars and back are metallic green and the tail is blackish brown. The chin and throat are metallic green and a narrow band of blue covers the upper breast. The lower breast has a broad band of maroon and the belly is black. The bill is black, the eyes are dark brown and the legs and feet are blackish. The female differs from the male in lacking the bright plumage colours, the upperparts being olive grey/brown and the underparts being pale grey/yellow, the throat and breast having some brown streaking.

Orange River White-eye *Zosterops pallidus* Gariepglasogie
A fairly common resident in western and southern parts of our range, frequenting all manner of woodland habitats including parks and gardens. They feed on insects and soft fruits, singly or in pairs and, during the non-breeding season, in small flocks. The head, neck, mantle and back are olive green/grey, the tail is blackish brown. The chin and throat are yellow, the sides of the breast and the flanks are pale rufous/buff. The centre of the breast to the belly is white/buff. The bill is black, the eyes are dark brown surrounded by a prominent white orbital ring and the legs and feet are greyish black.

Cape White-eye *Zosterops virens* Kaapse Glasogie
A very common resident in all woodland habitats, in thornbush country and in parks and gardens. They are usually seen singly or in pairs, feeding on fruits, nectar and a variety of insects. The upperparts are olive green and the tail is dark brown edged with green. The chin and throat are yellow, the upper breast is olive green along with the flanks. The centre of the breast and the belly are yellow. The bill is blackish, the eyes are dark brown with a prominent white orbital ring and the legs and feet are blue/grey. The sexes are similar.

Cape Sugarbird *Promerops cafer* Kaapse Suikervoël
A locally common species restricted to the southern part of our range, found in fynbos and anywhere in the vicinity of proteas and heathlands. They are a major pollinator of proteas, feeding on nectar as well as taking insects and spiders. An easy bird to identify with its long, flowing tail feathers that can be twice as long as the bird's body. The forehead is pale yellow, the crown, nape and mantle are dark brown with dark smudges and streaks. The lores are dark brown and they have a white/buff moustachial stripe and a black molar stripe. The breast is warm grey/brown dappled with darker brown streaks. These streaks extend on to the white/buff of the belly and the flanks. The undertail coverts are yellow. The bill is black, the eyes are dark brown and the legs and feet are blackish. The sexes are similar, but the female has a much shorter tail.

Black-headed Oriole *Oriolus larvatus* Swartkopwielewaal
A common resident found in a wide variety of woodland habitats as well as in parks and gardens. They forage mainly in the canopy of large mature trees, taking soft fruits, caterpillars and insects. The forehead, crown, face, chin, throat and breast bib are black. The nape, mantle, sides of the neck, sides of the breast and belly are bright chrome yellow. The scapulars and the back are olive green and the rump and uppertail coverts are olive yellow. The tail is olive at the base darkening to black towards the end and has a narrow yellow border at the tip. The primary flight feathers are black with grey edges, the secondaries are black with yellow edges. The bill is red, the eyes are red and the legs and feet are greyish. The sexes are similar.

Red-backed Shrike *Lanius collurio* Rooiruglaksman
A very common non-breeding migrant from the north arriving in November and departing in March. They can be found in open woodlands and dry thornbush country, usually singly, feeding on insects, reptiles, amphibians and some small birds. A black band runs across the forehead extends over the lores and encircles the eyes and ear coverts. The crown, nape and mantle are grey, the scapulars and back are chestnut and the rump and tail coverts are grey with a hint of chestnut. The tail is black edged with white. The cheeks, chin and throat are white, the breast and the flanks are whitish with a wash of pink, this pink is absent on the white/grey belly. The bill is black, the eyes are dark brown and the legs and feet are blackish. The female has the forehead and crow rufous, the neck is brown and the mantle and scapulars are rufous brown. The undersides are whitish with faint barring.

Magpie Shrike *Corvinella melanoleuca* Langstertlaksman
A locally common resident usually encountered in small flocks of up to ten birds. They feed on a variety of insects, small reptiles and small rodents, moving from bush to bush as a party. The entire plumage is black with a hint of blue, the exceptions being a white patch on the scapulars and white feathering at the base of the primary and on the tips of the secondary flight feathers. They have a long, flowing tail, which is around one and a half times the length of the body. The bill is black, the eyes are dark brown and the legs and feet are blackish. The sexes are similar.

Common Fiscal *Lanius collaris* Fiskaallaksman
A very common resident over most of the region, found in open grassland habitats with scattered scrub and bush. A very bold, confiding bird usually found singly or in pairs, they remain on territory for most of the year. They will feed on an array of insects as well as on reptiles and small to medium-sized birds. The forehead, crown, nape, mantle, upper cheeks and ear coverts are black. The chin, throat, breast and belly are white. The back and uppertail coverts are greyish and the tail is black edged with white. The bill is black, the eyes are dark brown and the legs and feet are blackish. The female is duller than the male and shows a wash of chestnut on the flanks.

Lesser Grey Shrike *Lanius minor* Gryslaksman
A common migrant visitor from the north. They are mainly to be found in acacia savannah areas and on cultivated farmland. They usually lead a solitary existence, feeding on large insects and some reptiles and small rodents. The forehead is black, forming a band, which extends above and below the eye to the ear coverts. The crown, nape and scapulars are grey. The chin, throat, breast and belly are white, the latter sometimes showing a wash of pink. The sexes are similar.

Southern White-crowned Shrike
Eurocephalus anguitimens Kremetartlaksman
A common species in the northern half of our region in dry woodlands, in bushes and thickets and in parks and mature gardens. They feed mainly on large insects and are found singly, in pairs or small parties. The forehead and crown are white. The lores are black and a black band extends from the rear of the eye broadening to cover the sides of the neck. The hindneck is white, the mantle, scapulars, back and rump are greyish buff and the tail is dark brown. The chin, throat and breast are white and the belly is greyish buff. The wing coverts and the primary and secondary flight feathers are dark brown with some light edging. The bill is black, the eyes are dark brown and the legs and feet are blackish. The sexes are similar.

Brubru *Nilaus afer* Bontroklaksman

A common resident found over most of Southern Africa, favouring mature acacia woodlands, mixed woodlands and parklands. They are secretive birds spending most of their time in deep foliage singly or in pairs. They feed on a wide array of insects including ants, caterpillars and beetles. The forehead is white and follows the line of the eyebrow to the ear coverts. The crown and upper nape are black, the lores are black and a band of black extends from the rear of the eye, broadening to cover the sides of the neck. The lower nape and hindneck are whitish, the scapulars are black and the mantle is black on the sides and white in the centre. The back is black with large white spots. The tail is black edged with white. The primary flight feathers are black with narrow white edges and the wing coverts are black with wide outer edges resulting in a prominent wing bar. The chin, throat, breast and belly are white and the flanks are rich chestnut. The bill is black, the eyes are light brown and the legs and feet are grey/black. The female differs from the male in having brown upperparts where the male is black and by having streaks of black on the underparts.

Black-backed Puffback *Dryoscopus cubla* Sneeubal

A common resident species found in a variety of woodland habitats. They are usually to be seen singly or in pairs and are quite secretive. They feed in the canopy, taking caterpillars, beetles and some fruits. The upperpart of the head, the nape, neck and mantle are bluish black. The entire underside is white with a wash of cream. The wing coverts are black, broadly edged with white, which shows as a prominent wing bar above the primary and secondary flight feathers, which are black narrowly, edged with white. The males have the ability to raise the feathers of the lower back during display. The bill is black, the eyes are red and the legs and feet are greyish black. The female differs from the male in having the black plumage areas less dense and creamy/grey not white plumage areas.

Brown-crowned Tchagra *Tchagra australis* Rooivlerktjagra

A common resident over much of the region, found in dry woodland habitats, thickets and areas of scrub. They are usually solitary or in pairs, feeding on insects of many kinds. The forehead, crown and nape are mid-brown. They have a white stripe extending from the base of the upper mandible following the line of the eyebrow to the ear coverts and bordered above and below by narrower black stripes. The mantle and scapulars are brown and the rump and tail are greyish olive/brown. The chin, throat, central breast and belly are greyish white, the outer breast and cheeks are greyish buff. The primary and secondary flight feathers are dark brown edged with rufous. The bill is black, the eyes are brown and the legs and feet are grey. The sexes are similar.

Southern Boubou *Laniarius ferrugineus* Suidelike Waterfiskaal

A common bird in southern and eastern parts of our region, favouring areas of dense woodland, thickets, forest edges and mature parks and gardens. They are rather secretive birds, spending much of their time skulking in deep vegetation, singly or in pairs. They feed on snails, caterpillars and birds' eggs and nestlings as well as on seasonal fruits. The upper portion of the head, the hindneck, mantle and the back and tail are dense black. The chin, throat and breast are white merging into pale rufous on the belly and flanks. The flight feathers and wing coverts are black with a broad white wing bar showing across the coverts. The bill is black, the eyes are dark brown and the legs and feet are slaty grey. The sexes are similar, the female being slightly duller than the male.

Tropical Boubou *Laniarius aethiopicus* Tropiese Waterfiskaal

A common resident in the north-eastern corner of our region where they inhabit areas of dense cover along riverbanks, in thickets, tall grasses and mature gardens. They are usually encountered singly, in pairs or in small family parties, skulking around in deep cover in a shy secretive manner. They usually feed low down in vegetation or even on the ground, where they forage through the leaf litter in search of termites, beetles, snails, small reptiles and a multitude of insect species. The upper portion of the head, the hindneck, mantle, back and tail are a dense black with a wash of blue. The underparts are entirely white with a wash of pink on the breast and flanks. The primary and secondary flight feathers and the wing coverts are black with a broad white wing bar running through the coverts. The bill is black, the eyes are dark brown/red and the legs and feet are greyish. The sexes are similar.

Crimson-breasted Shrike *Laniarius atrococcineus* Rooiborslaksman
A common resident in areas of dry grasslands and savannahs with scattered trees and scrub, occurring singly or in pairs. A rather shy bird, which is more often heard than seen. The head, nape, mantle, scapulars, back, rump and tail are black with a wash of blue. The wing coverts are black and the closed wing shows a prominent white wing bar, being the outer edge of the lesser coverts. The primary and secondary flight feathers are black. The chin, throat, breast and belly are a striking rich crimson. The bill is black, the eyes are dark blue and the legs and feet are blackish. The sexes are similar.

Bokmakierie *Telophorus zeylonus* Bokmakierie
A common resident in the south and west of our region, usually seen singly or in pairs and occasionally in small family parties. They inhabit grasslands with sparse trees and scrub, dry rocky hillsides, fynbos and mature parks and gardens. The forehead, crown, nape, hindneck and ear coverts are grey/blue, merging in to olive green on the mantle, scapulars, back and rump. The central tail feathers are olive green and the out feathers are black with a broad yellow tip. They have a bright yellow stripe extending from the base of the upper mandible following the line of the eyebrow to the rear of the eye. The chin and throat are bright yellow, the lores are black, the black extending across the cheeks, down the sides of the neck and forming a bib across the breast. The belly and flanks are yellow/olive green. The bill is black, the eyes are brown and the legs and feet are greyish, blue. The sexes are similar.

Grey-headed Bush-shrike *Malaconotus blanchoti* Spookvoël
A locally common resident in the north-eastern part of our range where they inhabit areas of thick bush and scrub. The head is a slaty blue/grey, the chin and the throat are bright yellow merging to chestnut on the breast then back to bright yellow on the belly and underparts. The mantle, back, wings and tail are olive green with some yellow spotting on the wing coverts, secondary flight feathers and the tip of the tail. The bill is black, the eyes are yellow and the legs and feet are bluish grey. The sexes are similar.

White-crested Helmet-shrike *Prionops plumatus* Withelmlaksman
A locally common bird of broad-leaved woodlands, savannah woodlands and open bush areas. They have a gregarious nature and are usually encountered in flocks of 20 or so birds. They are cooperative breeders with members of a flock helping to build a nest, incubate the eggs and to brood and feed the chicks. The forehead and crown are whitish/grey, the feathers being slightly elongated and forming in to a crest. The cheeks and ear coverts are white with a dark bar following the line of the coverts. A white collar extends from the hindneck around the sides of the neck and broadens on to the chin, throat, breast and belly. The mantle, back and tail are black, the outermost tail feathers showing white. The primary and secondary flight feathers are black with white inner edges, which results in a prominent white wing bar being visible on the folded wing. The bill is black, the eyes are yellow and the legs and feet are pale orange/red. The sexes are similar.

Retz's Helmet-shrike *Prionops retzii* Swarthelmlaksman
A common resident of broad-leaved woodlands, in the north and east of the region. The head, neck, breast and belly are black, the undertail coverts are white. The wing coverts are a dull brown and the flight feathers are black. The tail is black edged with a thin white border at the tip. The bill is bright red and they have bright red pronounced orbital rings surrounding their yellow eyes. The legs and feet are also bright red. The sexes are similar.

Fork-tailed Drongo *Dicrurus adsimilis* Mikstertbyvanger
A widely distributed common resident found in a range of habitat types such as dry woodlands, savannahs, plantations, parks and gardens. A very conspicuous bird perching on exposed tree branches, on posts and wires, from where they hawk for flying insects and occasionally swoop to the ground to snatch a tasty morsel, before returning to the favoured perch. The entire plumage is more or less black, with washes of blue/green on the upperparts and the breast and belly. The tail is deeply forked, the upper surface having a sheen of green. The primary and secondary flight feathers are dark brown. The bill is black, the eyes are rich ruby red and the legs and feet are blackish. The sexes are similar.

Cape Crow *Corvus capensis* Swartkraai

A common resident over the vast majority of the region, found in most habitat types. They are usually encountered singly, in pairs or, during non-breeding periods, in large flocks of several hundred unmated and immature birds. They are very territorial and stay within their chosen site year-round. They spend much of their time feeding on the ground, taking a wide variety of invertebrates as well as worms, frogs and lizards. A rather slender crow with the entire plumage black, the upperparts with a reflective sheen of green/violet. The bill is black the eyes are dark brown and the legs and feet are blackish. The sexes are similar.

Pied Crow *Corvus albus* Witborskraai

A very common bird throughout Southern Africa occupying many different types of habitat from grasslands and areas of bush and scrub to towns, cities, parks and gardens. They can be encountered singly, in pairs or in huge flocks of many hundreds of birds at rubbish tips and in the vicinity of abattoirs. They take a wide variety of food types including seeds, berries, cultivated crops, nuts, insects, fish, reptiles, young birds and small mammals. The plumage is mainly black with reflective sheens of iridescent violets, greens and blues, they have a broad white collar across the upper mantle, which extends around the neck and broadens to cover the lower breast and upper belly. The bill is black, the eyes are dark brown and the legs and feet are blackish. The sexes are similar.

White-necked Raven *Corvus albicollis* Withalskraai

A locally common resident in southern and eastern parts of our range, usually seen singly or in pairs. They prefer areas with mountains, hills, gorges, cliffs and rocky outcrops as well as towns and villages. They feed on a variety of small animals, reptiles, large insects, fruits and berries and will readily feast on dead road-kills and other forms of carrion, including farm stock. With the exception of a white collar on the hindneck and upper mantle, the entire plumage is black with reflective sheens of green and bronze. The heavy bill is black with a white tip, the eyes are dark brown and the legs and feet are blackish. The sexes are similar.

Common Myna *Acridotheres tristis* Indiese Spreeu

An introduced species now locally common in the east of our region and surviving well in villages, towns and large cities. They forage on the ground taking discarded human scraps, insects, earthworms, snails and fruits and seeds. The forehead, crown and nape are glossy black, the mantle, scapulars and tail coverts are greyish brown and the tail is black with a white tip. The cheeks and ear coverts are black with a wash of grey, the chin and throat are blackish merging in to dark rufous on the breast, belly and flanks, contrasting with the white of the undertail coverts. The flight feathers are black/rufous with a white wing bar, which is prominent in flight. The bill is yellow, the eyes are dark brown and are set in a patch of bare yellow skin and the legs and feet are yellow. The sexes are similar.

Common Starling *Sturnus vulgaris* Europese Spreeu

Introduced in the Cape Town area in the late 1800s, since when they have steadily spread north. They are equally at home in grassland areas and on cultivated farmland as they are in suburbia, being common in parks and gardens. They survive on a wide array of food items from seeds, insects, earthworms and small reptiles to discarded human scraps. The plumage has largely black coloration with iridescent lustres of green and purple. Many of the feathers are sharp pointed with the tips buff, this results in a speckled effect on all but the wings and head. The feathers of the throat are loose and stand out like hackles when they sing. The bill is yellow, the eyes are dark brown and the legs and feet are reddish brown. The sexes are similar.

Wattled Starling *Creatophora cinerea* Lelspreeu

A common resident throughout Southern Africa inhabiting open grasslands, pastures, cultivated farmland and open woodlands. They feed on insects of all kinds, snails and earthworms and fruits when available. The head, neck, mantle and the whole of the undersides are light grey. The tail and the primary and secondary flight feathers are black. In breeding plumage the male has a patch of bright yellow skin covering the ear coverts extending around the eye to the back of the crown. The forehead and chin are featherless and exhibit black wattles. During periods of non-breeding the wattles and bare skin are replaced with pale grey feathering. The bill is pale pink, the eyes are dark brown and the legs and feet are flesh pink.

Meves's Starling *Lamprotornis mevesii* Langstertglansspreeu

Local in distribution, being found only in the northern parts of our range in areas of mature woodlands where they usually appear in pairs or small parties, although at some roost sites numbers can reach 150 individuals. They feed on the ground, taking termites, beetles, ants and fruits, sometimes following elephants and other animal herds, feeding on the insects disturbed by the grazing beasts. The head, mantle and scapulars are iridescent greenish blue, merging into purple and bronze on the back, rump and uppertail coverts. They have a long, tapering tail of bluish/green. The lores and the ear coverts are black, the undersides are a mixture of iridescent blues, greens and purples with a narrow band of violet across the breast. The bill is black, the eyes are brown and the legs and feet are blackish. The sexes are similar.

Pied Starling *Spreo bicolor* Witgatspreeu

Found only in South Africa where they are common in open grasslands, cultivated fields and pastures, along coasts and in towns. They are encountered in small flocks of up to 20 birds. They work as a cooperative group during the breeding season, immature birds serving as helpers to the breeding adults. The bulk of the plumage is blackish with a reflective sheen of green. The belly and undertail coverts are white. The bill is black at the tip and yellow at the base, the eyes are white and the legs and feet are black. The sexes are similar.

Cape Glossy Starling *Lamprotornis nitens* Kleinglansspreeu

A common resident found in most areas of Southern Africa in savannahs, alongside water bodies and in parks and gardens. A gregarious bird forming flocks of up to 20 individuals which forage on the ground searching out ants, termites, grasshoppers, fruits and scraps from bird tables and picnic areas. The plumage is a metallic blue/green, the lores are black and the wrist joint of the wing shows a purple bar. Some feathers of the wing coverts show dark blue spots towards the tips. The bill is black, the eyes are yellow/orange and the legs and feet are blackish. The sexes are similar.

Red-winged Starling *Onychognathus morio* Rooivlerkspreeu

A common resident in the eastern portion of our range, favouring mountains, cliffs, rocky hillsides and towns and villages. They can be seen in very large flocks on fruiting trees and at favoured roosting sites. They feed on a wide variety of food items such as lizards, nestling birds, crabs, bees, fruits and some carrion. The majority of the plumage is violet blue and black, the exception being the primary flight feathers, which are a rich chestnut tipped with black, the chestnut mainly showing when the bird is in flight. The female differs from the male in having the head, neck, chin, throat and upper breast washed with dark grey and streaked with black. The bill is black, the eyes are deep red and the legs and feet are blackish.

Pale-winged Starling *Onychognathus nabouroup* Bleekvlerkspreeu

A common bird in the west, found in semi-arid mountains and on rocky hillsides and escarpments. They are usually encountered in pairs and small flocks. They forage in bushes and trees as well as on the ground and feed on fruits and nectar, grasshoppers, beetles, termites, ticks and ectoparasites, which they groom, from Mountain Zebras and Klipspringers. The entire plumage is gloss black with the exception of the primary flight feathers, which are creamy white with black tips. The bill is black, the eyes are orange and the legs and feet are blackish. The sexes are similar.

Red-billed Oxpecker *Buphagus erythrorhynchus* Rooibekrenostervoël

A locally common species, mainly in the north-east of our region, found in areas where game animals are present. They spend almost the whole of their time on and around herds of large ungulates on which they feed by removing parasites such as ticks and blood-sucking flies. They have needle-sharp claws that help them to hang on, sometimes upside down, as they search the animals' fur for a meal. The head, neck, mantle, back, wings and tail are earth brown, the breast and belly are buff. The bill is bright red, the eyes are red surrounded by a bright yellow orbital ring and the legs and feet are black. The sexes are similar. This species may be confused with the Yellow-billed Oxpecker (*Buphagus africanus*), which has a bright yellow base to the bill and a pale buff rump. It is not as common as the Red-billed.

Red-billed Buffalo Weaver *Bubalornis niger* Buffelwewer
A locally common resident in the north and west in areas of acacia grassland and thornbush country. They require tall, well matured trees in which to build their communal nests, most of which contain around 6 to 12 nesting chambers. They forage mainly on the ground, searching out a variety of insects as well as seeds and fruits. The plumage is entirely black, although the basal section of many of the feathers are white, which shows when the plumage is disarranged. The primary and secondary flight feathers are black narrowly edged with white. The bill is red, the eyes are dark brown and the legs and feet are blackish. The females are brown.

White-browed Sparrow Weaver *Plocepasser mahali* Koringvoël
A locally common species found in dry acacia woodlands and scrub and in parks and gardens often close to human habitation. The forehead, crown and face are grey/brown with a white stripe from the base of the upper mandible following the line of the eyebrow to the ear coverts. The nape, mantle and wing coverts are earth brown. A black moustachial stripe extends from the lores down the sides of the neck to the upper breast bordering the white of the chin and throat. The breast and belly are also white. The wing coverts are blackish edged with white and the primary and secondary flight feathers are dark brown/black. The rump is white and the tail is dark brown edged with white. The bill is black, the eyes are dark brown and the legs and feet are dull red. The sexes are similar.

Sociable Weaver *Philetairus socius* Versamelvoël
Found in dry savannahs and woodlands in the western portion of our range. They are extremely gregarious birds with up to 500 individuals pooling their efforts to build and maintain large nest structures in trees and on telephone poles. They feed on the ground taking small insects, seeds and some fruit. The forehead, crown and nape are grey/brown, the feathers of the mantle are dark brown with buff/white edges. The cheeks are creamy brown, the lores are black joined via the gape of the bill to a black bib on the chin and throat. The breast and belly are creamy brown, the feathers of the flanks and the primary and secondary flight feathers are dark brown edged with buff/white. The bill is grey, the eyes are dark brown and the legs and feet are brownish black. The sexes are similar.

Spectacled Weaver *Ploceus ocularis* Brilwewer
A fairly common resident in the eastern parts of the region, favouring areas of open woodland, forest edges and savannah grasslands. The forehead, crown and nape are golden yellow merging into olive green on the mantle and back. They have a black eye stripe extending from the base of the bill to the top of the ear coverts. The chin and throat are black, forming a short bib. The breast and belly are yellow and the wings are dull olive brown with greenish yellow edges. The bill is black, the eyes are yellow and the legs and feet are greyish black. The female lacks the black chin and throat bib of the male.

Cape Weaver *Ploceus capensis* Kaapse Wewer
Common in the south in areas of open grassland, fynbos, thickets and cultivated farmland. They are gregarious nesters, often building large colonies over water on overhanging vegetation, in reeds or attached to fence wires. The forehead, face, chin and throat are yellow with a soft wash of chestnut merging into yellow on the crown, nape, mantle back, rump and uppertail coverts. The tail is olive brown edged with yellow/green. The breast and belly are yellow often with orange/brown speckling. The wings are olive green/brown edged with green. The bill is black, the eyes are yellow and the legs and feet are flesh pink. The female lacks the bright plumage of the male, being generally olive green with grey/brown streaking; the eyes are also dark red not yellow.

Southern Brown-throated Weaver *Ploceus xanthopterus* Bruinkeelwewer
An uncommon local resident, found in reedbeds and stands of dense papyrus. They feed on seeds, fruits and insects. The breed in colonies with 100 to 300 nesting pairs. The entire plumage is a bright golden yellow, with a wash of pale olive yellow on the wings and tail. The chin and the throat are a rich chestnut brown. The bill is black, the eyes are red and the legs and feet are flesh pink. Females and non-breeding males lack the chestnut chin and throat and have a light wash of olive yellow on the head, mantle and back.

Southern Masked Weaver *Ploceus velatus* Swartkeelgeelvink
Common throughout Southern Africa in areas of open savannah, scrub, thickets and parks and gardens. They are a gregarious species, feeding together in small flocks, taking seeds, insects, nectar and bird table scraps. The forehead, face, ear coverts, chin and throat are black, the portion at the lower throat finishing in a point. The crown and nape are golden yellow merging in to the faintly streaked olive green of the mantle, back and tail. The breast and belly are golden yellow. The bill is black, the eyes are red and the legs and feet are dull red. The female lacks the bright colouration of the male, being mainly olive green streaked with grey.

Village Weaver *Ploceus cucullatus* Bontrugwewer
A common resident, usually found near water in the eastern part of our range. They are to be found in most open habitats from savannahs to coastal areas and parks and gardens. The face, ear coverts, chin and throat are black. The crown, nape, neck, breast and belly are yellow. The mantle, back and wing coverts are dark brown/black with bold yellow blotches. The primary and secondary flight feathers are dark brown/black edged with yellow. The bill is black, the eyes are red and the legs and feet are reddish brown. The female lacks the bold colouration of the male being mainly olive green, the wings and coverts being streaked with olive brown, the underparts are pale yellow becoming paler still on the belly.

Red-headed Weaver *Anaplectes rubriceps* Rooikopwewer
A locally common bird in broad-leaved woodlands, acacia savannah and in parks and gardens. The head, neck, chin throat and upper breast are bright scarlet red, the lower breast and belly are greyish white. The lores are black. The mantle, back and tail coverts are warm grey, the primary and secondary flight feathers are dark brown/grey edged with buff/yellow. The bill is pale orange, the eyes are red and the legs and feet are flesh pink. The female lacks the bright scarlet red plumage of the male, becoming brownish grey on the head with a wash of yellow.

Yellow-crowned Bishop *Euplectes afer* Goudgeelvink
A locally common bird of wetlands and marshes, flooded grasslands and papyrus swamps. They feed almost exclusively on seeds. The forehead, crown and nape are rich golden yellow, the mantle is dark brown/black and the back, rump and uppertail coverts are golden yellow. The tail is black. The face, cheeks, chin, throat and belly are black. A band of golden yellow extends across the breast and the flanks and undertail coverts are also golden yellow. The bill is black, the eyes are dark brown and the legs and feet are brown. The female lacks the striking plumage of the male, being mainly olive brown on the upperparts streaked with dark brown and whitish on the underside.

Southern Red Bishop *Euplectes orix* Rooivink
Common over much of the region in areas of tall wet grasslands, marshes and open areas close to water. The forehead, lores, cheeks, chin and upper throat are black. The crown, nape, back, rump and uppertail coverts are deep orange/red, the tail is blackish brown. The mantle is reddish brown. The lower throat and the upper breast are orange/red and the remainder of the underparts are black, with the exception of the undertail coverts, which are orange/red. The wings are dark brown narrowly edged with white/buff. The bill is black, the eyes are dark brown and the legs and feet are brownish red. The females lack the bright plumage of the males, the upperparts being mainly olive brown with dark brown/black streaks, the underparts being whitish with a wash of yellow/buff on the throat and breast.

Thick-billed Weaver *Amblyospiza albifrons* Dikbekwewer
A locally common species in eastern regions, found in wet habitats, swamps, marshes, and the edges of watercourses and lakes and ponds. The forehead is white, the crown, neck and mantle are dark brown merging with the black of the back, scapulars and tail. The chin and throat are dark brown with fine streaking and the breast and belly are blackish streaked with dark grey. The primary and secondary flight feathers are blackish, the base of the primaries being white forming a prominent wing patch. The heavy bill is black, the eyes are dark brown and the legs and feet are black. The female has the upperparts mainly warm brown streaked with brown/black. The underparts are buff/white with heavy dark brown streaks on the flanks.

Scaly-feathered Finch *Sporopipes squamifrons* Baardmannetjie
A common resident throughout most of the region in areas of acacia woodlands, scrub, thickets and dry riverbeds. The forehead and forecrown are black and white flecked and the lores are black. The hindcrown, cheeks, ear coverts, nape, mantle and rump are ashy brown and the tail is dark brown narrowly edged with white. The wings are dark brown broadly edged with white. The chin, throat, breast and belly are white and they show a prominent black molar stripe. The bill is pink, the eyes are dark brown and the legs and feet are flesh red/pink. The sexes are similar.

Red-billed Quelea *Quelea quelea* Rooibekkwelea
One of the most common birds in Africa, with non-breeding roosts often containing several million birds. They prefer dry habitats and can do severe damage to cultivated crops. In breeding plumage the male has the forehead, face, chin and throat black, although occasionally the head is rufous, lacking in non-breeding birds. The crown, nape, sides of the neck and the breast are buff with a wash of pink, the belly is whitish. The back, wings and tail feathers are dark brown edged with buff/white. The bill is red, the eyes are dark brown and the legs and feet are dull red. Breeding females resemble non-breeding males apart from the bill which changes from red to pale yellow.

Red-collared Widowbird *Euplectes ardens* Rooikeelflap
A common resident in the eastern section of our range, inhabiting savannahs with tall grasses, scrub and cultivated areas. In breeding plumage the male has a long flowing tail, almost the entire plumage is black, the exceptions being a scarlet breast band, buff edging to the wing feathers and the undertail coverts which are edged with white. The bill is black, the eyes are dark brown and the legs and feet are blackish. The female has the upper plumage dark brown edged and streaked with buff and the underparts are yellow/buff to white. In non-breeding plumage the male has similar plumage to the female but is larger and more heavily streaked.

Long-tailed Widowbird *Euplectes progne* Langstertflap
A common resident in the central-eastern part of our region, where they can be found in a variety of grassland habitats. During the breeding season the male has an exceptionally long tail. Apart from the lesser wing coverts being red, bordered with white/buff, the entire plumage is black. The bill is grey, the eyes are dark brown and the legs and feet are brown/black. In non-breeding plumage the male has a short tail, the forehead, crown and ear coverts are tawny brown, the chin and throat, breast and belly are whitish, with a wash of buff on the breast. They retain the red/buff patch on the lesser coverts, the back and flight feathers remain dark brown/black edged with buff. The female has similar plumage to the non-breeding male but lacks the red/buff of the lesser coverts.

Cut-throat Finch *Amadina fasciata* Bandkeelvink
A bird of dry savannah woodlands, scrub and large parks and gardens. They forage on the ground, usually in pairs, feeding on seeds and small insects. The forehead, crown and nape are pale buff, heavily barred with black. The chin is white and the throat has a red crescent running across it terminating at the ear coverts. The breast and belly are whitish with a wash of buff and a varying amount of dark barring. There is a rich brown patch on the centre of the belly. The mantle and scapulars are buff spotted with black. The bill is pale grey, the eyes are dark brown and the legs and feet are flesh pink. The female is similar to the male but lacks the red throat band.

Red-headed Finch *Amadina erythrocephala* Rooikopvink
A common resident found in areas of dry grassland, dense patches of thornbush and on cultivated farmland. The forehead, crown, nape, ear coverts, chin and upper throat are red. The lores are grey/brown, the sides of the neck and the lower throat are whitish. The upper breast is white with black barring. The lower breast and belly are cinnamon with bold white spots bordered with black. The wings are brown/grey edged with buff. The bill is grey, the eyes are dark brown and the legs and feet are reddish brown. The female differs from the male in having a plain buff/brown head.

Green-winged Pytilia *Pytilia melba* Gewone Melba

A common resident in areas of dry acacia savannah, open grasslands and thickets. They are usually in pairs or small family parties, foraging for seeds on the ground. The forehead and forecrown are bright red. The lores, ear coverts, hindcrown, nape and sides of the neck are brownish grey. The mantle, scapulars, wing coverts and rump are olive green, the tail is red at the base and brown/black towards the tip. The chin and throat are bright red, the upper breast is olive green, and the lower breast and belly are white with grey/brown barring. The bill is red, the eyes are deep red and the legs and feet are brownish red. The female differs from the male in having no red on the face, the entire head being grey/brown.

Red-billed Firefinch *Lagonosticta senegala* Rooibekvuurvinkie

A common bird in acacia savannah areas and in and around human habitations. The male has the entire head, neck, mantle, chin, throat and breast red. Generally a few white spots are discernable on the sides of the breast. The belly is sandy brown. The wing coverts and flight feathers are warm brown. The rump and outer tail feathers are red, the central feathers are brown. The female lacks the red plumage of the male with the exception of on the lores, the rump and tail are brown, and she also has spots on the sides of the breast and flanks. The bill is reddish pink, the eyes are dark red and the legs and feet are flesh pink.

Jameson's Firefinch *Lagonosticta rhodopareia* Jamesonse Vuurvinkie

A common resident in areas of scrub, thickets, tall grassy patches and cultivated farmland. They are usually in pairs or small parties. The forehead, crown, nape and mantle are red with a wash of brown. The rump and outer tail feathers are red, the central feathers are brown. The face, neck, chin, throat, breast and belly are reddish pink, the undertail coverts are dark brown/black. The wings are brown, the bill is black, the eyes are dark brown and the legs and feet are blackish. The female differs from the male in having the upper plumage greyish brown, the lores remain red and the underparts are dull pink on the breast, merging to grey on the belly and blackish on the undertail coverts.

Shaft-tailed Whydah *Vidua regia* Pylstertrooibekkie

A common bird in areas of acacia savannah and dry grassland habitats. In breeding plumage the male has extremely long thin central tail feathers that broaden towards the tips. The forehead and crown are black, the nape and hindneck are pale orange. The sides of the neck, ear coverts, chin, throat, breast and belly are pale yellow/brown and the undertail coverts are brown. The mantle, back, wings and tail are black. The bill is orange/red, the eyes are dark brown and the legs and feet are red. The plumage of the female is subdued compared to the male, having the upperparts buff with dark brown streaks and the underparts are light buff/white.

Long-tailed Paradise Whydah *Vidua paradisaea* Gewone Paradysvink

A fairly common bird of dry acacia woodland and savannah. In breeding plumage the male has long broad black tail feathers. The forehead, crown, ear coverts, face, chin and throat are black. The nape is yellow, the breast is chestnut and the belly is buff. The mantle and wings are black. The bill is black, the eyes are dark brown and the legs and feet are blackish. The females and non-breeding males lack the flamboyant plumage of the breeding males having the upperparts grey/brown streaked with brown/black. A whitish stripe follows the line of the eyebrow and the outer edge of the ear coverts merging with the white of the chin and throat. The underparts are whitish buff.

Pin-tailed Whydah *Vidua macroura* Koningrooibekkie

A common resident in open woodlands, dry grasslands and mature parks and gardens. The forehead and crown are black. A collar extends from the nape around the neck, broadening over the face, chin, throat, breast and belly. The mantle and back are black, the rump is white and the wings are black with a white wing bar running across the lesser coverts. The central tail feathers are black and very elongated, the bill is red, the eyes are dark brown and the legs and feet are greyish black. The female and non-breeding male look similar, the upperparts being buff with blackish streaks, they have a dark brown stripe on the side of the crown and a less obvious stripe through the eye. The underparts are buff/white, the bill is black in the breeding season and red at other times.

Blue Waxbill *Uraeginthus angolensis* Gewone Blousysie
A common resident over much of the region, found in small flocks in areas of dry open acacia woodland and savannah. The forehead, crown, nape, mantle and back are ashy brown. The rump and tail are blue. The face, ear coverts, chin, throat and breast are blue merging to grey over the belly to the undertail coverts. The bill is greyish, the eyes are red and the legs and feet are pink/brown. The female is similar to the male but slightly duller in colour.

Violet-eared Waxbill *Granatina granatina* Koningblousysie
An inhabitant of dry acacia woodlands, scrub and thickets. Usually found singly, in pairs or small family parties. The forehead is bright blue, the lores, chin and throat are black and the cheeks and ear coverts are violet. The crown, nape, mantle, scapulars, breast and belly are rich chestnut and the undertail coverts are black. The wings and the tail are brown/black, the rump and uppertail coverts are blue. The bill is red, the eyes are dark red surrounded by a red orbital ring and the legs and feet are blackish. The female differs from the male, being less colourful and having the underparts buff, not chestnut.

Swee Waxbill *Estrilda melanotis* Suidelike Swie
A fairly common species in the east and south of the region, inhabiting evergreen forests, damp woodlands farms and gardens. The forehead, crown, nape and sides of the neck are grey. The mantle, scapulars and wing coverts are olive green and the rump and uppertail coverts are bright red, the tail is black. The lores, face, chin and throat are black, the breast is grey and the belly is buff. The upper mandible is grey and the lower is red, the eyes are rich red and the legs and feet are black. The female differs from the male in having the chin and throat whitish grey, not black, and having slightly more subdued plumage.

Common Waxbill *Estrilda astrild* Rooibeksysie
A very common resident over most of the region in areas of tall grass and other types of rank vegetation, around farms and in parks and gardens. They have a bright red eye stripe and a smudge of bright red in the centre of the belly and on the undertail coverts. The head and all upperparts are pale grey/brown finely barred with dark brown. The cheeks are greyish buff, the chin and throat are buff/white and the breast and belly are buff/brown all finely barred with dark brown. The bill is red, the eyes are brown and the legs and feet are blackish. The sexes are similar, the females being slightly less colourful.

Bronze Mannikin *Spermestes cucullatus* Gewone Fret
A common resident in the eastern part of our range, found in areas of long grasses and rank vegetation alongside riverbanks, roadsides, on farmland and in parks and gardens. The forehead, crown, cheeks, chin and throat are brownish black with a sheen of bronzy green. The neck, mantle and back are brown, the rump and uppertail coverts are greyish white finely but distinctly barred with dark brown and merging to black on the tail. The breast is white merging to grey on the belly and undertail coverts, which are finely barred with dark brown/black. The flanks are heavily barred with brown/black. The bill is black, the eyes are dark brown and the legs and feet are blackish. The sexes are similar.

Village Indigobird *Vidua chalybeata* Staalblouvinkie
A fairly common resident in the north-east in woodlands and acacia savannah, scrub, farmland and gardens. They can be seen in pairs during the breeding season and in small to medium-sized flocks during other periods. They forage on the ground after seeds and small insects. Almost the entire plumage of the male is black with blue and green reflective sheens often visible. The primary flight feathers often show a little brown and the underwing coverts sometimes show grey. Two races occur, the southern race has a red bill, the north-western race has a white bill, the eyes are dark brown and the legs and feet are reddish. Females and non-breeding males have the upperparts brown, streaked with dark brown/black. The crown has a pale central stripe bordered by a dark brown stripe. The underparts are whitish grey, darker on the sides of the breast and flanks and with a wash of buff.

Cinnamon-breasted Bunting *Emberiza tahapisi* Klipstreepkoppie
A common resident found in woodlands, along side dry riverbeds, on rocky hillsides and on open ground with scrub. They are usually encountered in pairs or in small family parties, foraging on the bare ground, seeking out seeds and small insects. They have a central white stripe extending from the forehead to the nape along with a white superciliary stripe and a black moustachial stripe, which collectively give the whole head a black and white striped appearance. The throat, breast and belly are cinnamon/rufous. The mantle, scapulars and the back are brown with black streaking, the primary and secondary flight feathers are dark brown edged with buff. The bill is yellow, the eyes are dark brown and the legs and feet are brownish. The sexes are similar, the female having duller plumage than the male.

Cape Bunting *Emberiza capensis* Rooivlerkstreepkoppie
A locally common species inhabiting rocky mountainsides, open grasslands and areas of scrub and thornbush. They can usually be encountered singly, in pairs or small family parties, foraging on bare earth, seeking out seeds and small insects including caterpillars and termites. The forehead, crown and nape are greyish brown with black streaking. They have a white superciliary stripe, a black stripe from the lores extending through the eye to the ear coverts and a black moustachial stripe. The chin and throat are white, the breast is grey merging into white on the belly and undertail coverts. The mantle and scapulars are grey/brown with dark brown streaks and the primary and secondary flight feathers are dark brown edged with buff and rufous, the wing coverts also show broad rufous edging. The bill is grey/black, the eyes are brown and the legs and feet are blackish. The sexes are similar, the female being slightly duller than the male.

Golden-breasted Bunting *Emberiza flaviventris* Rooirugstreepkoppie
A common resident over most of the region in dry woodlands, open grasslands with scrub and thornbush, cultivated farmland and gardens. They are usually seen in pairs or in small flocks of 10 to 20 birds, often mixed with other bunting species. The head is black with two broad white stripes, one above and one below the eyes. The chin and throat are yellow, the breast is a rich golden yellow and the belly is whitish/yellow. The mantle and scapulars are rufous, the back, rump and uppertail coverts are greyish brown, and the tail is brown/black. The wing coverts are blackish brown edged with buff and tipped with white forming a wing bar. The primary and secondary flight feathers are dark brown/black edged with buff. The bill is greyish yellow, the eyes are dark brown and the legs and feet are brownish pink. The sexes are similar, the female being slightly duller.

Cape Canary *Serinus canicollis* Kaapse Kanarie
A common resident in the south and east of our range, found in grasslands with thin woodland and scrub, as well as in fynbos, plantations and in parks and gardens. They occur singly, in pairs or in non-breeding flocks of several hundred birds. They forage on the ground, taking seeds and some small insects. The forehead is yellow, the crown is olive green/yellow, the nape and the sides of the neck and the mantle are grey. The chin, throat and upper breast are yellow with a wash of brown, becoming paler on the lower breast and the belly. The undertail coverts are yellow. The primary and secondary flight feathers and the wing coverts are blackish brown edged with yellow and olive green. The bill is grey/yellow, the eyes are brown and the legs and feet are grey/brown. The sexes are similar, the female having duller facial coloration.

Yellow-fronted Canary *Serinus mozambicus* Geeloogkanarie
A common resident in the east and north of the region, found in open woodlands, acacia scrub, plantations, on cultivated farmlands and in parks and gardens. They spend much of their time foraging on the ground, often with other related species, taking seeds, insects, nectar and some fruits. The forehead, crown, nape and mantle are greyish green, finely streaked with dark brown. They have a yellow superciliary stripe below which is a dark stripe which extends from the lores through the eye to the ear coverts. The cheeks, chin and throat are yellow. They have a dark molar stripe. The sides of the breast are olive green, the remainder of the underparts are bright yellow. The wing coverts and the primary and secondary flight feathers are black/brown edged with olive green. The bill is grey/brown, the eyes are dark brown and the legs and feet are blackish. The sexes are similar, the female having slightly paler plumage than the male.

Yellow Canary *Serinus flaviventris* Geelkanarie
A common bird over most of the region, inhabiting areas of dry acacia woodland, savannah scrub, sand dunes, on cultivated farmlands and in gardens. They can be seen in pairs during the breeding season and in small flocks at other times. They forage on the ground, often with other species, taking seeds, termites, ants and crustaceans. The forehead is bright yellow from which flows a yellow superciliary stripe which runs to the side of the nape. The crown, nape, ear coverts, mantle and back are olive green with fine dark brown streaking. The entire underparts are bright yellow with a wash of olive green on the sides of the breast. The wing coverts and the primary and secondary flight feathers are blackish brown edged with olive green. The bill is greyish yellow, the eyes are dark brown and the legs and feet are grey/black. The female lacks all the bright plumage coloration of the male, being predominantly a mixture of olive browns and greens with dark brown streaking.

Brimstone Canary *Serinus sulphuratus* Dikbekkanarie
A common resident in the eastern parts of our range, inhabiting damp woodlands, savannahs, the margins of rivers and streams and in rank vegetation. They can be encountered singly, in pairs or in flocks of around 10 individuals foraging on the ground, often with other related species, seeking out seeds and fruits. The forehead, crown, nape and ear coverts are olive green finely streaked with dark brown. They have a bright yellow superciliary stripe and the cheeks, chin and throat are also bright yellow. An olive green molar stripe merges with a broad band of olive green which covers the breast and upper flanks. The belly and undertail coverts are bright yellow. The primary and secondary flight feathers are dark brown/black edged with yellow and green. The bill is greyish pink, the eyes are dark brown and the legs and feet are brownish. The sexes are similar, the female having slightly duller plumage than the male.

House Sparrow *Passer domesticus* Huismossie

An introduced species, now a common resident over the whole of Southern Africa. They can be encountered on farms, particularly around buildings, in towns, cities and villages and in parks and gardens. A gregarious bird usually found in flocks of 20 to 30 individuals. They feed on the ground and in trees and bushes on a wide variety of food items including seeds of many types, berries, insects and human scraps. The forehead and crown are grey, the lores are black and a band of chestnut extends from the rear of the eye joining with the rufous feathering of the nape and mantle. The ear coverts and cheeks are off-white. The chin and throat are black, widening to form a bib on the upper breast. The remainder of the underparts are off-white. The wings are dark brown, the primaries edged with buff, a pale patch on the wing coverts creates a whitish wing bar and the lesser coverts are rufous. The rump is grey and the tail is dark brown/grey. The bill is greyish, the eyes are dark brown and the legs and feet are flesh brown. The female is far duller than the male and lacks the grey and chestnut head, which is replaced with olive brown. She also lacks the black bib and throat, this becoming off-white.

Great Sparrow *Passer motitensis* Grootmossie

An uncommon species found in dry acacia woodlands and scrub. They can usually be seen in pairs but will occasionally mix with other sparrow species at watering holes. They usually forage on the ground, taking mainly seeds and small insects. The forehead, crown, central nape and upper mantle are slaty grey, the sides of the nape and area surrounding the ear coverts are rufous. The lores are black, joining around the base of the bill with the black chin and small throat bib. The remainder of the underparts are greyish white. The flight feathers are dark brown, narrowly edged with buff, the wing coverts are dark brown broadly edged with rufous, the rump is rufous and the tail is dark brown. The bill is blackish, the eyes are dark brown and the legs and feet are greyish. The female has duller plumage than the male and lacks the black throat bib.

Yellow-throated Petronia *Petronia superciliaris* Geelvlekmossie

A fairly common resident in the north and east of the region, inhabiting woodlands, river courses, and areas around human settlements. The forehead, crown and nape are brown, the remainder of the upperparts are brownish grey. The chin and throat are white and they show a prominent white superciliary stripe and have a yellow spot in the centre of the lower throat. The breast and belly are off-white. The tail and the primary and secondary flight feathers are dark brown edged with buff. The bill is grey, the eyes are dark brown and the legs and feet are grey/black. The sexes are similar although the yellow throat spot is often more difficult to see in the female.

Southern Grey-headed Sparrow *Passer diffusus* Gryskopmossie

A common resident over much of Southern Africa, favouring areas of open acacia woodland, grasslands and villages and gardens. They are usually in pairs but outside the breeding season they often gather into larger flocks. They forage on the ground for seeds and insects, berries, fruits and human food scraps. The entire head is ashy grey. A small white patch is visible on the chin and the centre of the throat, the breast and belly are grey with a hint of brown. The mantle and scapulars are mid-brown, the back and tail coverts are brown and the tail is dark brown edged with buff. The wing coverts are dark brown broadly edged with rufous and the inner feathers are tipped with white resulting in a prominent wing bar. The flight feathers are dark brown narrowly edged with buff. The bill is black, the eyes are dark brown and the legs and feet are brown/black. The sexes are similar.

Cape Sparrow *Passer melanurus* Gewone Mossie

A common resident over most of the region in dry acacia woodlands, open grasslands, scrub, cultivated farmland and in parks and gardens. They are very gregarious in non-breeding periods, gathering together into flocks of up to a 100 or so individuals, foraging on the ground or in low bushes for seeds, fruits and insects. The forehead, centre crown and nape are black, a broad band of white extends from the rear of the eye circling the ear coverts and curves on to the sides of the lower throat. The ear coverts, cheeks, chin and throat are black and are connected to a black bib covering the upper breast. The remainder of the underparts are white. The upper mantle is grey and the lower mantle, scapulars, back, and rump are rufous, the tail is brown/black. The wing coverts are blackish brown edged with buff and tipped with white resulting in a wing bar. The bill is black, the eyes are dark brown and the legs and feet are black. The female is duller than the male and lacks the black head markings and breast bib.

Southern African Hedgehog *Atelerix frontalis* Krimpvarkie

A species that occurs in two separate areas within our range, one in Namibia and a second running north from the east of Cape Province to Botswana and Zimbabwe. They avoid areas of high rainfall, preferring semi-arid habitats, grasslands, areas of scrub and suburban parks and gardens. They are generally nocturnal in habits, but can be encountered during the daytime, particularly following rainstorms. They forage for a wide variety of food types including, earthworms, insects, bird's eggs and nestlings, lizards, fungi and various fruits. An unmistakable mammal, covered in a dense mass of dark brown spines with white tips. The forehead, eyebrows, temples, sides of the neck and underparts are covered in dense off-white fur. When threatened they will roll into a tight spiny ball, presenting a formidable defence to any would-be predator.

Chacma Baboon *Papio ursinus* Kaapse Bobbejaan

The commonest and largest of Southern Africa's primates, found over most of the region. Their pelage is grizzled grey above with lighter underparts. The tail is roughly the same length as the body usually extending upwards for a few centimetres, before curving downwards at a sharp angle, giving the appearance of being 'broken'. The head is large with small, close-set, brown eyes beneath a protruding eyebrow ridge. The long muzzle is black and devoid of fur. The mouth contains a formidable set of canine teeth. The males are considerably larger than the females and have a mane of darker fur on the neck and shoulders. They feed throughout the day, both on the ground and in trees, taking fruits, leaves, buds, grasses, insects, lizards and occasionally other mammals. They are a very gregarious species, living together in troops varying in number from just a handful to well over one hundred individuals. A female will carry a newborn beneath her during daily foraging, but as the youngster grows it soon adopts a 'jockey style' position. At night they roost together in trees or on rock ledges to avoid predation, principally from leopards.

Vervet Monkey *Cercopithecus pygerythrus* Blouaap

A common species, widely distributed over the region but much less common in western areas, where they are largely absent from dry desert habitats. They are usually to be found in areas of savannah woodlands. A very agile and slender primate with long limbs and a well-developed system of both visual and vocal communications. The coat colour is subject to some regional variation, but is usually grey/brown with a wash of olive on the back and the crown of the head. The black face has a fringe of white hair on the cheeks and across the eyebrow line. The chest and underparts are whitish and the lower parts of the limbs are greyish with black feet. The eyes are a deep rich brown, the tail, which is about the same length as the head and body, is greyish with a black tip. The small ears are black. Males have brightly coloured genitalia, the powder blue scrotum and bright red penis are displayed to indicate a willingness to mate. An adult male is about 20% larger than the female. They live in troops varying in number from just a few up to 50 or more. They eat fruits, berries, invertebrates and bird eggs and nestlings, they will readily eat cultivated crops and are considered a pest by most farming communities.

Samango Monkey *Cercopithecus mitis* Samango-aap

A rare localised species found in the east of the region preferring moist forest habitats. A large robust primate, which has a thick coat of blue/black fur with an olive wash on the back and the crown of the head. The back, face and hind legs are flecked with silver/grey. The close-set eyes are amber in colour. The small ears are black edged with grey. The tail is longer than the combined length of the head and body and is olive/grey at the base and black towards the tip. They are usually encountered in troops of between 10 and 30 individuals, feeding among the trees and occasionally on the forest floor on vegetation, insects, birds eggs and young, seeds and cultivated crops.

Pangolin *Manis Temminckii* Ietermagog

A widespread solitary mammal which, as a result of its nocturnal habits, is rarely seen. They prefer open savannah habitats and rocky hillsides. These unmistakable mammals are heavily protected with large overlapping scales and when threatened roll into a tight ball thereby presenting an almost impenetrable barrier to would-be predators. They can also emit a foul smelling waxy secretion from the anal glands when threatened. The small ears have soft hair linings, the eyes are small and set either side of the long pointed nose. They live either in self-excavated burrows or commandeer holes vacated by other burrowing mammals. They have no teeth and eat mainly ants and termites, which they extract from nests using their long sticky tongues, having first broken into the nests using their powerful claws and front legs.

Thick-tailed Bushbaby *Otolemur crassicaudatus* Bosnagaap

A scarce species found in thickets and dense woodlands and forests in the east and northeast of the region. This nocturnal primate has a rounded head, large ears, stout limbs and huge forward-facing eyes. The coat is thick and fluffy and varies in colour from overall grey with a white tip to the tail, to dark brown with a blackish tip to the tail. The underparts are off-white and the short, pointed face has dark patches along the sides of the muzzle and around the eyes. The thick bushy tail is longer than the combined length of the head and body. They are expert climbers and have well-adapted fingers and toes for this purpose. Small family groups will maintain a territory of several hectares, feeding on vegetation, fruits, berries, insects and occasionally small birds and reptiles.

Lesser Bushbaby *Galago moholi* Nagapie

Widely distributed in forest and woodland habitats, they can be found across most of the northern part of the region but are by no means common. This charming little nocturnal primate is about half the size of the Thick-tailed Bushbaby. They have a rounded head, short muzzle, large eyes and substantial pointed ears. They have a soft, fluffy grey coat covering the body and the tail, with a wash of yellow on the flanks and both the fore and hind limbs. The underparts are whitish. They have dark patches around the eyes and the insides of the ears are pink. They have a conspicuous light stripe extending from the forehead down the muzzle towards the nose. The tail is longer than the combined length of the head and body and is bushy towards the tip. They can be encountered singly, in pairs or in small family groups. They feed mainly on tree gum which exudes from areas of striped tree bark, they have a particular liking for the gum of acacia species. They will also feed on insects and fruits.

Cape Hare *Lepus capensis* Vlakhaas
Widely distributed in the western and central parts of our region, preferring open dry savannah habitats. They have a coat of grizzled brown fur, becoming almost white on the belly and occasionally with a wash of yellow on the cheeks. The legs are long and slender, the hind legs, being nearly twice the length of the forelegs, allowing the animal to run and jump at high speed. The legs are covered with pale rufous fur. The ears are very long, dark around the edges and tipped with black. They have long white whiskers and large, prominent golden brown eyes. The tail is short and fluffy, white below and black above. They feed on a wide variety of vegetation and graze mainly during the night. They can be easily confused with the Scrub Hare.

Scrub Hare *Lepus saxatilis* Kolhaas
Found over the whole region apart from the far west and north-west. This is the commonest hare of the area and is easily confused with the Cape Hare with which it is similar in many respects and habits, however all the body features of the Scrub Hare are noticeably larger. Viewed in profile the head is less rounded and they often have a patch of white fur on the forehead. There can be much variation in pelage colour throughout the range, but generally speaking the upperparts are greyish brown with black flecking, while the underparts are white. They also have a reddish patch on the nape. They are mainly active during the night, but can often be encountered during the early morning and late evening.

Ground Squirrel *Xerus inauris* Waaierstertgrondeekhoring
They are inhabitants of the drier more arid western and central parts of our region. They prefer areas that have hard subsoil into which they can construct their underground burrows, which they inhabit in groups of around 6 to 30 individuals. They have a thick coat of coarse hair, the head and back varying in colour from brown to light tawny. The hair on the underside of the body is pale grey, almost white. The bushy tail, which is roughly the same length as the body, is a mixture of grey and black. The ears are small and a ring of white fur surrounds the large dark eyes. A white stripe extends along the sides of the body from the rear of the forelimbs to the thighs. The feet have very long claws which are used for digging. They feed mainly on grasses and seeds but will occasionally take termites and other insects.

Tree Squirrel *Paraxerus cepapi* Boomeekhoring
Tree Squirrels are a very common inhabitant of the drier savannah grasslands and woodlands, in the north and north-east of our region. A diurnal species which varies in colour from sandy to dark brown, with lighter underparts. The flanks and limbs often have a wash of rufous. The tail, which is bushy and almost as long as the body, is often slightly darker in colour. They are usually seen singly or in pairs, scampering along the ground from tree to tree, feeding on a wide variety of plant material and occasionally on insects. They nest in tree holes, especially holes excavated by woodpeckers. They often form into small family groups and, when threatened by a predator, all members of the colony will become agitated, making harsh 'clicking' sounds and flicking their tails above their heads.

Porcupine *Hystrix africaeaustralis* Ystervark

A common species found throughout the whole region, with the exception of the coastal desert areas of Namibia. They are the largest rodents in Southern Africa and are unmistakable with their covering of black and white quills which provide a formidable defence against most predators. They have a large head and a thick neck, from which grows a long, backward facing mane of bristles. The legs and tail, although substantial, are often hidden from view when the animal is in motion, by the spread and fall of the quills. They have a series of hollow quills on the tail which they vibrate when threatened as a warning to predators to stay clear. They have poor eyesight but excellent senses of hearing and smell. They are nocturnal, foraging at night singly or in family parties; they spend the daylight hours in caves or burrows. They have long, sturdy claws for excavating burrows and for unearthing food items such as roots and tubers. They will occasionally feed on carrion and often come in to conflict with farmers for eating cultivated crops. They are often recorded gnawing bones for the calcium content.

Cape Fox *Vulpes chama* Silwervos

They can be found over much of the region other than in the northeast and east. They inhabit mainly open country from grassland plains to semidesert scrub and are mainly nocturnal. The body is slender and the legs are long, and they have a coat of grizzled black and grey, with a beautiful silvery sheen. The flanks and underparts are light yellow. The tip of the bushy tail is always black. The head is typically fox-like with large pointed ears and a black nose and whiskers. They are predominately nocturnal, spending the daylight hours in caves, burrows and crevices amongst boulders. While preferring to eat small mammals, reptiles, birds and carrion, they will also eat insects and wild fruits.

Bat-eared Fox *Otocyon megalotis* Bakoorvos

Widespread in western and central areas, their preferred habitats are open semi-arid country and grasslands where they are active during the early morning, late evening and throughout the night. The coat has a slightly shaggy appearance and is uniform greyish/yellow paler on the flanks and on the underside. The lower portion of the legs are black, as are the tips of the enormous rounded ears, the nasal area of the muzzle and the tip of the large bushy tail. The eyes are set in patches of black fur which are joined across the bridge of the muzzle, giving the animal the appearance of wearing a 'highwayman's mask'. The body is rounded at the rear and higher in the hindquarters than at the shoulders. They feed mainly on invertebrates and live in dens which they excavate for themselves.

Springhare *Pedetes capensis* Springhaas

An uncommon species found over most of the region, they are mainly solitary animals and are members of the rodent family. They have a uniform light sandy coloured coat, with a black tip to their long bushy tail. They have well-developed hind legs and short forelegs, reminiscent of a kangaroo. They are nocturnal and live in burrows which they excavate using powerful claws on both their hind and forelegs. They have a thick muscular neck supporting their short head. They also have big eyes, and large ears. They feed mainly on the underground stems and roots of grasses but will also take fresh surface grasses and some herbs and fruits.

Black-backed Jackal *Canis mesomelas* Rooijakkals
A common resident throughout most of the region, inhabiting areas of dry scrub, savannah grasslands and open acacia woodlands. The body is slender, the legs are long and the head is fox-like with large pointed ears. The head, the lower portion of the body and the ears are pale rufous in colour. Along the hindneck and back runs a saddle of black fur, flecked with a variable amount of silver/white. The tail is bushy, pale rufous and white edged with a black tip. The underparts are whitish and the flanks are buff/yellow. Although they scavenge for a lot of their food, they will regularly catch small mammals and birds.

Side-striped Jackal *Canis adustus* Witwasjakkals
They are found only in the north and east of the region in areas of damp woodlands. The coat is a mixture of rufous, grey and black. The body is sleek with long legs and a busy tail which is blackish with a pronounced white tip. The side stripes, from which it gets its name, vary in prominence from animal to animal but are usually clearly discernible as a whitish line edged with black extending from the shoulder, along the body towards the base of the tail. The muzzle is blunter than other jackal species and the ears are smaller. They have a varied diet of small mammals, birds, invertebrates and wild fruits.

Wild Dog *Lycaon pictus* Wildehond
In recent years Wild Dog packs have become an increasingly rare sight. Restricted to the north and east of the region, they live a nomadic lifestyle covering vast distances within their home range. The coat pattern and coloration shows great individual variation, but is usually that of dark brown/black with irregular blotches and patches of tan, cream and white. They have a long slender body, long legs, large rounded ears and a bushy, white tipped tail. The head is rather short and broad, with powerful jaws. They are highly gregarious, living in large family groups and will hunt cooperatively most small to medium-sized plains game animals. Once a victim has been selected the pack will pursue it mercilessly until the prey is totally exhausted; often the chase will cover several kilometres.

Cape Clawless Otter *Aonyx capensis* Groototter
They are to be found in the eastern part of our range, usually in areas associated with water. The coat is dense with a silky appearance. They have a dark brown coat covering their upperparts and have off-white fur on the throat and underbelly. They are characterized by white facial markings that extend downward from the cheeks towards the throat and chest area. They have partially webbed paws with, as its name suggests, clawless fingers. The tail is thick at the base, tapering to a pointed tip. Their large skull is broad and flat and the ears are very small. Adults can measure 130 cm in length including the tail and weigh 12 to 14 kg. They are mainly solitary and feed on fish and other aquatic life.

Honey Badger *Mellivora capensis* Ratel
Found over most of the region Honey Badgers are mainly nocturnal. A robust, stocky animal with thick, loose skin, a long body and short, sturdy legs. They have a reputation for their tenacity and courage if attacked and will put up strong resistance even when confronted with predators as large as lions. The coat consists of short, coarse hair, the colour of which is evenly divided into two sections. The crown of the head, the tail and the upper portion of the body are greyish/white, while the lower portion of the body is jet black. Younger animals are brownish. The head is large with small eyes and ears and very powerful jaws. The front paws have large robust claws, which aid the badger in digging, in ripping bark from dead trees in pursuit of grubs and in breaking into bees nests in search of honey.

Banded Mongoose *Mungos mungo* Gebande muishond

Common in the north and east of the region in open savannahs, forests and grasslands, especially near water. A sturdy mongoose with a broad head and a pointed face typical of the family. The hindquarters are rounded and higher than the forequarters. The tail is quite long, about half the length of the body and tapers to a pointed tip. The coarse coat is grey/brown with a series of dark brown, almost black vertical stripes on the back and hindquarters. The lower portion of the legs and the tip of the tail are black. The ears are small and the feet are well equipped with long claws. A highly social diurnal animal that lives in groups of 10 to 30 individuals. They often make their homes in termite mounds. They forage as a group searching out most forms of invertebrates, small birds and rodents, reptiles and occasionally carrion.

Slender Mongoose *Galerella sanguinea* Swartkwasmuishond

Widespread throughout the region in all but the very south, the Slender Mongoose favours a wide variety of habitat types from forests and woodlands to savannah grasslands and thickets. They have a long slender body, short legs, a long pointed face with a red tip to the nose. The coat colour would appear to vary as a result of the type of habitat occupied, being darker in forest and mountainous areas and lighter in drier more open locations. The coat is made up of very fine hair varying in colour from light grey to darkish brown and rufous often becoming paler on the underside. The tail, which is almost as long as the body, has a black tip. They are mainly solitary and diurnal, they are good climbers but forage mainly for food on the ground where they catch invertebrates, small birds and mammals and occasionally they will take wild fruits.

Dwarf Mongoose *Helogale parvula* Dwergmuishond

A species that favours the savannah habitats to the north and east of the region, they are often seen, in large family groups, on or near termite mounds. As its name implies, this is the smallest mongoose in Southern Africa. The fine coat can be variable in colour from reddish brown to grizzled grey, often lighter below and with darker legs and feet which are short with long claws. The tail is about half the length of the body and tapers to a point. They have a broad head and a pointed face, small ears and light brown eyes. They are most active in the early morning and the late evening, when they forage mainly on the ground. They feed mainly on insects, but will also take snakes, lizards and spiders.

Yellow Mongoose *Cynictis penicillata* Witkwasmuishond

Found over most of the western region, in areas of open and lightly wooded savannahs. The body colour is brownish to reddish yellow, becoming lighter on the underbelly and chin. They have a long, thick bushy tail with a white tip and a series of faint black streaks. They are most active in the early morning and the late afternoon and will often continue foraging throughout the night. They live in hierarchical groups of around 30 to 40 individuals, led by a dominant breeding pair. They will often stand upright on their hind legs when alarmed, or when looking for food, which consists mainly of insects, some reptiles and small birds and occasionally carrion.

Meerkat *Suricata suricatta* Stokstertmeerkat

Sometimes known as the Suricate, their preferred habitat is the more open arid areas in western and central parts, where there is hard stony soil, into which they can create a complex of tunnels as a 'homebase' for their group. The hair is rather coarse and is grey/brown to white/grey, often with a yellowish tinge. Extending down the entire length of the back are a series of irregular brownish black bands. The eyes are surrounded by dark bare skin and fur, creating a contrast with the light, almost white, fur of the eyebrows and cheeks. The tail has only a thin covering of black hairs, tapers to a point and is shorter than in other closely related species. A very gregarious animal, often seen standing on its hind legs, using the tip of its tail as an extra support, on the look out for predators. They feed mainly on insects, birds' eggs, lizards and snakes, even the most venomous being taken.

Large Spotted Genet *Genetta tigrina* Rooikolmuskejaatkat

Their preferred habitat is the higher rainfall areas of woodlands and forests, in the east of the region. The body is long and sleek, the legs are short and the paws have sharp, retractile claws. The short coat is greyish/yellow boldly marked with a black dorsal stripe, either side of which extend several rows of large black spots. These spots are occasionally edged with rufous-coloured hairs. The short, pointed face has white patches on the upper cheeks and around the nasal area. They have large, honey-coloured eyes and pointed ears, the insides of which often show as naked pink flesh. The sides of the muzzle are black. The bushy tail is almost as long as the body and is ringed alternately with grey and black bands, terminating in a black tip. They are nocturnal and have a varied diet of amphibians, reptiles, small birds, mammals and wild fruits.

Small Spotted Genet *Genetta genetta* Kleinkolmuskejaatkat

While having a wide distribution over most of the region, they prefer drier forests and adjoining grassland habitats, the Small Spotted Genet is very similar to the Large Spotted in appearance, size and weight. However, the ears are larger, the spots are smaller and the last ring on the tail is greyish white not black. Like the Large Spotted, they are nocturnal, hiding themselves away during daylight hours. They are excellent climbers and are usually seen singly or in pairs:, they often take up residence in safari lodges and become quite tame.

Striped Polecat *Ictonyx striatus* Stinkmuishond

Found over most of the region, these small solitary carnivores are easily identified. They are strictly nocturnal and have a pointed snout with white patches on the forehead and cheeks. The long body hair is black with two pronounced white stripes, running from the crown of the head onto the hindneck and continuing down the flanks to the tail, along either side of the body. The tail, which is white and bushy, is held horizontally when trotting but vertically if stressed. If cornered or threatened in any way they will eject a foul-smelling secretion as a form of defence. They feed mainly on insects and small rodents.

Civet *Civettictis civetta* Siwet

They are to be found only in the north and northeast of the region. A short-legged, nocturnal animal of sturdy build. The general coat colour is grizzled grey, marked with a varied selection of spots and stripes. In motion the head is carried low and the shoulders are lower than the hindquarters. The coat is shaggy and loose, with the semblance of a mane extending from the neck to the root of the tail. A black dorsal stripe extends from the crown of the head to the tail, which is ringed with alternate bands of grey and black and terminates with a black tip. The throat, chest and lower portion of the face and all the limbs are black. Two bands of black fur extend from the ears, down the side of the neck, to the chest. They are generally solitary, and hunt at night, preying on a wide variety of mammals, birds, reptiles, and insects as well as taking some wild fruits.

Brown Hyaena *Hyaena brunnea* Standjut

Their preferred habitats are the drier savannahs in the central and northwestern parts of the region. They are predominantly nocturnal. Less substantial in build than the Spotted Hyaena but similar in shape, they have distinctly longer front legs than back legs. They have long, shaggy coats with course hair which is a mixture of browns and black, around the neck and shoulders the fur is buff in colour. An erectile mane extends down the neck and the back. The undersides are buff/brown, and the legs have alternate bands of black and buff. The dark tail is short and bushy. The ears are long and pointed and they have very powerful jaws and strong teeth for crunching through bone. They feed on carrion and left-overs from the kills of other predators as well as taking small mammals, insects and some wild fruits.

Spotted Hyaena *Crocuta crocuta* Gevlekte hiëna

Confined to the northern half of the region where scattered populations are found in their preferred habitat of open savannah, active mainly at night, when their eerie calls can be heard. A substantial animal, with well-developed forequarters, a large broad head with rounded ears and extremely powerful jaws. The hindquarters are substantially lower than the forequarters resulting in a rather ungainly gait. The coat has an unkempt appearance with short hair and the semblance of a mane covering the lower neck and shoulders. They are grey/yellow in colour heavily marked with irregular black spots. The underside and chest are lighter and the lower portion of the legs are black. The tail is of medium length with a black tip, the powerful muzzle is dark. A most successful predator, which can hunt as a pack, but will also readily scavenge. They are well known for crushing bones in order to extract the marrow content.

Aardwolf *Proteles cristatus* Aardwolf

These timid and inoffensive carnivores are mainly nocturnal and are found over most of the region. A thick mane of hair extends along the length of the back, from the rear of the ears to the tail. The head has a long dark muzzle and large pointed ears. The legs are long and slender. The tail is long and bushy with a black tip. The colour of the coat is yellowish brown with yellow/white fur on the throat, cheeks and underparts. The body has an irregular pattern of broken near vertical black stripes and the forelimbs are banded alternately with yellow/brown and black fur. Like hyaenas, the Aardwolf has a sloping back, being higher at the shoulders than at the hindquarters. They are very specialised feeders, eating mainly termites.

African Wild Cat *Felis lybica* Vaalboskat

Found over the entire region, mainly solitary and generally nocturnal. The African Wild Cat is the distant ancestor of the present day domestic cat. The coat is buff/grey with warmer shades on the face, behind the ears and on the belly. There are marked variations to coat colour in differing parts of the region, animals found in arid areas are more sandy with reddish marking, while those from the wetter regions are blue/grey in colour with grey/black markings. The legs, the tail and, to a lesser extent the body, are blotched, barred and striped with black. The relatively long tail has several black rings and terminates with a black tip. They feed mainly on rodents and other small mammals, birds, reptiles and insects.

Serval *Felis serval* Tierboskat

The Serval favours areas of tall grass, often close to water, in savannah and montane grasslands mainly in the north and east of the region. This medium-sized, long-legged cat has a narrow head with broad, long rounded ears, the backs of which are black with a pronounced white spot towards the centre. The coat colour is yellow/buff boldly and irregularly marked with black spots and bars. The chest and underparts are off-white. The tail is short and has alternate black and yellow/buff rings. They are generally nocturnal, but are also often active during the early morning and late afternoon. They are solitary, living on small mammals, reptiles and birds.

Caracal *Felis caracal* Rooikat

Suited to many different habitats, they can be found over most of the region. A tall, slender cat with a broad, flat head, large eyes and pointed, triangular ears with long tufts of black fur flowing from the tips. The backs of the ears are black; the insides are white edged with black. The coat colour varies from tawny/red to sandy yellow. The chest, underside and insides of the legs are white, with some faint spotting usually discernible on the lower portion of the legs. The tail is relatively short. They have well-developed hindquarters, which slope down to the shoulders. They are nocturnal, often active around dusk and dawn. They live a more or less solitary existence and feed on small to medium-sized mammals such as Rock Dassie and hares, as well as taking birds, which they catch by means of a prodigious leap as they take flight.

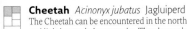

Cheetah *Acinonyx jubatus* Jagluiperd

The Cheetah can be encountered in the northern parts of our range, preferring habitats of open and lightly wooded savannahs. They have a lean, slender body, which is very flexible, they possess a powerful chest and have long legs – an animal built for speed. The coat is yellow/buff and covered with a multitude of black spots. The head is comparatively small with small ears and orange eyes. They have prominent black stripes extending from the inner corners of the eyes to the mouth. The tail is long, spotted at the root and terminating in a series of black and white rings and ending with a white tip. A mane of coarse hair is often discernible on the lower neck and shoulders, particularly in younger animals. Being the world's fastest mammal, the cheetah is usually able to run down its prey using its superior speed which it can only sustain for a relatively short period. All cheetahs are known to be genetically similar, but mutant variations do occur and in southern Zimbabwe, eastern Botswana and northern Transvaal the beautiful King Cheetah is occasionally seen; the golden fur is heavily blotched and marbled with black.

Lion *Panthera leo* Leeu

Lions are found mainly in protected areas across the north of the region. They are the largest and most powerful of Southern Africa's cats. The head is very broad with a short muzzle and small, rounded ears, the backs of which are black. The coat, with the exception of the mane, is very short, and is a sandy yellow colour, often with faint spots, which are most noticeable in younger animals. The mane, only present on males, is variable in colour from pale buff to black and covers the neck and shoulders. Unlike other cats, lions are social animals, living in prides of 30 or more individuals, the bulk of which are females with their young, and each pride has a dominant male. Lionesses do the vast majority of the hunting, taking small to medium prey individually and taking larger prey animals by pride members cooperating in setting an ambush, stalking into position and surrounding the chosen victim.

Leopard *Panthera pardus* Luiperd

Apart from the Northern Cape and Free State provinces of South Africa the Leopard is found over the whole region. They are a muscular, thickset cat with short, powerful limbs. The head is broad with a muzzle of medium length, strong jaws and long, white whiskers. The ears are small and round, the backs of which are black with a prominent white marking in the centre. The coat is yellowish/tan and is covered with black/brown spots, grouped in rosettes on the body but generally solid black on the head and lower legs. In some individuals the close grouping of the spots and rosettes gives an impression of a much darker pelage. The chin, throat and underside are off-white. There can be a great deal of regional variation in coat colour. The tail is long, spotted from the root to the centre but terminating with a series of black and white rings. Largely nocturnal, they prey on many mammal species, which they will often carry high into a tree to avoid the attention of other predators.

Aardvark *Orycteropus afer* Erdvark
A rather bizarre animal also known by the name of 'Antbear', they have a very wide distribution over most of the region but nowhere are they common. These short-legged mammals would be difficult to confuse with any other creature. They are grey to light brown in colour, with a sparse covering of bristly hair; long pointed ears help to provide them with excellent hearing. They have an elongated muzzle, with a soft flexible snout and a long sticky tongue which they use to secure their food. They also have a well-developed sense of smell, but rather poor eyesight. The tail is long and thick. They are shy, solitary and strictly nocturnal; they feed almost exclusively on ants and termites.

African Elephant *Loxodonta africana* Olifant
They are confined to a narrow strip extending from the northwest, across the region to the east where they can be found as far south as the Kruger Park. Quite unmistakable, they are the world's largest land mammals. The trunk is unique, being not only a nose, but also acting as an additional limb, with an extremely sensitive and flexible tip. The trunk is used for drinking and gathering food. Their eyesight is poor, but their senses of smell and hearing are very acute. The large ears contain a network of blood vessels which, by constant flapping, helps them to regulate their body temperature. The tusks grow throughout the animal's life. They have six pairs of molar teeth, with two being in use at any one time. As one pair becomes worn and of little more use, they move forward in the jaw to be replaced by the second set. That pair are then replaced by the next set and so on until all six sets have been used up – at this point the elephant will have attained a great age and will eventually die of starvation. The soft cushioned undersides of their feet enable almost noiseless movement. Elephants eat a wide variety of vegetation from grasses and herbage to bushes and trees. During periods of extended drought, they can do considerable damage to trees in their quest for food.

Rock Dassie *Procavia capensis* Klipdassie
They are widespread over most of the region where their preferred rocky habitat can be found. Often known as the Rock Hyrax, they can be easily mistaken for a rodent. However, this family is thought, by some, to be the closed living relative to the elephant. They live in large extended family groups. The body is round and the head is short with a blunted snout and stiff grey whiskers. The ears are rounded and the legs and tail are short. The feet have specially adapted paws, the bottoms of which act like suction pads, aiding the animal as it runs among rocks and stones. The coat is dense and varies in colour from light to dark brown, the shoulders and legs are often lighter in colour. They frequently have a patch of pale ochre/brown fur along the centre of the back. The underside is yellowish white. Like all dassie species they have large incisor teeth. They are diurnal and feed on a wide variety of plant foods.

Tree Dassie *Dendrohyrax arboreus* Boomdassie
An inhabitant of the lowland evergreen forests and thickets of the eastern coastal region, where they mainly live a solitary life. The body is round; the head is short and pointed with stiff grey whiskers, rounded ears and dark prominent eyes. The coat consists of dense, soft fur and varies in colour from pale grey/brown to dark brown sometimes with whitish spots on the back. The belly is yellowish white as is a variable amount of the dorsal area. They have pale eyebrows and whitish edging to the ears and lips. The tail is not very long, the legs are short and slender and the feet have specially adapted pads to aid them when climbing. They are diurnal and feed on a wide variety of vegetation including leaves, shoots, buds, twigs, fruits and seeds.

Burchell's Zebra   *Equus burchelli*   Bontsebra

Found across the far north of the region from west to east spreading south as far as Swaziland. The distinctive markings make the zebra easy to identify. Broad blackish stripes, vertical on the neck and shoulders and horizontal on the rump and legs are set against an almost white body colour. The stripes continue down the legs to the hooves, cover the head, face and the stiff hair of the mane, each animal having a pattern as unique as a fingerprint. The ears are large. The tip of the muzzle, around the nose and mouth, is black and sometimes tinged with brown. A broad black stripe follows the line of the spine from the base of the mane to the root of the tail. The stripes of young animals are usually brown rather than black and have a shaggy appearance. Look for 'shadow' stripes between the heavy broad stripes on the hindquarters as the easiest feature with which to distinguish Burchell's Zebra from other races. They are primarily grazers but will occasionally browse leaves and shoots from a variety of trees and bushes. An animal of open plains, grasslands and hills and mountains, where they roam in large herds often numbering thousands, but generally they are found in smaller family groups of 6 to 20 animals consisting of a dominant stallion of at least 5 to 7 years old, with a number of mares and foals. They are dependent on water and are rarely found far from a permanent source. They are active throughout the day. At the approach of danger adults may present a collective defence for themselves and other herd members, particularly the young.

Cape Mountain Zebra   *Equus zebra*   Kaapse bergsebra

As their name implies, this species is generally found on slopes and plateaus in mountainous areas of the southern Cape. The smallest member of the zebra family they can be distinguished from other zebra species by their larger ears and by the presence of a dewlap, or fold of skin on the throat. The coat has evenly spaced vertical black and white stripes on the neck and the body, changing to broader horizontal on the hindquarters. A pattern of short, closely grouped stripes are present on the rear above the root of the tail. The legs are striped horizontally all the way to the hooves. They are most active in the early morning and late afternoon and although they are generally grazers they will occasionally browse from bushes and trees.

Hartmann's Mountain Zebra   *Equus hartmannae*   Hartmann se bergsebra

Confined to the mountainous areas of western Namibia, this subspecies is differentiated from its close relative, the Cape Mountain Zebra, by its larger body size, smaller ears and narrower black stripes on the white body. The legs are striped horizontally for their entire length. They are a shy animal and are mainly active during the early morning and late afternoon. Being grazing animals and requiring a constant water supply, they will dig for water in dry riverbeds during times of drought.

White Rhinoceros   *Cerototherium simum*   Witrenoster
There are scattered populations over the whole region in protected areas. The White Rhino is the world's second largest land mammal – the African Elephant being the largest. The animal's name has nothing whatever to do with colour, but is a corruption of the Afrikaans word 'Weit' meaning 'wide' and refers to the shape of the mouth which has a broad upper lip, this being the most obvious difference between the two rhinoceros species. Far bigger and heavier than the Black Rhino, the head is large, square-shaped and carries two horns. The front horn is the larger of the two, averaging 80 cm in length; the rear horn is shorter and thicker. The ears are large and oval in shape with pointed tips, the eyes are small and the eyesight is rather poor. The huge body is covered with a thick hide of pale grey skin. The tail is short, terminating with stiff hairs. They feed by grazing, using the wide mouth and strong lips to crop short grasses. They will feed throughout the day and night, but usually seek shelter from the hot midday sun. They will drink several times a day if water is readily available but during the dry season they can survive by drinking every three to four days. In spite of their bulk they are surprisingly quick and manoeuvrable.

In some parks staff have been experimenting with different anti-poaching measures, one of which involves sedating and then removing the rhino's horn. This procedure in no way harms the rhino, but does decrease the possibility of them falling foul of the poacher's gun.

Black Rhinoceros   *Diceros bicornis*   Swartrenoster
As a result of heavy poaching, scattered populations are now only found in protected areas. A relic of prehistoric times, the rhinoceros is almost unmistakeable. The Black Rhino is distinguished from the slightly larger White Rhino, by the narrow mouth and prehensile upper lip. The head is large and carries two horns, the larger front horn measuring on average 60 cm. The ears are rounded and are fringed with tufts of dark hair. The eyes are small and the eyesight poor, but the senses of smell and hearing are very acute. The huge body is covered with a thick hide of grey skin, although due to the rhino's predilection for wallowing in mud, their coloration can appear variable. The tail is short and tipped with stiff hairs. In spite of their bulk the Black Rhino is very manoeuvrable and capable of a top running speed of 50 kph. They are far more aggressive and bad-tempered than the White Rhino. They feed mainly in the early morning and late afternoon, seeking shade or a mud wallow during the hottest midday period. Although they are capable of surviving for several days without water, they will drink and wallow daily when possible, often travelling many miles to an available source. During periods of drought they will often dig for water in dried-up riverbeds. Rhino's are solitary animals although females are usually accompanied by their most recent offspring.

Bush Pig *Potamochoerus porcus* Bosvark

An animal of forests, woodlands, thick bush, and other areas offering sufficient cover and water, they are best seen in the east of the region, with small populations also in the far south. Bush Pigs are typical hogs, with a long face and a short rotund body. The snout is blunt, the eyes are small and the ears are pointed. The coat is long and coarse and varies in colour from reddish to dark brown. Along the back the hair is longer, forming a dorsal crest. The head has a conspicuous pattern of black and white markings which are extremely variable and in some instances the whole head appears white. The tail is long and thin, measuring up to 40 cm in length. The hooves have four toes. Very young animals have a spotted pelage of buff on dark brown, but these spots are replaced, at about six months old, by a rufous brown coat and the longer hair of the dorsal crest. Males are larger and heavier than females. Bush Pigs are gregarious animals living in family groups usually consisting of a boar with several sows and offspring, numbering on average 15 to 20 pigs in all. The boar is the dominant family member, leading and protecting his group. Bush Pigs are omnivorous, eating a wide variety of vegetation as well as insects, reptiles, birds' eggs, seeds and fruits which they search out by rooting around and digging with their snouts.

Warthog *Phacochoerus aethiopictus* Vlakvark

An animal of open savannahs and woodlands, they are common in suitable habitats over most of the northern half of the region. They have little in the way of fur, just a few bristles and whiskers on the body of grey skin. They do, however, have a long grey/black mane of hair on the neck and shoulders. Coloration can vary greatly due to their habit of wallowing in muddy pools. The tail is long and thin, measuring up to 50 cm. in length and is carried vertically when running. They have a large flat face on which are found two sets of 'warts', one set immediately below the eyes and the other on the sides of the face between the eyes and the mouth. They have tusks, which emerge from the mouth in a semicircle outwards and upwards. The tusks and warts are less prominent in the sow than in the boar. They live in family groups consisting of a boar, a sow and the offspring from several litters. They can be found during daylight hours grazing, which they often do while kneeling on their front legs. During the hottest part of the day they will seek shade or cover. They feed mainly on short grasses, but will take leaves, roots, fruits and tubers.

Hippopotamus *Hippopotamus amphibius* Seekoei

Hippos are animals of rivers and swamps across much of the north-east and as far south as Natal. Second in weight only to the elephant, this unmistakable amphibious mammal has a bulbous body, short legs and a large head which broadens at the muzzle. The eyes, ears and nostrils are placed high on the head in order to remain clear of the water when the animal has its body submerged. The coloration is pink, grey/purple and brown. The body is devoid of fur, having just a few bristles on the tail, head and face. The tail is short and thick. They have well-developed incisor teeth which are used when fighting and serve no purpose at all with regard to feeding, which is accomplished by use of the large lips in a ripping motion. In isolated cases hippos have been recorded feeding on the rotting flesh of other animals. During the daytime they usually remain partially submerged to avoid the effects of overheating, sunburn and dehydration. At night-time they leave the water to graze, preferring short grassy pastures. They will usually gather together in herds of 10 to 50 animals, but during periods of drought densities can increase dramatically.

Giraffe *Giraffa camelopardalis* Kameelperd

An inhabitant of bush and lightly scrubby plains across the north of the region. The world's tallest animal, reaching heights over 5 m. The immense neck, sloping body and long legs aid easy identification. The coat pattern is that of irregular brown blotches on a yellow/buff background. The coat colour has a tendency to darken with age. The underparts are light with faint blotches and spots. A mane of stiff hair extends from the nape, down the neck to the shoulders. The tail is long and thin, terminating in an abundance of long black hair. The amount and size of horns is very variable, but normally they possess a principle pair on the upper forehead and signs of a much smaller pair on the crown. In addition they often have a single knob of horn in the centre of the lower forehead. Females are smaller than males. They feed by browsing to a height denied to all other herbivores. They will strip leaves and shoots from even the most thorny trees and bushes with ease, by use of prehensile lips and a very long 45 cm tongue.

Buffalo *Syncerus caffer* Buffel

Found over a wide range of habitats from dense forests and woodlands to open plains, from the central north and east. An enormous bovid of strong, solid build with short legs and cattle-like appearance. The sparse coat is short and blackish in colour; young animals have a thicker browner coat. The stout muscular neck supports a large head with a wide muzzle and large ears on the sides of the head, beneath massive horns which spread outwards and downwards from a thick broad base before arcing upwards and inwards. The horn size and shape is variable and dependent on age, the old mature bulls carrying the prize sets; they are much reduced in the female. The tail is long, terminating in a tassel of black hair. They are gregarious, living in herds of 20 to 40 animals. They are primarily grazers but in forest habitats will browse leaves and shoots.

Kudu *Tragelaphus strepsiceros* Koedoe

Found over most of the region where there are thickets and areas of bush and scrub. The males having magnificent horns with two and a half to three spirals and measure up to 180 cm in length. The smooth coat is bluish grey to fawn with the sides of the body boldly marked with white vertical stripes, varying in number from 6 to 10. The head has a dark muzzle with white upper lip and chin and a conspicuous white stripe running from eye to eye across the bridge of the muzzle. A growth of longer hair extends down the centre of the back from the neck to the tail. The males have long hair growing along the throat and down the neck to the chest. The tail is of medium length, grey above, white below and with a black tip. The female is of smaller build, very occasionally having horns. They are usually found in small family groups browsing leaves, shoots and occasionally grasses.

Eland *Taurotragus oryx* Eland

An antelope of open plains and lightly wooded areas, they occur across much of the region. They have a hump on the shoulders and a dewlap at the base of the neck which generally becomes more pronounced in older males. General coloration is tawny fawn to grey, the sides of the body being faintly marked with light vertical stripes, bolder on the shoulder than at the rear. Males have a crest of hair on the forehead and a mane on the nape. Horns are present in both sexes. They have several tight twists and range in length from 60 to 100 cm, generally thinner but longer in the female, sloping backwards following the profile line of the forehead. The tail is long, terminating in a tuft of black hair. Gregarious by nature, herd sizes can vary from a few individuals to 500 or more. They feed on a variety of vegetation.

Sitatunga *Tragelaphus spekei* Waterkoedoe

A very secretive and shy aquatic antelope of marshes and swamps confined to Okavango and Chobe. An antelope with a shaggy medium length coat of drab grey/brown fur, often faintly marked with vertical stripes along the back and on the hindquarters. Some faint spotting also occurs on the flanks. The head has white patches on the cheeks and on the muzzle below the eyes. There are two white patches on the front of the neck, one on the throat and the other lower down towards the chest. The horns, which are only found on the males, are long, with spiral twists and measure up to 90 cm in length. The hooves are specially adapted to support their weight in wet habitats, being long and splayed at the tips. The animal has a hunched appearance with hindquarters higher than forequarters. The female is smaller than the male and usually has a coat more chestnut in colour. They feed mainly at dawn and dusk, as well as through the night, when they venture into surrounding grassland and wooded areas to feed on grasses and swamp vegetation. They spend much of their time partially submerged and are very good swimmers. At the approach of danger they will often immerse themselves completely, all but for the tip of the nose. They often create well-trodden platforms of reeds and vegetation, on which to rest, by trampling and turning. They also maintain a network of paths through the reedbeds. Local hunters often make use of these well-defined pathways along which they place wire snares.

Bushbuck *Tragelaphus scriptus* Bosbok

An animal of forest edges and dense thickets found in the north, the east and along an eastern coastal strip from Mozambique to the Cape. They are one of the most elegant of Africa's antelopes, with rounded hindquarters slightly higher than the shoulders. The colour of the coat varies greatly from yellowish chestnut through reddish brown to dark brown. The underparts of the male are black. They have a dorsal mane of longer hair running from the shoulder to the tail. The head is lighter in colour with a dark band extending along the muzzle and a white cheek patch. The body has white vertical stripes and spots, mainly on the hindquarters and the back. The tail is bushy, white underneath, with a black tip. The horns are almost straight, with a single spiral, varying in length from 30 to 57 cm and they only occur on the male. They usually live singly or in pairs, but occasionally in small family groups. They are extremely secretive, hiding away during daylight hours in dense cover, feeding mainly during the night. Their main food consists of leaves and shoots, but they will dig for roots and tubers. They will also associate with troops of baboons and monkeys, feeding on the fallen fruit shaken from the trees by the primates as they feed. When alarmed by the approach of a predator, the bushbuck's usual response is to freeze, in the hope of being overlooked.

Nyala *Tragelaphus angasii* Njala

A species confined to the northeast of our region, in areas of savannah woodlands, scrub and thickets, usually close to water. The males have dark brown coats with long, shaggy hair on the underside of the neck, along the length of the underbelly and following a line down the spine from the shoulders to the root of the tail. The tops of the legs are black, the lower portions are buff/tan and the hooves are black. They have a rufous patch on the forehead and a broken white stripe across the upper muzzle. They also have two white spots on the cheeks just below the ears and a series of white vertical stripes flowing down the sides of the body; these stripes become fainter as the animal ages. The horns, which are only present on the males, are quite substantial and are lyre-shaped with white tips. Females have a yellow/rufous coat with a series of vertical black lines along the sides of the body. They are predominantly browsers.

Gemsbok *Oryx gazelle* Gemsbok

An inhabitant of the more arid central areas of the northwest, this large elegant and very distinctive antelope has a short coat of grey/fawn, a black horizontal stripe running across the lower flank and black bands around the forelegs just above the knee joints. The facial markings are very conspicuous; a broad black stripe runs down the side of the face through the eye to the lower cheek. The horns are long and straight measuring up to 110 cm. The forehead has a black patch as does the upper muzzle. The hair on the lower muzzle is white, contrasting strongly with the black nostrils. A black line extends under the chin and around the upper throat from ear to ear. A thin black stripe extends down the centre of the neck from the throat to the chest and from the back of the neck along the spine to the root of the tail. The tail consists of long black hair. They feed mainly on grasses but will also browse trees and bushes and will occasionally eat desert melons and tubers for moisture. When water is available they will drink daily but they are capable of surviving for long periods without drinking.

Roan Antelope *Hippotragus equinus* Bastergemsbok

An antelope of open and lightly wooded areas found in the north and northeast of the region. A large antelope with sloping shoulders and powerful neck and forequarters, its coat coloration varies from dark rufous to reddish/fawn contrasting with the black and white head and face markings. The ears are long and narrow with tufts of long hair becoming dark at the tips. A well-defined mane of dark hair extends from the upper neck to the shoulders; a similar growth of hair is present on the underside of the neck extending down the centre of the throat. The legs are rufous, the forelegs having irregular black patches. The horns are heavily ringed and curve backwards in a sickle shape; the length varies from 55 to 100 cm, and they are less well formed in the female. They live in small herds of about 20 animals. They feed mainly on grasses and occasionally browse leaves and shoots from trees and bushes. They are very dependent on water and rarely venture far from a readily available source.

Sable Antelope *Hippotragus niger* Swartwitpens

An inhabitant of dry woodland, bush and grasslands in the north and northeast of the region. This large and magnificent antelope has very powerful forequarters. The male has a glossy black coat, white underparts and a striking head of black and white markings. White hair covers the chin and the tip of the muzzle, from where broad white bands extend up the sides of the muzzle terminating on the forehead. The crown of the head and the outside of the ears are light chestnut, the inside of the ears are white. They have a pronounced mane of stiff hairs extending from the neck to the shoulders and a long black tail. Females and young are often paler and more chestnut in colour than the males. The horns are very long, measuring up to 154 cm in length, sweep backwards in an arc and are heavily ridged; they are less well developed in the female. They are found in herds of 10 to 20 animals on average. They are primarily grazers, taking grasses and herbs, but occasionally they browse trees and bushes for leaves and shoots. They are heavily dependent on water.

Waterbuck *Kobus ellipsiprymnus* Waterbok

An animal found in the north and northeast, favouring savannahs and open woodlands and thickets. A large antelope with a shaggy coat of grizzled grey/buff, the back and lower legs are darker, becoming almost black. The ears are large, with black tips. Facial markings are limited to a white stripe extending from the eyebrow along the sides of the muzzle to just below the eye and a white patch around the nasal area and the lips. They have a white collar extending across the throat almost from ear to ear. On the rump is a pronounced white crescent shape. The tail is of medium length and has a dark tip. The horns, present only in the male, are heavily ringed and curve backwards, upwards and forwards towards the tips, they measure up to 95 cm. Waterbuck inhabit woodlands and clearings usually close to water, where they feed mainly on grasses and herbs. They will also occasionally feed on the foliage of trees and bushes, particularly during periods of extreme drought. They are dependent on water and will drink every day or so. The waterbuck is mainly active during the early morning, late afternoon and early evening. They are usually found in small groups consisting of a bull with several females and young, numbering on average 5 to 10 animals in all. Herds of bachelor males may be encountered consisting of 6 to 40 individuals. Males are at least 4 years old before they are able to establish themselves as master bulls. When pursued by predators waterbuck will flee and attempt to hide themselves in bush cover or long grass, but there have been many reports of them taking refuge in water, submerging completely all but for the nostrils.

Red Lechwe *Kobus leche* Rooi-lechwe

Restricted to the Okavango and Chobe floodplain. This swamp-loving antelope is well adapted to its environment. They have splayed hooves which help spread their weight on boggy ground. They have powerful hindquarters and have an unusual bounding gallop when running on flooded ground. They are also powerful swimmers. Only the male has horns which, when fully developed, are long, ridged and sweep slightly backwards and upwards in a smooth arc, measuring up to 85 cm. The coat is a rich rufous with white underparts and the neck has a shaggy mane. The front of the forelegs are black and the tail has a black tip. The nostrils and the mouth are outlined with a narrow band of white fur. They are territorial animals and a dominant male will gather up to 30 females into his harem. Fights between males are common and usually start with a ritual of low horn sweeping; as this becomes more serious the powerful swings of the vicious horns can inflict fatal wounds. Lechwe graze waterside grasses and sedges as well as aquatic weeds.

Puku *Kobus vardonii* Poekoe

An animal of rivers and marshes, they are found only in the Chobe River area of Botswana. They can easily be distinguished from Red Lechwe by their smaller size and the absence of the black bands down the front of the legs and a more brightly coloured coat. The horns of the males are significantly smaller measuring only 50 cm. While occupying a similar habitat they make more use of the grassy, drier areas further from the swamp. They live in small herds of 6 to 30 individuals. Alpha males will hold as many as 20 females within the herd as well as some bachelor males which are tolerated in the herd by the alpha male as long as they remain submissive. Any young bachelor attempting to mate with a female will be driven from the territory by the alpha male.

Mountain Reedbuck   *Redunca fulvorufula*   Rooiribbok

An inhabitant of rocky hillsides and mountainous areas in the east and the south of our region. A small antelope with a shaggy coat of grey/fawn, the head and neck are tinged with rufous/brown; the chest and belly are white. The eyebrows, throat, chin and lips are faintly marked with off-white, as is the short, bushy tail. A gland of dark skin is clearly visible below the ears on the sides of the head; a dark line extends down the centre of the muzzle from the eyes to the nose. Horns are only present in the male and are short, heavily ringed and arc forward, measuring about 32 cm. Females are usually larger and often greyer in colour than the males. An antelope that inhabits steep riverbanks, slopes and terraces of hills and mountains they are gregarious animals and gather into small herds of 3 to 10 animals, sometimes larger herds occur. These herds, usually consisting of females and young, occupy the territory of a single resident male while other males tend to form small bachelor groups. They are active in early morning and late afternoon as well as during moonlit nights. They feed by grazing grasses and herbage.

Reedbuck   *Redunca arundinum*   Rietbok

Reedbuck are to be found in the north and east of the region, in areas of tall grasses and reedbeds. These medium to large antelopes vary in colour from pale yellow/brown to grey/brown, with a white underbelly and black forelegs. They also have a small black spot below their ears. The tail is short and bushy, yellow/brown above and white below. Males have ridged horns of around 35 cm, which grow backwards and then curve forwards. Reedbucks live in valleys and upland areas, where they eat grasses and reeds, as well as browsing bushes when times are hard. Mature Reedbuck males are territorial, living with a single female, which they follow at all times to prevent any contact with rival males. Non-breeding females and young males are usually solitary, except in the dry season, when they sometimes form herds of up to 20 individuals. They are diurnal but inactive during the heat of the day.

Grey Rhebok   *Pelea capreolus*   Vaalribbok

These graceful antelopes favour rocky mountain slopes, hillsides and rocky screes in the south and central areas of our range. Their coat is brownish grey in colour with pale underparts, the body having long woolly hair which insulates them against the cold of their high altitude habitat. The eyes are ringed with white, and the lips and chin are also white. They have very long, pointed ears. Only males have horns, which are narrow vertical spikes, with a slight forward curve, measuring up to 28 cm in length. They usually live in small herds of around 20 individuals but can be encountered as solitary males, or in family parties. They are primarily grazers, but they will browse on occasions.

♂

♀

Black Wildebeest   *Connochaetes gnou*   Swartwildebees

The distribution of the Black Wildebeest is restricted to the south central grasslands. They are smaller in size and weight than the Blue Wildebeest. The head is black with a broad muzzle. The horns spread forwards and upwards from a heavy broad base; female horns are similar but smaller, they can measure up to 75 cm. The coat is dark brown/black in colour and is short and sleek during the summer and longer in the winter, the long, shaggy tail is white. As a species they were brought to the verge of extinction by hunters in the nineteenth century; in more recent times the numbers have been increasing steadily in protected areas, but herd sizes are small in comparison to the Blue Wildebeest. They feed on the grasses of the highveld plains and will occasionally browse; they are never far from a supply of fresh water.

Blue Wildebeest   *Connochaetes taurinus*   Blouwildebees

A species likely to be found in the north central and northeast of the region. A large antelope with the forequarters higher than the hindquarters giving the appearance of a pronounced 'slope' from front to rear. They are greyish in colour with a mane of long black hair on the neck and shoulders and a beard of hair on the neck and throat, the coloration of the beard varies greatly from almost pure white to black. The neck, shoulders and, to a lesser extent, the flanks show dark vertical stripes. The head is large and broad with a completely black face. The horns are present in both sexes, measuring between 40 and 70 cm in length and from a flat base curve outwards, downward then upward, not dissimilar in shape to those of the Buffalo. The black bushy-tipped tail is extremely long almost touching the ground. They are mainly found in large herds and are active throughout the day, usually seeking shade during the hot midday period. They eat mainly grass and will drink twice a day if possible.

Red Hartebeest   *Alcelaphus buselaphus*   Rooihartbees

A species found in grassland and savannah habitats in the northwest of the region. This is a large antelope, characterised by its 'sloping' appearance, being higher in the forequarters than in the rear. The coat is brick red with black on the shoulders and legs and with a pale upper rump. The head and face are long and narrow with large pointed ears. The horns are set high on the head and rise straight upward, curve forwards then sharply backwards, they are deeply ringed and are present in both sexes, measuring up to 60 cm. The tail consists of medium-length black hair. The female is similar to the male but is usually paler in colour is less distinctly marked and has smaller, slimmer horns. These gregarious animals can be found in herds ranging from just a dozen to many hundreds. They feed mainly on grasses, but will occasionally browse from shrubs and bushes.

Lichtenstein's Hartebeest   *Sigmoceros lichtensteinii*   Lichtenstein se Hartbees

Due to over hunting their numbers have been greatly reduced and they are now mainly to be found in reserves in the northeast of the region, in their preferred habitats of savannah woodlands and floodplains. They are similar to the Red Hartebeest but lack the black markings on the legs and are more yellowish in colour with a lighter underbelly. The head has a less elongated appearance. They are diurnal and live in small family herds made up of females with calves with a single male acting as herd leader. The males can often be seen standing on the top of termite mounds, keeping an eye open for predators, while the other members of the herd feed in greater safety. They feed mainly on grass, but will occasionally browse from bushes.

Impala *Aepyceros melampus* Rooibok

Widely distributed in the northeast of the region this very graceful medium-sized antelope has a long neck, a smooth short coat of rufous brown, being paler on the lower flanks and with white underparts. The males carry magnificent, wide-set, lyre-shaped horns that curve backwards, sideways then upwards; they are heavily ringed and can grow to over 90 cm in length. The upper lip, chin, throat and eyebrows are white. The inner ears are white tipped with black. The nose is black and forms a characteristic 'Y' shape. A vertical black line extends down the hindquarters from the root of the tail. Just above the heel of the hind legs there is a tuft of long black hair. The tail is of medium length with a black stripe on the upper side. The female is smaller than the male and lacks horns. They feed mainly on short grasses.

Black-faced Impala *Aepyceros melampus petersi* Swartneusrooibok

Restricted in distribution to the northern region of Namibia. Their appearance is similar to the Impala, generally darker in colour; the upper body often lacks the rich reddish brown, being a duller brown. The tips of the ears are darker and the tail considerably longer and bushier. The most obvious difference is a black line which extends along the centre of the muzzle from the nasal region to the forehead. They have a similar diet to the Impala, favouring short grasses, and they also feed on acacia seed pods when available.

Bontebok *Damaliscus dorcas dorcus* Bontebok

A species found only in the South Western Cape region. One of the most beautifully marked and attractive antelope. They are level backed with a coat that is short and glossy, dark red/brown above, contrasting with the white belly and lower legs. The rump is white as is the root of the tail, the remainder of the tail is black. A band of white extends from between the horns down the forehead broadens between the eyes and continues to the nasal region. The insides of the ears are white and the backs are red/brown. Both sexes have horns which rise straight up, spread sideways and back, then forward and inwards. They are ridged for most of the length, measuring up to 40 cm. They are primarily grazers, but will browse occasionally.

Blesbok *Damaliscus dorcus phillipsi* Blesbok

Found only in the central southern part of the region. They are very simular in size and shape to the Bontebok but have a coat which is uniform reddish brown in colour. The undersides and the insides of the ears are off-white. They have a band of white extending downwards from between the horns, broadening between the eyes and contiuing to the nasal area. The tail is white at the root and black towards the tip. Their horns can be up to 50 cm long and are heavily ridged. They can gather into large herds and are selective grazers.

Tsessebe *Damaliscus lunatus* Tsessebe

They have a patchy distribution in the north and northeast of the region. This large antelope with a pronounced 'slope' is higher in the forequarters than at the rear. The coat is short and glossy, dark chestnut brown with bluish black patches extending from the lower shoulders down the forelegs to just above the knees and from the rump down the back legs terminating just above the hock. The same bluish black hair extends down the centre of the long narrow face, from the forehead to the tip of the muzzle and on the backs of the ears. The horns are 30 to 60 cm in length and appear in both sexes but are larger on the male. They are heavily ringed and angle backwards, outwards and upwards towards the tips. The tail is of medium length, terminating with tufts of long black hair. They feed almost entirely on grasses and herbage.

Suni *Neotragus moschatus* Soenie
Restricted in distribution to the north and northeast of the region, this very small antelope
has hindquarters that are higher than the shoulders. They are reddish brown above with pale
underparts. They have a conspicuous linear preorbital gland which extends from the eye down
the line of the face. Only males have horns which rise from just above the eyes sloping back in
the same plane as the muzzle and are ridged almost to the tips, measuring up to 13 cm. They
are found in pairs or small groups. They are secretive and difficult to locate in thick forest
habitats, where they browse on a wide range of plant material.

Damara Dik Dik *Madoqua kirkii* Damara Dik Dik
Confined to the northwest of the region, this small delicate antelope has a grizzled yellow/grey
coat. The head, neck and shoulders sometimes show a flush of rufous brown. White patches
encircle the large dark eyes and the males have short, spiky horns, measuring up to 11 cm. The
hair on the forehead is long and can be raised in a crest when alarmed. The elongated nose is
a distinctive feature, serving as a very effective cooling device. They have prominent preorbital
scent glands. Female Dik Dik are slightly larger than males. They inhabit arid regions with
bush or scrub cover. Dik Dik live in pairs and are very territorial. The boundaries are marked
by a succession of dung/urine sites, which are re-stated daily by both males and females. They
are active during both the day and night, but seek shade during the hottest period of the day.
They are primarily browsers, but will take fresh grasses following rains.

Klipspringer *Oreotragus oreotragus* Klipspringer
Widespread throughout much of the region, but restricted to steep, rocky hill sides and screes,
as well as isolated kopjes and high mountains. A small, strongly built antelope, with a wedge
shaped head and a thick coat of olive/yellow and grey hair which has a slightly speckled
appearance. The muzzle is washed with brown. The large rounded ears are white-lined with
prominent black markings. They have dark preorbital scent glands which are very pronounced.
The legs are sturdy, terminating in black hooves which are specially adapted for rocky ground,
giving the animal the appearance of 'standing on tiptoe'. The tail is very short. Only the male
has horns which are upright, measuring up to 15 cm. They live in pairs or in small family
parties and can often be seen standing atop a rock or boulder keeping a sharp lookout for
predators. They feed on leaves, shoots and berries, taking fruits when available and very
occasionally grass.

Springbok *Antidorcas marsupialis* Springbok
A common species found in open grasslands in the west of the region. They are pale cinnamon
brown above, with a dark chocolate stripe along the flanks. They have white underparts, white
insides and backs to the legs and a white rump patch. The tail is white at the base and black
at the tip. The face is white with a black band through each eye extending to the nose. Horns
are present on both sexes, rising upwards, then outwards and backwards before turning in at
the tips. They are ringed along the whole length, measuring up to 49 cm. They can be found in
large herds sometimes in excess of 1,000 animals, mainly grazing on open grassland; they will
also eat roots and melons for moisture.

Oribi *Ourebia ourebi* Oorbietjie
An antelope of open grassland in the north-east of the region, this is a small, slender-built antelope with long legs and neck; the hindquarters are rounded and slightly higher than the forequarters. They have large pointed ears. They have preorbital scent glands which appear as patches of bare black skin on the upper cheeks. The coat consists of silky fine hair, reddish to fawn above and white below. The chin is white and the dark eyes contrast strongly with the white eyebrows. The legs are reddish/fawn with tufts of slightly longer hair at the knee joints. The horns, which feature in the male only, have rings on the lower third, are curved backwards and grow to a length of about 19 cm. The rufous tail is very short and has a black tip. Females are slightly larger than males. The males will establish and defend territories forcefully, marking their territories by the use of six different scent glands found about the body. When alarmed the Oribi will emit a loud shrill whistle and will commence a 'stotting' performance, springing into the air with legs held rigid. They are predominantly grazers, feeding on short grasses and using taller grasses for cover while resting.

Steenbok *Raphicerus campestris* Steenbok
They are widespread over the whole region, favouring areas of dry, partially wooded grasslands. This small, slender antelope has a reddish fawn coat covering the upper body and is whitish on the underbelly and on the insides of the legs. The horns, which are present only in the male, are straight spikes, measuring about 19 cm in length. They have long legs and the appearance of being higher at the hindquarters than at the shoulder. They have a pale patch around the eyes, contrasting with dark areas surrounding the preorbital scent glands. A triangular patch of black fur extends up the muzzle from the black nose. The young have a heavier, fluffier coat than the adults, but retain the same coloration. They graze on grass and browse trees, bushes and shrubs, as well as scraping with their hooves to expose roots and tubers. They are able to survive without water, obtaining their entire fluid requirement from their food. Usually diurnal in habit, they are most active during the mornings and late afternoon.

Sharpe's Grysbok *Raphicerus sharpei* Sharpe se grysbok
A small, shy and retiring antelope found in the northeast and east of the region. They have a slightly hunched posture. The coat is a buff tawny colour with white flecks and paler underparts. There is a darkish band extending from the nostrils along the muzzle, which tapers and disappears at the level of the eyes. Horns appear only on males, they are short, smooth and straight, sloping backwards in the same plane as the face, measuring about 10 cm. They have large rounded ears. Mainly solitary or in pairs, they prefer woodland savannah with thickets. They are nocturnal but may also be seen at dawn and dusk. They mainly browse on leaves and wild fruits, but will also eat tender new grass.

Blue Duiker *Philantomba monticola* Blouduiker

They are restricted to small populations in the southeast coastal region, with another isolated group situated in Mozambique, this is the smallest antelope in Southern Africa, measuring a mere 30 cm to the shoulder. The coat colour is dark brown with a distinct bluish sheen, the underparts are much lighter and the tail is black edged with white. Glandular scent pits are noticeable on both sides of the face below the eyes. Both sexes have short horns, measuring 3 to 5 cm; these can often be hidden by tufts of hair. They are usually solitary but sometimes can be found in pairs, they are very secretive and browse in dense forest and coastal habitats, taking leaves fruits and berries.

Common Duiker *Sylvicapra grimmia* Gewone duiker

Found over the whole region, this is the largest of the three duiker species found in Southern Africa. They have long legs and large ears. Only the males have horns which are pointed and grow up to 18 cm in length. The pelage coloration ranges from grizzled grey to yellowish brown with a black streak running from the top of the russet forehead to the nose. The underparts are white tinged with grey and the legs are grey having a black band just above the hooves. The short tail is black above and white below. Females are generally larger than males. They are mainly solitary and diurnal preferring woodland habitats with scattered bush and scrub, they avoid arid desert regions, as well as areas of open plains and dense forest. They feed mainly on the leaves and shoots of bushes, as well as tree bark, fruits and seedpods; rarely do they eat grass. They also consume insects and other animal matter from time to time, including frogs, small mammals and birds. Duikers obtain the vast majority of their water requirement from their food and are able to survive for very long periods without drinking.

Red Duiker *Cephalophus natalensis* Rooiduiker

They are confined to the east and northeast of the region. Midway in size between the Common and Blue Duiker, the main distinguishing features are their chestnut-red colour and a head with a crest of black and chestnut bushy hair. The ears are rounded with the outside edges fringed with black hair. A prominent scent gland along the sides of the muzzle appears as a black line. Both sexes have horns which are straight and lie backwards along the line of the face; the males' are bigger and can grow to 16 cm in length. These secretive and mainly solitary antelopes prefer dense thickets and forest habitats, where they are most active at dawn and dusk. They feed on fallen fruits and will graze fresh grasses as well as browsing from bushes and shrubs. A regular water supply is an important requirement.

Common Dolphin *Delphinus delphis* Gewone Dolfyn
Found in all the coastal waters of the region. They have a streamlined body with an elongated, pointed beak. They are dark grey/black above and pale grey below. The flanks have an hourglass pattern, the front half of which is brown/grey, the rear half being pale grey. They have a prominent upright dorsal fin, pointed flippers and a horizontal tail which helps make it a very agile swimmer, frequently jumping clear of the water, and they often enjoy riding the bow waves of ships. They are found in small to large family groups and will often feed cooperatively by surrounding fish shoals.

Great White Shark *Carcharodon carcharias* Witdoodshaai
They can be found in all coastal waters, not common but best seen where they are baited for the tourist trade. They are torpedo shaped with a robust conical snout, grey blue above, white below and often have a mottled appearance. This colouration makes it difficult to spot as the darker shades blend in with the sea from above and below. The dorsal fin is large; there is a second dorsal fin which is much smaller. The pectoral fins are sickle shaped and prominent. The upper lobe of the caudal fin protrudes almost vertically into the air, while the lower lobe is a similar size and extends horizontally, giving the appearance of a symmetrical half moon. The gill slits are conspicuous. The teeth are large, wide, triangular and with saw-tooth edges; when the shark bites, it shakes its head from side to side, helping the teeth saw off large chunks of flesh. They will feed on most marine species.

Cape Fur Seal *Arctocephalus pusillus* Kaapse pelsrob
The Cape or Brown Fur Seal is found along the west coast from Namibia, extending south as far as the Cape of Good Hope. Both sexes have a large broad head with small but visible ears and a pointed snout with long whiskers. The male has a mane around the shoulders. The body fur is dark brown, the under fur is lighter and has a hint of rufous. They grow up to 2.2 m in length and weigh around 200 to 360 kg. Females are grey to light brown with a dark underside and light throat. They grow up to 1.7 m in length and weigh on average 120 kg. Pups are black at birth but turn grey with a pale throat after moulting. They feed on fish, squid and crustaceans and are often seen resting on rocks sometimes in large groups. Breeding colonies can number many thousands.

Bottlenose Dolphin *Tursiops aduncus* Stompneusdolfyn
Resident year-round in the coastal waters of Southern Africa, where they are best seen in the east of the region, they are larger than the Common Dolphin. The body colour is mid-grey on the back, becoming paler on the underside. A thin pale line extending from the eye to the flipper is often visible. The dorsal fin is prominent and hooked. These dolphins are often seen in large groups which can average between 20 and 120 animals. They seem not to be disturbed by boats and often bow ride, back-splash and summersault alongside sailing vessels. They hunt collectively feeding on fish and squid. A second Bottlenose dolphin species, *Tursiops truncates*, is also found in the region, it is noticeably larger with a shorter beak and is not generally encountered inshore.

Killer Whale *Orcinus orca* Swartwalvis

Although not common, the Killer Whale, which is also know as the Orca, has been recorded off the coasts of the whole region. Their distinctive markings make them easy to identify. The head is blunt and rounded with a conspicuous white patch behind the eye and throat. The back, apart from a grey saddle behind the dorsal fin, flanks and undertail area are black. The belly is white, which extends onto the flanks behind the dorsal fin. The flippers are large and paddle shaped. The dorsal fin is prominent and can be 2 m tall on adult males, while the female is smaller. They live in family groups and feed on squid, fish, birds, seals, sharks, dolphins and even other whales.

Southern Right Whale *Eubalaena australis* Suidelike Noordkaper Walvis

Most sighting are recorded between June and November, when they can often be seen in sheltered bays as they return north from the Antarctic to calve and mate. The body is stocky and fat, smoothly rotund and without a trace of a dorsal fin or any ridge along the back, which makes it unlikely to be confused with any other whale species. They can weigh 65 tonnes and measure 16 m in length. They are mostly black in colour but some individuals have a mottled appearance. The head is covered in hard warty growths which form unique patterns, which help scientists to identify individuals. The head is large and runs smoothly into the body with no suggestion of a neck; the long, narrow highly arched jaw is designed for the suspension of baleen plates, which can measure up to 2 m.

Humpback Whale *Megaptera novaeangliae* Boggelrugwalvis

Most sightings are recorded from June to January as the whales migrate along the east coast to calve and mate in the waters off Mozambique and Madagascar. They have a broad rounded head with a string of fleshy tubercles or knobs in place of the median ridge and further rows of knobs, all of which have protruding hairs, along each edge of the jaw. The body is heavily built, blackish in colour and narrows to the tail, the throat has white grooves. The flippers are very large, mottled black above and white below. The dorsal fin is small. The tail is heavily scalloped on the trailing edge, dark above and light beneath. Look out for the distinctive spout, which has a broad bushy balloon appearance and can reach a height of 3 m.

Fin Whale *Balaenoptera physalus* Rorkwal walvis

The world's second largest whale, the Fin Whale is most likely to be seen during the winter months in deep waters surrounding our region. The long streamlined body is dark grey to brownish black and has a long flat head with a narrow rostrum and with a large diagnostic white patch on the right side of the lower jaw, the left side of the jaw being grey to black. The slightly hooked dorsal fin is small and set three-quarters of the way along the back. The flippers are small and tapered and the tail is wide, pointed at the tip and notched in the centre. They can weigh up to 80 tonnes and measure up to 27 m in length, females being larger than males. They are extremely fast swimmers and are quite gregarious, often living in small groups of six to ten individuals. They are thought to live for around 90 years. The world population of Fin Whales has been much reduced as a result of hunting and it is now considered to be an endangered species.

Grass Jewel *Chilades trochylus*

A small butterfly found over much of the region. The upperside is grey/brown in colour, but there can be considerable differences in colouration between those individuals encountered in dry habitats compared to those found in wet areas with heavy rainfall. At the rear of the hindwings there are three orange marginal spots, inside which are black dots. The underside of the wings are grey/brown spotted with prominent black dots and a multitude of white arcs. The orange marginal markings on the upperside are replicated on the underside with the addition of shining blue arcs edging the black dots. The body is brown with a white abdomen; the antennae are ringed in alternate black and white hoops.

African Monarch *Danaus chrysippus* Suidelike melkbos skoenlapper

A very common, medium-sized butterfly found over much of the region. The body is black, speckled with numerous white spots. The main portion of the wings, both the upper and undersides are a rich tawny/golden yellow, while the wing tips and edgings are black with a series of white spots and dashes. There is a great deal of colour and pattern variation within this species. Generally speaking the African Monarch is to be found in areas of open grassland and gardens. A very active daytime flier, usually to be seen sipping nectar from flowering plants. It rests with its wings closed but can often be found sunning on the ground with its wings wide open in order to expose as much surface area as possible to the warming rays of the sun. They are also often to be seen in large groups on patches of wet or damp ground, extracting moisture and mineral traces from the earth.

Natal Acraea *Acraea natalica* Natalse rooitjie

A large butterfly, with a wingspan of 5.5 to 6.3 cm. A very common species throughout the eastern regions of Southern Africa. The head and forward section of the body is black with a varying number of white spots; the rear of the body is yellowish/pink. The upperside of the wings are mainly yellowish with a wash of salmon pink, and a scattering of black spots. The very tips of the wings, the shoulders and the trailing edge of the hind wings are black. The underside of the hindwings are a rich reddish orange with a scattering of black spots. The rear edges of the hindwings are black into which are set prominent white patches that follow the curvature of the wings. The underside of the forewings are golden /yellow with black edgings. The colouration of the male is brighter than that of the female.

Neobule Acraea *Acraea neobule* Dwaaleselrooitjie

A common species throughout the dryer central and western regions of Southern Africa. A slow-flying, solitary species usually encountered in areas of open grassland. The body is black with white dots. The upperside of the forewings are pale golden yellow at the base, fading across the wings to become almost transparent at the wing tips/edges. The upper side of the hind wings are golden yellow with a black terminal band set into which are a series of prominent yellow dots. The underside of the wings almost mirrors that of the upperside. The males are generally brighter than the females.

Yellow Pansy *Junonia cebrene* Geelgesiggie

A very common species over the whole of Southern Africa. The body is black on its upper side and white below. The upperside is black with large yellow/orange circular areas towards the tips of both forewings and hindwings. The wing edges are slightly waved. In the centre of the wings on either side of the body is a large blue/violet circular mark. The undersides of the forewings are yellow with a small black eye spot. The undersides of the hindwings are predominantly grey becoming brown towards the edges.

Long-tailed Blue *Lampides boeticus* Lusernbloutjie

A very widely distributed species throughout Africa. It is mainly to be found in areas of grassland, gardens and woodland edges. It has a wingspan of 3.5 to 4.2 cm, the females being larger than the males. It is a strong, rapid flyer. The upperside of the male is blue with a narrow brown border edging the wings. The long tails, from which it gets its name, appear from the rear of the hindwings. There are black dots on the wings at the base of the tails. The upperside of the female is mid-brown with a flush of blue on the wing areas closest to the body. The underside is mid-brown with a multitude of white arc markings – a white stripe runs across the hindwing towards the rear edge from which protrude the tails, at the base of which are two black dots surrounded by orange.

Brown Veined White *Belenois aurota* Grasveldwitjie
This species is the most common of the white butterflies and is found throughout the region. It is indeed common throughout the whole of the African continent. The male is white on the upperside with the apex and forewing outer margins brown/black and with a series of dark spots along the outer margin of the hindwing. There is also a large comma-shaped mark midway along the forewing. The female is white with the apex and outer margins of both the forewing and the hindwing brown. The brown/black comma-shaped mark midway along the forewing is broader in the female than in the male. On the forward edge of the hindwing is another brown/black mark and the veins of the hindwing are picked out in brown/black. The underside of the male is white with yellow streaks at the base of the hindwing. The veins of both the forewing and the hindwing are picked out in brown/black. The female is similar but has far more yellow on the underside of the wings. This species often migrates, particularly in December/January and can be seen on the wing at all times of the year.

Painted Lady *Vanessa cardui* Sondagsrokkie
One of the most common butterflies in the world with a distribution reaching around the globe to all places other than South America, Australia and the polar regions. A true long distance migrant, found in areas of open grasslands and meadows. The upperside is orange, the apex of the forewings are brown/black with a series of white spots. The hindwings are orange spotted with a series of black dots and both the forewings and hindwings are thinly edged with white. The underside of the hindwings is a mosaic of cryptic browns, with a series of eye-spots towards the rear of the hindwings. The underside of the forewings are orange towards the rear; this area seldom shows when the butterfly is at rest.

Common Joker *Byblia ilithyia*
A common species in the eastern part of our range. There are two species of *byblia* occurring in Southern Africa and they can be easily confused. The Common Joker can be distinguished from the Joker *Byblia anvatara* by the orange area in the centre of the hindwing carrying a series of small black dots. They are usually to be found in areas of open grassland where they fly slowly within a metre or so of the vegetation. The upperside of the male is a rich orange colour with a black jagged border along the leading edge of the forewing. A similar jagged line extends out across both the forewing and the hindwing from the area of the thorax. Yet another black jagged line extends around the rear edge of the hindwing and continues onto the forewing for about half of its width. The female is similar to the male but is lighter in colour.

Blue Pansy *Junonia oenone* Blougesiggie
A common species in the eastern half of our range where it appears throughout the year. They are found in open areas and usually settle on rocks or on open bare ground. The males are territorial and they defend their ground with vigour, chasing away any other males that stray into an already occupied area. The upperside is black with two very prominent iridescent blue spots in the centre of the hindwings. The forewings are bordered with white and a series of white marks appear in the apex area. The hindwings are edged with a double white border. Both the forewings and the hindwings carry two orange spots with blue/black centres. The undersides of the wings are a cryptic mixture of browns. The hindwing is pale brown at the base becoming darker towards the centre and the trailing edge. The forewing has brown margins and areas of orange throughout, little of the orange shows when the butterfly is at rest.

Striped Policeman *Coeliades forestan* Witbroekkonstabel
A large member of the skipper family, this species is common in eastern and central parts of our range. They are extremely fast fliers and are more active during the early morning and late afternoon. They can be encountered on the wing throughout the whole year. The upperside of the forewings is a uniform mid-brown with a hint of orange near the inner margins. The upperside of the hindwing has a broad brown border around the outer margins with pale orange centres. The underside of the forewings varies from mid to dark brown with a flush of white towards the rear centre. The undersides of the hindwings are pale to dark brown with a broad white diagnostic band running from the forward centre edge of the wing and stopping short of the trailing edge. There is bright orange fringing along the anal angle of the hindwings and around the head and upper legs. The abdomen is striped black and white. The sexes are similar.

Water Monitor *Varanus niloticus* Leguaan

Also known as the Nile Monitor, this is Southern Africa's largest lizard, which can measure up to 2 m in length and can be encountered along riverbanks, in swamps and marshes and in most other wet habitats. They have a body colour of black which is irregularly marked with bands, spots and speckles of bright yellow, the juveniles are often brighter than the adults. They are extremely good swimmers and climbers and prey on a wide variety of small animals and birds, as well as on reptiles, fish, amphibians and other aquatic life forms. They are partial to crocodile eggs and will also scavenge on carrion.

Nile Crocodile *Crocodylus niloticus* Nyl Krokodil

A species that is so easily recognised it hardly requires a detailed description. They can grow to a length of around 6 metres and can be found in the rivers and lakes of game reserves and other areas in the north and northeast of our region; a most formidable aquatic predator. They are a dull olive colour above and pale yellow below. They are mainly nocturnal in habits and spend much of the day submerged in shallow water. They can also often be seen basking on sandbanks at the water's edge. They feed on fish and other water dwelling animals, as well as ambushing land-based mammals as they come to drink. They lay eggs in nests at the water's edge which hatch after about 85 days. Once hatched the young are protected by the parents during their early stages of development. The hatchlings will take around 15 years to reach maturity. It is thought that they may live for around 100 years.

Rock Monitor *Varanus albigularis* Likkewaan

A large lizard, inhabiting arid, rocky habitats in central and eastern parts of our range as well as central areas of Namibia. They have a rather dull body colour made up of browns, olives and greys and show a variable amount of spotting and banding. They forage during the day for insects, taking millipedes, grasshoppers and crickets as well as taking lizards and small mammals. If they are threatened they may lash out with their tail and attempt to bite their aggressor. Although not poisonous, any bite is likely to become badly infected.

Ground Agama *Agama aculeate* Distant se stekelkoggelmander

A species found over much of our range apart from in the northeastern region and in coastal areas. They prefer savannah and semi-arid grasslands and can often be seen early in the day basking on rocks. They can grow to around 20 cm in length. The body colour is a mosaic mixture of browns, greys and buffs; the breeding males often develop bluish heads. They have a relatively large ear hole. They will principally feed on ants and termites, but will no doubt take other small insects. They live in holes and crevices among rock piles and will dig holes in sandy soils into which they will deposit their eggs.

Spiny Agama *Agama hispida* Stekelkoggelmander

A species inhabiting dry semidesert areas in the southwest. They show considerable colour variation ranging from grey/brown to bright green, the breeding males often having blue heads, the females remaining plainer in colour. Short spines are visible along the length of the body from the nape to the tail. They have small ear holes compared to other closely related species. They feed on ants, termites and other small insects and will lie in ambush rather than chase would-be meals.

Flap-necked Chameleon *Chamaeleo dilepis* Gewone Groot Verkleur-mannetjie

A species found over much of our region except for the far west and south. They inhabit areas of savannah with light woodlands, scrub and thickets. Like many chameleons, the Flap-necked is famous for its ability to change colour in response to factors such as light intensity, climate as well as to emotions such as fear and aggression. Colouration changes are generally more pronounced in males than in females. They will feed on a variety of insects which are captured by thrusting out a long sticky tongue, hauling in the prize neatly stuck on the tip. The tongue can be as long as the body and is kept coiled in the base of the mouth ready for action. The ability to swivel their eyes independently of each other ensures pinpoint accuracy.

Peringuey's Adder   *Bitis peringueyi*   Namib-duinadder

An endemic species found only in the deserts of Namibia. A relatively small but extremely dangerous species. The head is short and rather flat, with the eyes situated on top of the head, which is a helpful adaptation when hunting. They will bury themselves in the sand leaving only the eyes exposed – a perfect ambush position. They will strike at lizards, gecko's and any other passing reptiles, inflicting a venomous bite which almost immediately renders the victim immobile. The body colour is pale buff to chestnut, overlaid with a series of fine grey and brown spots and flecks. They move over loose sand by adopting a motion of 'side-winding'.

African Rock Python   *Python sebae*   Luislang

The largest snake in Southern Africa with some individuals measuring in excess of 7 m. They are a non-venomous species that kills by constriction. They have a body colour of pale buff, overlaid with blotches of brown, olive and tan along the back and the sides, the latter being generally paler in colour. They prefer areas of savannah and woodlands, usually close to water. Reproduction occurs in the spring, when females lay up to 100 eggs in a tree hollow, a termite mound or similar, the female coils herself around them for warmth and protection. They feed mainly on small mammals, but will occasionally take larger prey, such as impala or other similar-sized herbivores. All prey is swallowed whole. Although non-venomous they should be treated with respect, as they will readily bite if molested.

Cape Cobra   *Naja nivea*   Kaapse Kobra

A species found in the southwestern portion of our range. Colouration varies considerably from location to location, ranging from a uniform yellow ochre to a dark chestnut brown, often with dark brown flecking. When threatened they will raise the head and front section of the body off the ground and spread their broad hood as a warning. Failure to respond to this signal will result in a 'strike' with alarming speed and the infliction of a highly venomous bite. They are active mainly at dawn and dusk, hunting small mammals and other snakes. They are good climbers and can cause havoc in Sociable Weaver colonies, taking young birds from nests.

Black Mamba   *Dendroaspis polylepis*   Swart Mamba

A large agile snake found in the northern and eastern parts of our range. The body colour is dull grey, with an occasional hint of olive. The inner mouth is black, from which it gets its name. They feed mainly on rodents and dassies by injecting one of the most virulent nerve poisons known to exist. They can grow to 3.5 m in length and usually live in termite mounds, tree cavities, in rock crevices and in abandoned porcupine holes.

Puff Adder   *Bitis arietans*   Pofadder

A large, thick-bodied adder which can be encountered throughout our region in all habitats other than deserts and high mountain ranges. They have a triangular head and a short tail, the thick body can have a girth of up to 30 cm. The body colour is a mosaic of buffs, browns, blacks and yellows, which affords a tremendous camouflage when they are at rest in leaf litter or other dead vegetation. They feed by lying in ambush, waiting for small mammals, birds, amphibians, lizards and other snakes to approach close enough for the adder to 'strike'. The injected venom soon takes effect. They account for many bites to humans, being sluggish they fail, unlike most snakes, to react to the vibrations created by approaching human footfall; this often results in the adder being trodden on, which in turn results in a nasty bite.

Brown House Snake   *Lamprophis fuliginosus*   Bruin Huisslang

Found throughout the whole of Southern Africa, they are an extremely adaptable species and can be found in a variety of habitat types including human settlements. They are reddish brown in colour and often become darker with age. They have a stripe of yellow extending from above the eye down the body for just a short way. They are mainly nocturnal and feed on rodents and other small mammals as well as lizards.

Angulate Tortoise *Chersina angulata* Ploegskaarskilpad
Found in the southwest of our region, in dry, sandy areas, in scrub and in fynbos. The upper part of the carapace is light yellow in colour with wide black edges to the scutes or scales, while around the lower portion of the shell, triangular decorations of alternating yellow and black are prominent. The legs are yellow and brown and have strong claws. They have a greatly enlarged gular plate, the part of the lower shell under the head, which males use as a weapon to ram and overturn other males in disputes over dominance. They weigh, on average, 1.5 kg and have the strange habit of drinking through their nose. They feed on a wide variety of plant material as well as taking snails and fungi. Females lay single egg clutches and can produce six such clutches during a season.

Serrated Hinged Terrapin *Pelusios sinuatus* Groot waterskilpad
A large terrapin, found in the northeastern corner of our range, in permanent water bodies such as rivers and lakes. They have an elongated black oval carapace which is serrated at the rear, more so in juveniles than in adults. The broad head is olive black in colour with a pointed snout, the chin, throat and underside of the neck are yellow. The remainder of the exterior limbs are greyish. They can often be seen basking in large numbers on logs, rocks and sand banks. In the spring they excavate tunnels, sometimes as far as half a kilometre from water, into which the females will deposit up to 30 soft-shelled eggs. If threatened or handled they may exude a foul-smelling liquid as a form of defence.

Leopard Tortoise *Geochelone pardalis* Bergskilpad
The largest tortoise in Africa, found over most of the region. The carapace has a yellow base colour, which is overlaid with black spots and blotches, not dissimilar to the coat pattern of the leopard, hence its name. They can grow to weights in excess of 28 kg and are long lived, being recorded in captivity at 50 years or more. They feed on a wide range of plant material, often travelling great distances in search of good grazing. They are active for most of the day, but usually seek shade during the hot midday period.

Tent Tortoise *Psammobates tentorius* Tentskilpad
A most attractive tortoise, found in southern and western parts of our range. They show great variation in shape and colour. They usually have black and yellow radiating patterns on each scute or plate, but some individuals can be almost plain brown in colour. The head, neck and limbs are greyish brown. The females are larger than males and lay clutches of one to three eggs, burying them in the sand, usually between September and January – the young will hatch in April or May. They have a vegetarian diet which includes mesembryanthemums and other succulents, as well as grasses, sedges and herbaceous plants.

Giant Girdled Lizard *Cordylus giganteus* Reuse gordelakkedis
The largest of the Girdled Lizard species, they are restricted in distribution to the central and eastern parts of the Orange Free State in South Africa and surrounding areas. A species easily recognised by its heavily spined body and tail, they have a series of elongated spines around the back of the head and on the neck. They are yellow/buff in colour with dark banding and blotching. They live in colonies, each digging a burrow, usually on sloping ground – they are under considerable threat as a result of habitat destruction, as grasslands are ploughed to produce maize crops; they also suffer from illegal collecting for the pet trade. They are known by local people as the Sungazer from their habit of sitting in their burrow entrances soaking up the warming ray of the sun. They feed on insects such as grasshoppers, beetles and termites.

Wedge-nosed Desert Lizard *Meroles cuneirostris* Wig snouted woestynakkedis
A species restricted to the southern Namib Desert where they can be found on dune hummocks with sparse vegetation. They are reddish/orange above, finely speckled with yellow along the entire length of the body. They are off-white on the underside. The thighs and the hind limbs are boldly marked with dark, almost black, blotches.

Striped Skink   *Mabuya striata*   Gestreepte Skink Sefeleko

A very common species found throughout Southern Africa with the exceptions of the extreme south and the Namib Desert, frequenting rocky outcrops, trees and urban areas including human dwellings. They measure around 20 cm in length. The body colour shows some variation from location to location, but is usually bronze/black or dark brown with two broad bands of pale brown/buff on either side of the body, extending from a position just above the eye and running the length of the body to mid tail. The chin and throat are also pale brown/buff. Breeding males develop an orange/yellow throat. They can often be seen in the early morning on top of a rock or other exposed position, soaking up the warming rays of the sun.

Common Barking Gecko   *Ptenopus garrulous*   Grond Geitjie

A common species in central and western parts of our region. They are nocturnal and spend the daytime hidden away in burrows, becoming active at dusk when the males start to call in order to attract females. This is done from the burrows and amplifies the sound which, as its name suggests is reminiscent of a dog barking. The body colour is variable but is usually reddish/buff or greyish/yellow and is finely speckled and blotched with pale buff, dark brown and black. The chin and the throat are yellow. Females will lay several clutches of one or two eggs during the course of the summer. They feed on ants, termites and other small insects.

Karoo Toad   *Bufo gariepensis*   Karoo Skurwepadda

A common species found in central and southern parts of our region. They breed in streams, ponds, waterholes and other water bodies in areas of Karoo scrub and grasslands. They exhibit considerable variation in body pattern and colouration, in the central part of our range they are buff with irregular blotches of dark brown, while further south they are usually dull brownish/yellow. In the northern part of their range the ground colour barely shows at all, resulting in a dark brown version. The skin appears rough and dry with the back and the sides of the body bearing a whole series of warty bumps. They feed on a wide range of insects.

Red Toad   *Schismaderma careens*   Rooirug-skurwepadda

A common species in the northeastern part of our region. They are found in areas of open woodlands and savannahs, in or close to permanent water bodies such as lakes, rivers and man-made dams. They are also often to be found in urban gardens and ponds .The upper body colour is dull orange/red, while the sides of the body and the underparts are off-white with a hint of yellow with spots and smudges of dark green and black. They carry two dark spots on the back which aid identification. They lack the large warts present in most other toad species and have a relatively prominent tympanum. The tadpoles of the Red Toad are distinctive in having a flap of skin around the crown of the head.

Giant African Bull Frog   *Pyxicephalus adspersus*   Afrikaanse brulpadda

Found in the central regions of Southern Africa, this is the largest frog to occur on the continent, weighing in at around 2 kg. The females are generally about half the size of the males. They can be encountered in a variety of open habitats, they are extremely good burrowers and can stay underground for many months to emerge after heavy rains to join a breeding frenzy. The upper body is green in colour with a series of raised skin folds that are usually lighter in colour. The chin and throat are off-white and the flanks are yellow. Should you attempt to handle a full grown male you can expect a fearsome bite from tooth-like projections set into the lower jaw. They have great appetites and will feed avidly on large insects, other amphibians as well as on small mammals and reptiles. If threatened they will often inflate their bodies like balloons to intimidate the aggressor.

Raucous Toad   *Bufo rangeri*   Gestreepte Skurwepadda

A species of toad found in southern coastal regions and in central and eastern areas. They breed in rivers, ponds and other bodies of standing water in both grasslands and in wooded areas. The body colour is pale buff on the back, becoming paler on the flanks and the underparts. The entire body is covered in dark brown/black blotches and speckles. They have pairs of dark symmetrical patches on the back which sometimes join across the dorsal line of the spine.

Sharp-nosed Grass Frog *Ptychadena oxyrhynchus* Gevlekte graspadda

A species found in a variety of habitats including savannahs, swamps, marshes, cultivated farmland, rural gardens and bodies of standing water from large lakes to small pools. They have limited distribution along a strip running north to south along the east coast. The body colour consists of a series of yellows and buffs, with dark brown/black speckles and blotches. They have a pointed snout and the body has a series of raised ridges within the skin. The back legs have several black bands along their length. They have a large tympanum and within the frog world is one of the most accomplished of 'jumpers', launching themselves great distances with their large rear legs. They feed on a variety of insects, particularly grasshoppers and crickets.

Cape Sand Frog *Tomopterna delandii* Gestreepte Sandpadda

A small burrowing frog, found in central Namibia and the Western, Eastern and Northern Cape Provinces. A frog of swamps, marshes, ponds, rivers and other bodies of standing water, but they can also be encountered in more arid habitats. They have the look of a toad rather than that of a frog, particularly in the manner in which they move. The base body colour is off-white, overlaid with smudges of olive green/brown along with black spots and blotches. They usually have an off-white line running the length of the spine from the tip of the nose and an additional line running along the side of the body from the rear of the eye.

Painted Reed Frog *Hyperolius marmoratus* Gestreepte rietpadda

A very common frog found in the eastern and northern parts of our region where they can be found breeding in almost any form of standing water, from large lakes to small pools. A species that shows extreme variation in body colour and markings as a result of geographic distribution. Those from the south tend to be spotted, in central areas they tend towards mottled patterns, while in the north they are usually striped in a range of differing colour forms. Within these geographic forms there is further variation, some individuals being rather plain. They are good climbers and can often be found during the day resting on reed stems or on other vegetation. They become active at night as the males commence calling to attract females.

Common River Frog *Rana angolensis* Gewone graspadda

A reasonably common species, found in central and eastern parts of our range, where they breed in streams, lakes, pool and most other bodies of standing water. The upper body colour varies from green to brown overlaid with a series of black spots and blotches. The sides of the body are mid-brown with some white spots and stripes, the underside is white. They have a series of raised ridges running the length of the back and they have a pointed snout.

Cape River Frog *Rana fuscigula* Kaapse graspadda

A species encountered in central and southern parts of our region, where they breed in any large, still body of water as well as in rivers and streams. They show considerable variation in body colour from green to brown being overlaid with dark spots and blotches, a light ventral strip is usually present. They have powerful back legs and are extremely good jumpers. They are generally more tolerant of cold weather and low temperatures than other frog species, often staying active throughout the cooler months of the year.

Common Caco *Cacosternum boettgeri* Blikslanertjie

Found in southern, central and eastern parts of our region, in marshes, on floodplains, wet grasslands and in shallow pools. They are often found in huge breeding groups during and following wet weather. They have long bodies and small heads, the limbs are quite slender and the fingers are unwebbed. They show considerable colour variation, ranging from pale brown to bright green; they also exhibit a variety of overlaying stripes, spots and bands.

Emperor Dragonfly *Anax imperator* Keiser naaldekoker
A very large dragonfly, usually to be seen patrolling well-vegetated ponds, pools and other water bodies on the look out for a meal, which usually consists of aerial prey such as flies and mosquitoes, although they will occasionally take larger items such as butterflies and damselflies. The male has green eyes with a hint of blue, a green thorax and a sky blue slightly decurved abdomen with black dorsal markings along the upper surface. Unlike the male, the abdomen of the female is green.

Scarlet Darter *Crocothemis erythraea* Slanghalsvoël
A stunning dragonfly found in areas with standing shallow water such as pools, ponds, floodplains and drainage ditches. The male is a vivid scarlet in colour and has a flattened abdomen and when at rest sits with his wings swept forward. The veins along the forewings are red and all of the wings have a patch of yellow at the base, this patch being larger on the hindwing than on the forewing. The female has subdued colouring when compared to the male, being pale amber in colour with a conspicuous pale stripe running along the thorax between the wings. She too has the yellow patches at the base of the wings.

Elegant Grasshopper *Zonocerus elegans* Korthoringsprinkane
As the name suggests this grasshopper is extremely pleasing to the eye. The antennae are black with orange rings, the eyes are red and the other body parts are a fantastic mixture of yellows, reds, blues and black. They are very gregarious and lay their eggs communally in the autumn where they remain in the ground for about six months, hatching in the following spring. The nymphs then take a further three months to attain maturity. They are considered by farming communities to be pests, as they can inflict serious damage to crops such as cotton, cocoa and coffee as well as to fruits and vegetables. If threatened they can emit a foul yellow fluid.

Armoured Ground Cricket *Acanthroplus discoidalis* Langhoring sprinkaan
A flightless species found in Namibia, Botswana and South Africa. A rather bland species with the body colour a mixture of browns, however, there is some variation within the species, some showing more in the way of greens. The body is wide and the thorax has a series of very sharp spines, coupled with strong biting jaws they present quite a problem to would-be predators. They have yet another method of defence: the ability to eject 'insect blood' from their bodies, this is a toxic substance which predators find most distasteful. They can eject over a distance of around 30 cm. Yet another defence strategy involves the regurgitation of their stomach contents. They are regarded as pests by farmers for their destruction of millet and sorghum crops.

Common Green Mantis *Sphodromantis gastrica* Hottenttotsgot
A creature characterised by its 'praying' posture, keeping the front legs raised in readiness to pounce on any likely victim. They blend extremely well with their surroundings and will lay in ambush for other insects which may pass by close enough to be snatched. The body colour shows some variation but is usually bright green. They can grow to 7.5 cm in length, the females being larger than the males. As in most mantis species the male is often the victim of sexual cannibalism, the female devouring the male after mating.

African Honey Bee *Apis mellifera scutellata* Heuningby
Found throughout the region with the exception of the southwestern corner. A species with the abdomen showing alternative yellow and black bands. The thorax is brown/black with a buff fringe. They are often known as' Killer Bees' and, although their sting is no more potent than the European species, they tend to attack a perceived threat with more bodies and with greater persistence. People have died from incurring 100 to 300 stings, although it is estimated that 500 to 1000 is the lethal dose for adults. The African Honey Bee may well be threatened in the near future, by the introduction of the Cape Honey Bee into the northern parts of our range. Cape Bees parasitise colonies of African Bees, causing death to the original occupants.

Bush Locust *Phymateus viridipes* Sprinkaan

A species capable of long migratory flights, growing in length to around 7 cm. The body colour and the forewings are green, while the hindwings are red and dark blue. The wings are well hidden when the locust is at rest, appearing as a burst of colour as they launch themselves in to the air. The shield or body plate covering the neck area is covered in small raised spots which are tipped with bright red.

Red Locust *Nomadacris septemfasciata* Rooi sprinkaan

A species found in wet habitats such as floodplains, swamps, marshes and damp grasslands. The overall body colour of this large locust is a mixture of browns and yellows. Females are larger than males, measuring up to 8.5 cm in length. Its name refers to the colour of the hindwings, which are only visible when in flight. When food and shelter are in good supply, red locusts remain sedentary, but where suitable habitats are reduced the locusts change their behaviour and become very gregarious, forming in to enormous swarms moving through the landscape looking for food. During these periods, enormous amounts of damage can be done to cultivated crops and pasturelands. Swarms can cover in excess of 20 km a day.

Dune Ant *Camponotus detritus* Mier

Dune ants construct simple nest structures among the roots of vegetation in desert sand dunes with the expansion and relocation of colonies taking place regularly. The head and thorax are black, the abdomen is pale yellow with bold black patches in the centre of each body section. They feed on honeydew excreted by aphids as well as on pollen, nectar, some animal faeces and rotting carrion. They obtain moisture from condensing fog.

Matabele Ant *Megaponera foetens* Matabele miere

An ant with all black body colour, although the tip of the abdomen often has a hint of dark brown. Within this species, reproduction is undertaken by a lone queen. Matabele ants are named after Matabele Warriors who, in times passed, advanced across the plains, wiping out villages as they went. The ants form into dense columns in their thousands to raid the nests of termites, they position large soldiers with powerful jaws on the flanks while the workers attack the termites. Bites from matabele ants can be extremely painful, just a small number of bites can cause paralysis.

Darkling Beetle *Onymacris unguicularis* Toktokkie

An all black species found in the Namib Desert, also known as the 'Fog-basking Beetle'. This name refers to the beetles' drinking method; the beetle stations itself on a dune ridge, with its back legs straightened and its front legs bent with the head down. The overnight fog condenses on the beetle's body and forms into drops which trickle down to the mouth parts. This behaviour makes it possible for the darkling beetle to survive in such a harsh environment, one of the world's driest temperate deserts. They feed on wind-blown seeds and plant material which gathers on the lee-side of dune ridges.

Dung Beetle *Scarabaeoidea sp.* Miskruier

Also known as the Scarab Beetle, this species feeds at least partially, if not exclusively, on animal faeces. Dung Beetles exist in a variety of habitat types, including deserts, savannahs, grasslands and woodlands. They locate dung by smell and will mould a portion of it into a ball before rolling it in a straight line, regardless of obstacles, to a pre-selected location, where they will bury it, either as a food store for later, or as a brooding ball into which the female lays a series of eggs – the ball sustaining the young hatchlings. This constant burying of dung balls can much improve the nutritional value of the soil and is also an effective method of seed dispersal.

Index